Life As Living Ceremony

An Essence Sculpture Art Book

Mary Saint-Marie
Sheoekah

...behold Life as an enactment of the Eternal...
...live Life as an enactment of the Eternal...

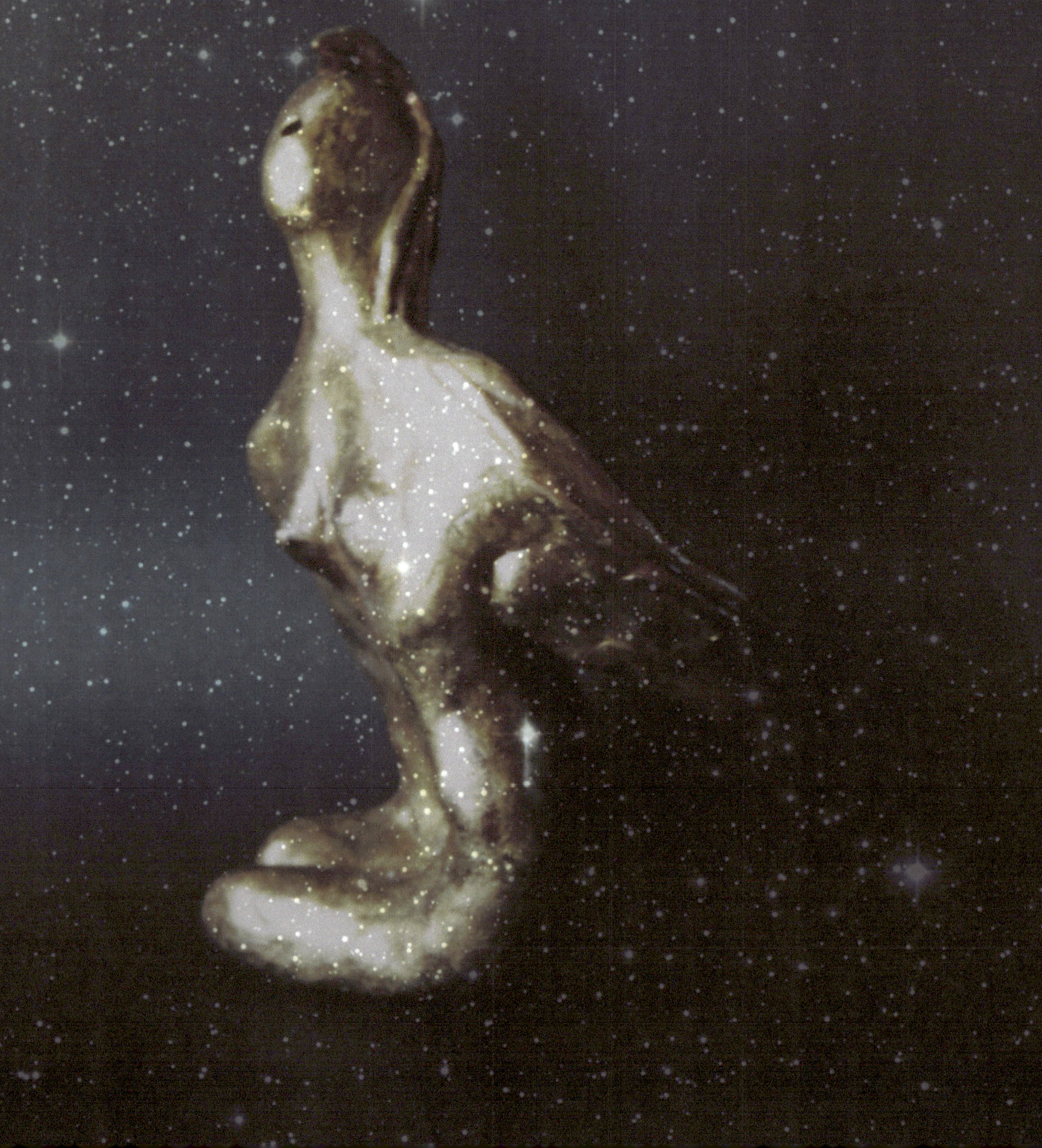

Life As Living Ceremony

Published by Ancient Beauty Studio, www.marysaintmarie.com

ISBN: 978-0-692-84517-2 (sc)

All artwork by Mary Saint-Marie

Front Cover Art: *Serpent-Priestess-SHE*

Back Cover Art: *Warrior-Priestess-SHE…in flight…*

Book Design, Editing, and Layout by Aaron Rose, Mount Shasta, California

Photographs of the artist: Rebecca Allen

Credit for NASA Public Domain Image of M35: Atlas Image obtained as part of the Two Micron All Sky Survey (2MASS), a joint project of the University of Massachusetts and the Infrared Processing and Analysis Center/California Institute of Technology, funded by the National Aeronautics and Space Administration and the National Science Foundation.

Publications by Mary Saint-Marie:

Galactic Shamanism
The Holy Sight
Messages from the Silence
Nectar of Woman
The Sacred Two
The Star-Stone Ones
The Animating Presence
The Monitor and Laughter of the Gods
Art As Consciousness
The Oracle and the Dreamer
Life As Living Ceremony

This book is dedicated to the Blue Kachinas.
This book is dedicated to the Realm of Purity.
This book is dedicated to the purity of the earth and of the sky.

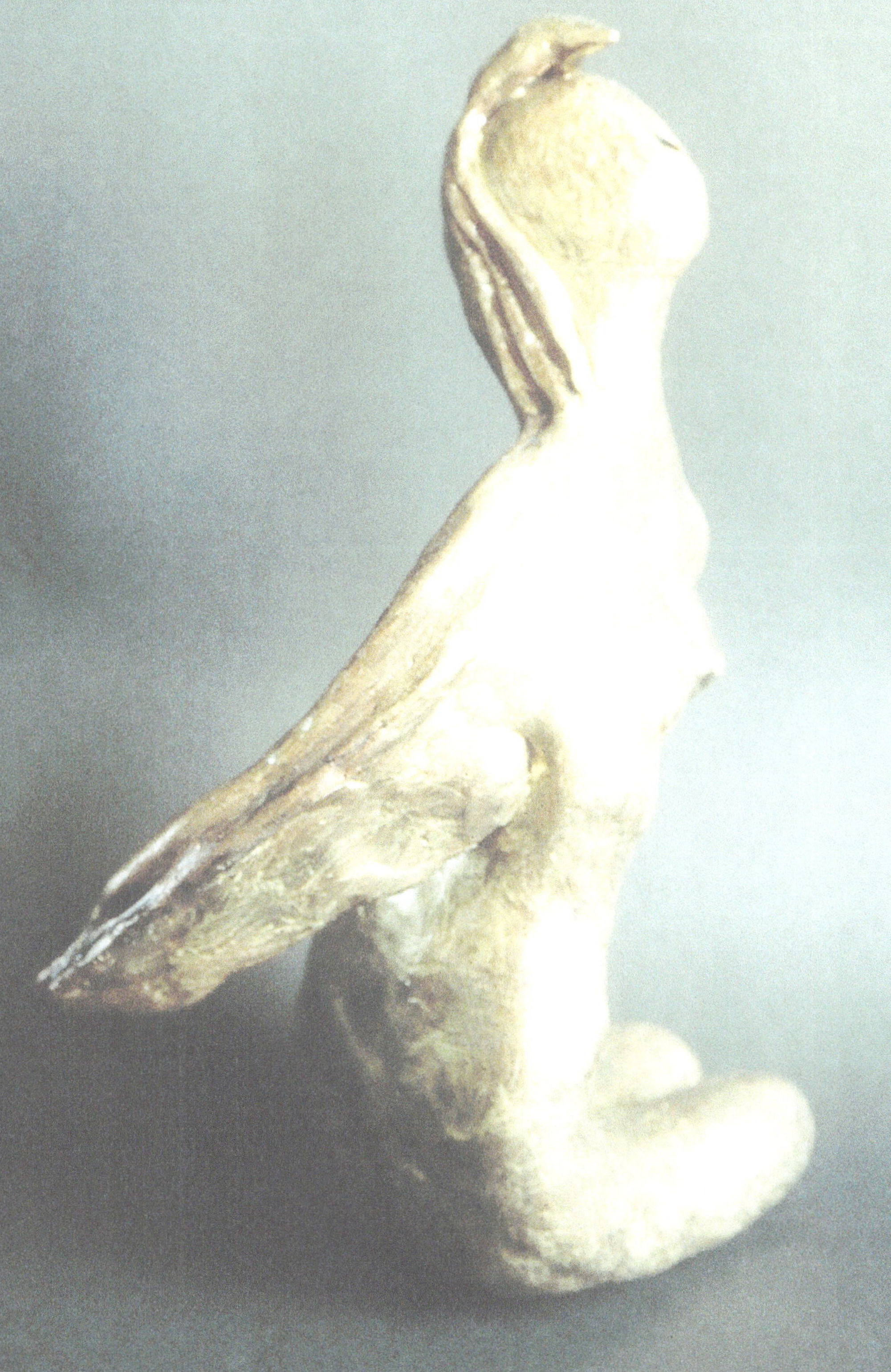

Contents

Second Phase: Kachina Cactus Gardens

Third Phase: Figures in Living Ceremony

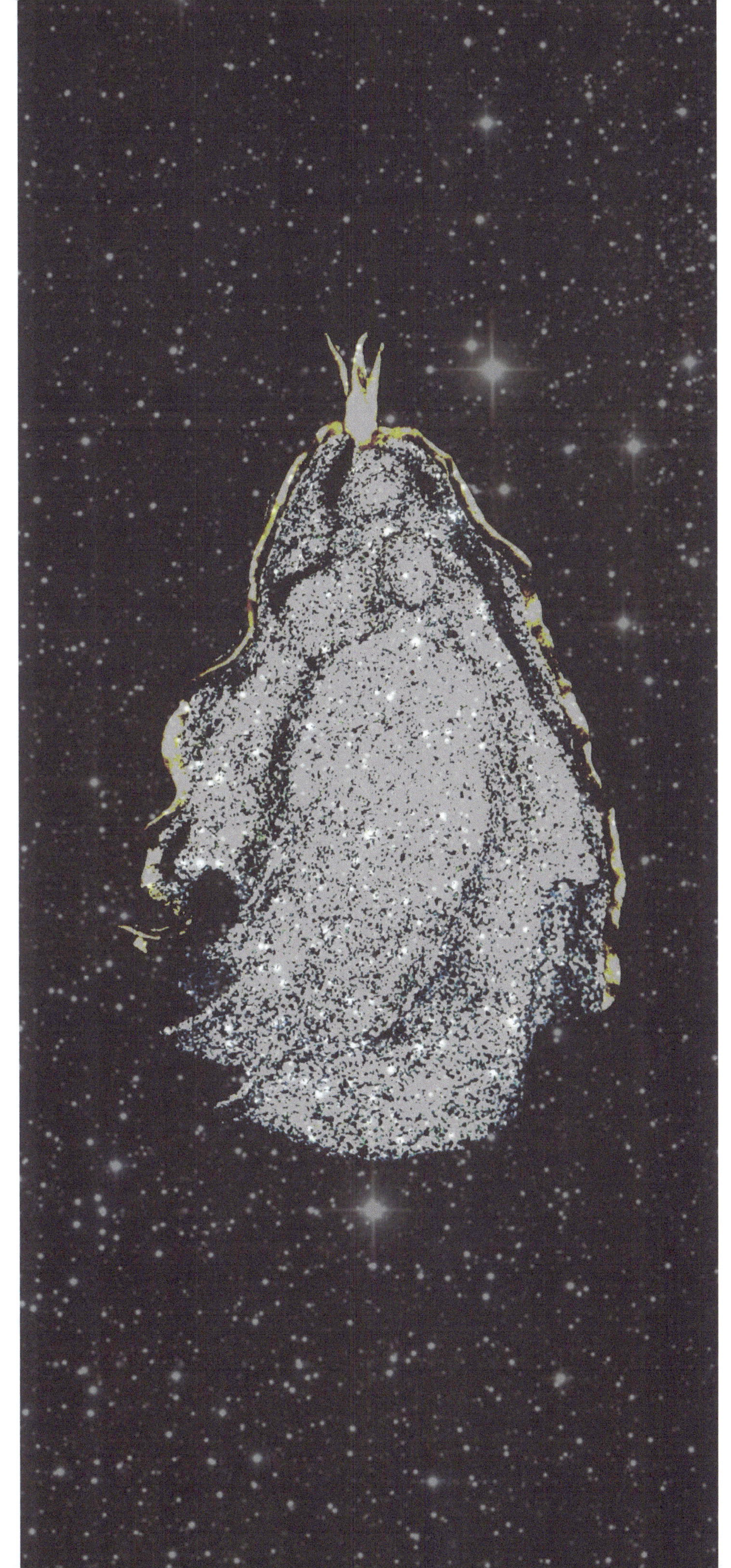

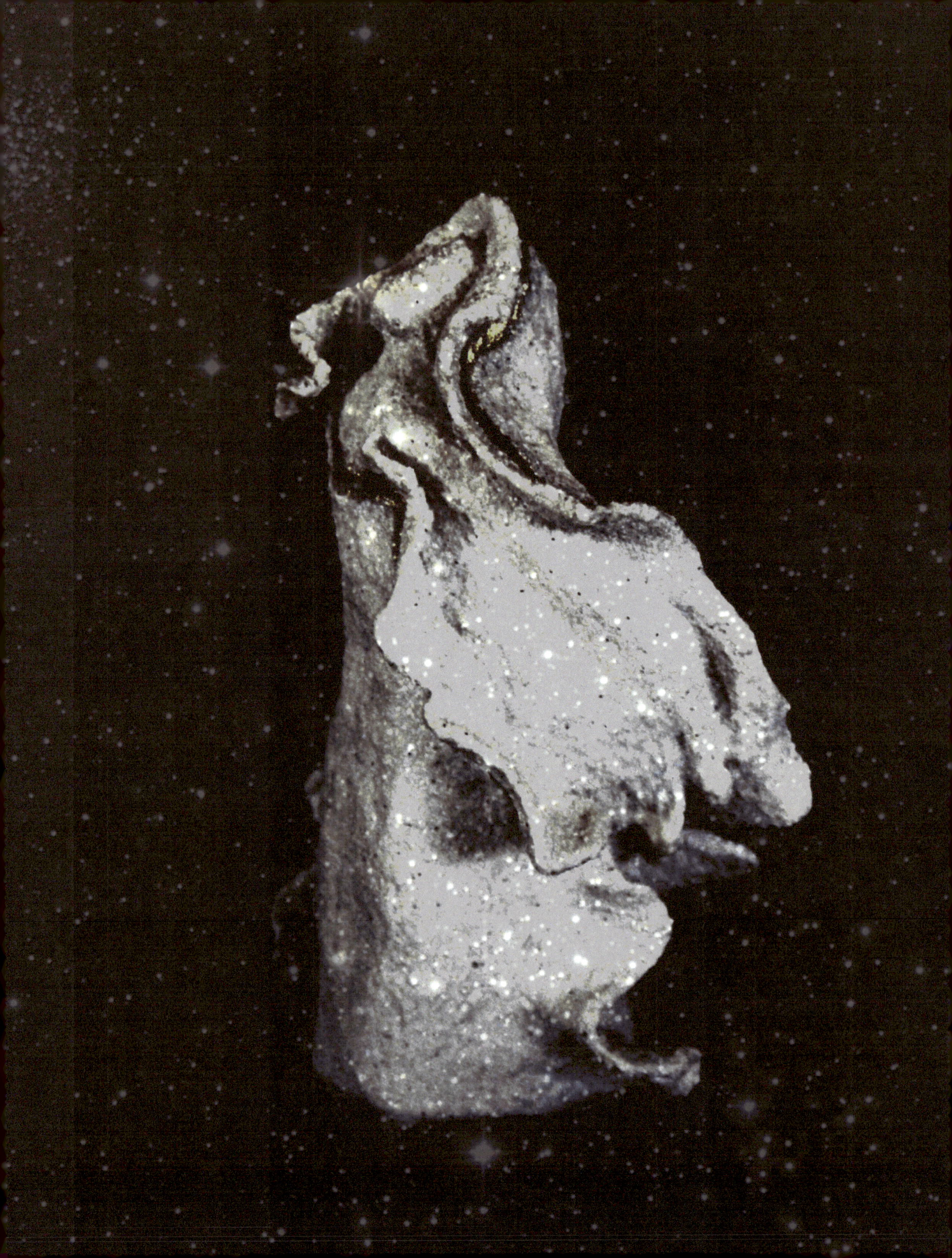

Acknowledgments

I am in such gratitude each time I have the time and space to enter deeply into the creative process to paint, to write, to create a book, to sculpt. The creative process is such an opportunity to enter into the Timeless Realm with no interruptions and distractions. It is such a sacred gift.

I am in such gratitude when I see the potential for all in this world to be in the deepest Soul Expression. The expression of each one's Perfection. Perfection accepted, felt, demonstrated, and manifest!

I thank the Blue Kachinas for opening me to the Realm of Purity, outside the reaches of the ever human mind. I thank them for shaking my world to the core. I thank them for inspiring the sacred ceremonial kachinas and gardens. And I thank them now for the inspiration to create this unexpected book that allows the sharing in yet another form.

I thank Spirit for yet another experience of allowing the Invisible to arrive as the visible. The Unseen...seen. The Formless One...in form.

I thank the Universal Life, God, for the exaltation and ecstasy of the Essence-world experienced as creation. Art form.

I thank my daughters, Kimberly and Rebecca, who had now grown up, as I began this sculpture phase of creation. I was now left with time for moving beyond mother-of-the-home to experiencing the energy of Mother of the World-Home. It was sometimes a bumpy ride. Yet creating always brings us back to the Single Purpose.

I thank my precious granddaughters, Maya and Ella, for being in my life. Already, their writing, their art, their creations and enthusiasm for life constantly inspire me!

I thank my friends. All of you add to my days and to my nights, as I continually plunge deep into meditation and solitary creation.

I thank all of the Earth's precious materials I use in creation. Together...we manifest.

Thanks is given to the young challenged Hopi man who took me to Grandmother Carolyn to gain understanding of this profound experience with the Blue Kachina Realm.

I thank Grandmother Carolyn, Hopi elder, that invited me into her home to help me understand my "visitation" from the Blue Star Kachinas. Thank you, Grandmother, for the wisdom given, the stories given, and the guidance given. Manna.

I thank Aaron Rose for continuing to gift me with his gifts of book design and editing. And the continued laughter during the process. And I thank Aaron for his ability to attune to the soul of the book and listen to its whisperings.

I thank my dear friend, Laura Daen, who was spending time with me during the summer of this Blue Kachina visitation. I thank her for always believing in what I have to share out into the world.

Introduction

As we each deepen into ourSelf, our true expression comes forth. Unique. And often it does even startle us. It is such a different expression. One might even ask, "How does this fit into the world, as I have known it?"

It may take time and dedication and a deep spiritual determination to bring the understanding to light. One may call it focus or concentration, but what it really is...is an inward calling.

As I began to deepen in meditation, there were times when the realms of the original archetypes began to open. I had no idea that they were even there to desire. As these experiences continued to happen, I could feel these images through and as my very being. The essences that they embody are experienced. Exhaltation comes!

In some ways it seems mysterious, but in other ways it is a simple unveiling. I experience some of the original archetypes in a way that is raw, real, primordial. Devoid of scholarly layerings. Devoid of historical layerings. Naked. And innocent.

I simply experience the primal energy of the higher realms. I feel the purity of Christ Presence. It is original. Virgin.

This experience is not personal. It is Impersonal. It is there for all of us as we open to and realize the Oneness.

The Blue Kachina is known by the Hopi peoples. The experience that I had was opening into a Realm of Purity (Christ Consciousness) that the mind cannot conceive.

In the Emptiness, the higher realms are revealed...
In the Purity of the heart, the higher realms do dwell...

It is important to note the following:

In meditation, one must simply open to the Source and allow. Be the One Presence that Already Is. Be empty. An awaiting vessel.

Whatever is there, revealed, is a gift. It is unique. It arrives from the withinness. One receives the gift from the Infinite and then begins to give. This allows one to give into the world the gifts that are given to us individually.

This giving is the principle of abundance in action. It is giving and receiving. It is the Universal Law of Balance in all of nature. This is the Law of Love. The Law of Love expressing. Yin and Yang. Masculine principle and feminine principle, in balance. It is the dancing of the Dance of the One.

This Law of Balance is the very simple and inviolate principle that humanity has chosen to mainly ignore for the last 6,000 years. This Law of Balance is the nature of the universe. It is unalterable.

Now is the time for the return. Now is the time for the return to the principle.

It is simple. It is inexorable. Unstoppable.

And comes...Life as Ceremony.
Life as Living Ceremony.
Life as spontaneous Living Ceremony.

It is the Living Ceremony of the One...come as the Many.

awa tey ewa tey
Now is the Time.

Note about the photography in this book:

These sculptures and many others were created in Mount Shasta. Once a group of figures was created, I was on the road, traveling to the next art exhibit.

The photos that I took were only for my own personal records. They were never intended to be in a book. That is the simple story of the photo shots.

In 2016, long after I had created these pieces, I was deeply inspired to share these sculptures in book form.

The images of the sculptures are intended to unveil the essence world. The Invisible as the visible. The Unmanifest...as manifest.

The viewers and the viewed become the 'viewing'. Viewing, as a state of consciousness, is a powerful practice. The viewer is then invited to feel into this essence world and allow the feeling of the vastness of awareness to be realized.

*Note that there is representation of the Infinite manifest as the feminine principle and the masculine principle through the artist. Our receptive and feminine nature opens to the essence world. Vision is seen, heard, experienced or simply intuited or known. And creation, the masculine principle, begins to sculpt, create, design and on! The yin and yang of creation. In balance.

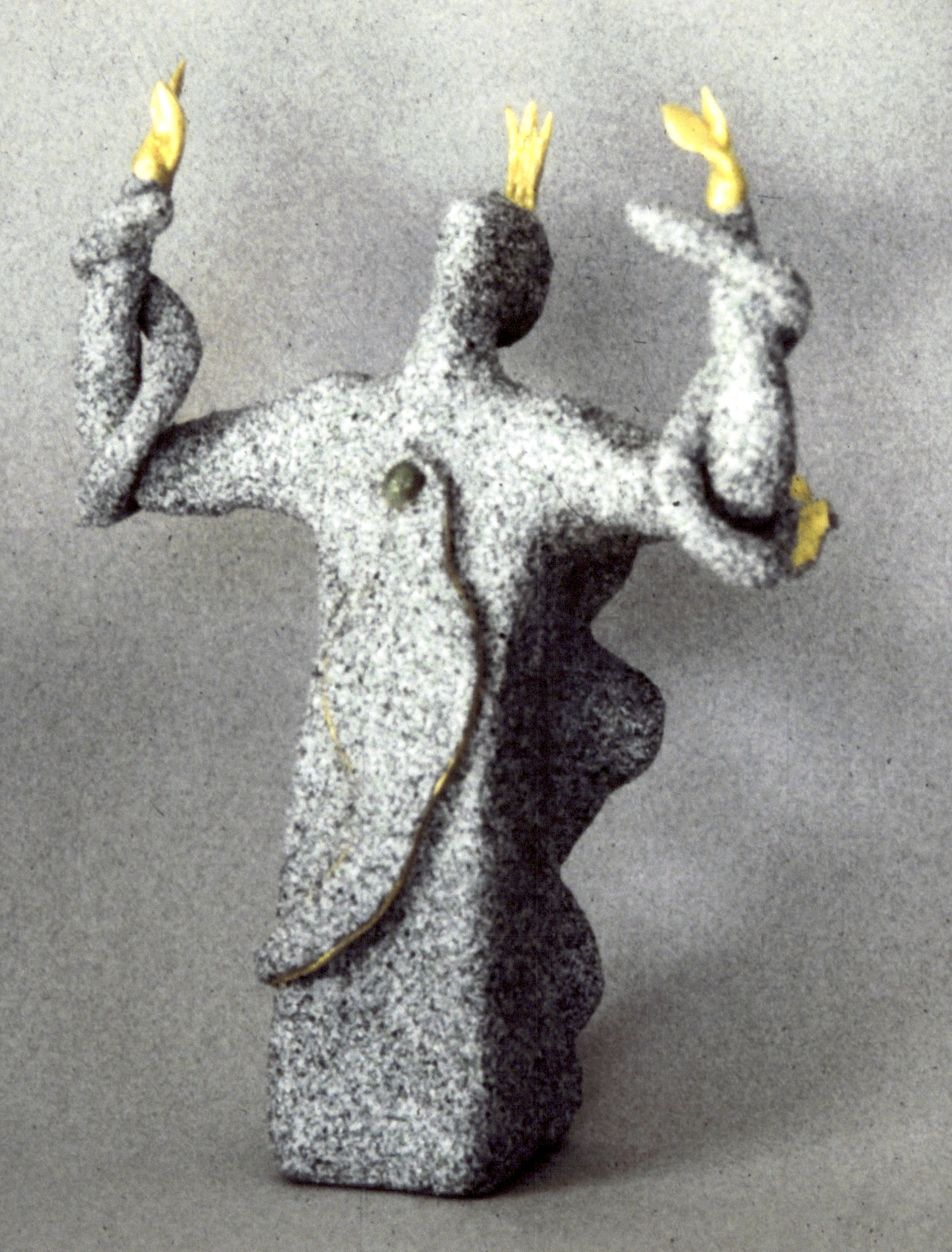

Preface

Life As Living Ceremony is the spontaneous, flowing and creative Life, that is always new, always fresh, always changing.

Life As Living Ceremony does celebrate beauty, purity, and eternal love in every moment.

Life As Living Ceremony does celebrate the Oneness with the Earth and with everyone, everything, and everyplace.

Life As Living Ceremony does celebrate one's own unique way of being in this world.

Life As Living Ceremony does ever celebrate the Undivided One.

Life As Living Ceremony IS an opening to and allowing of the sacred, animating current of life.

Life As Living Ceremony IS an Enactment of the Eternal.

It is a way of Being.

It is beyond the concept of a practice.

It is freedom lived.

Part 1:

Essays

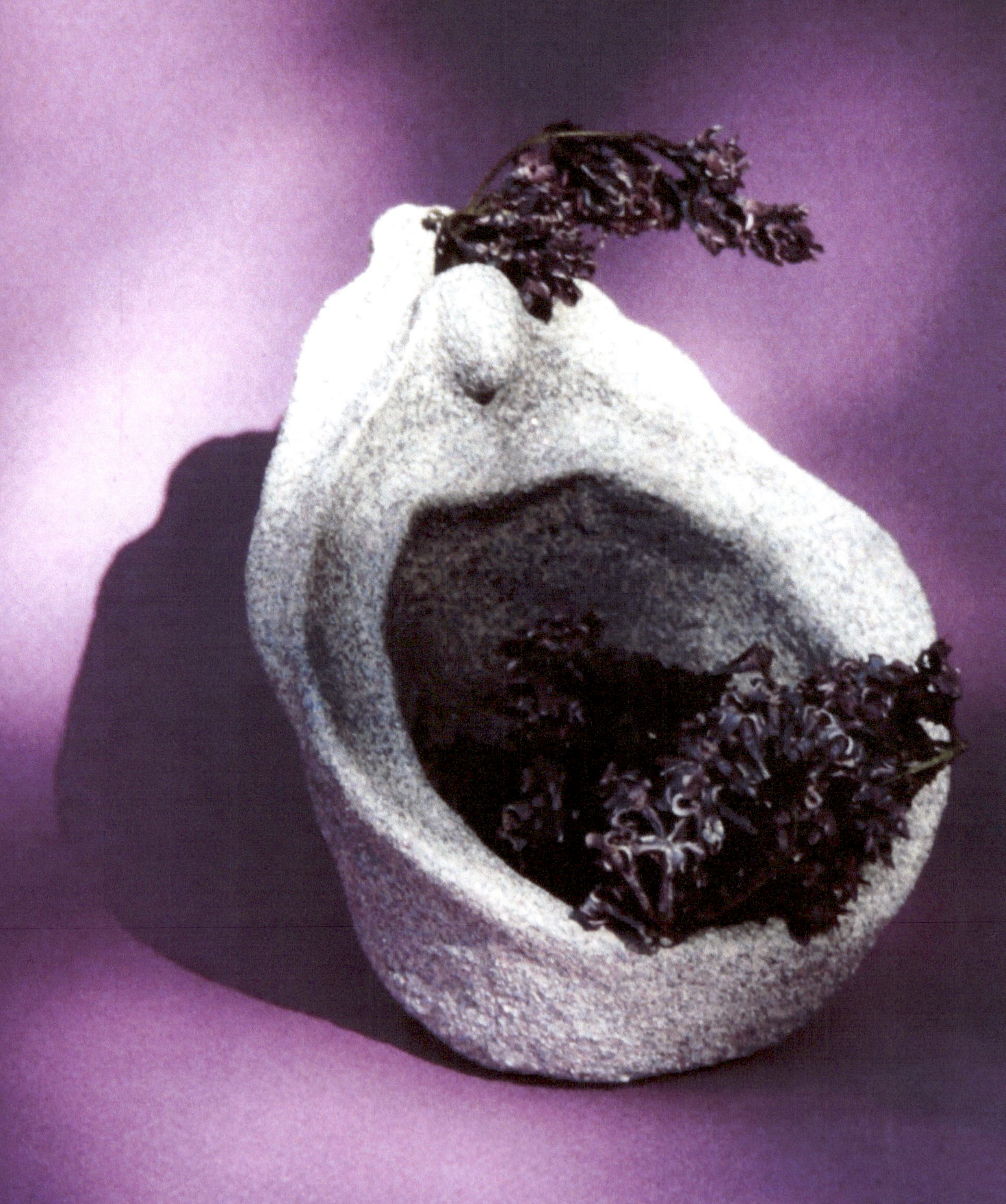

The Birth of the Kachina Sculptures

It began like this. In June of 1987, just before the Harmonic Convergence, I was uplifted, during meditation, into the Realm of the Blue Kachinas.

Not long after that, I was finding myself creating kachina-like sculptures that reflected the type of Supreme Energy that I experienced during the upliftment. It could be called also...a Visitation.

The sculptures began to come spontaneously, with no design or preplanning. I would just get quiet and empty, and in feeling the essence of the art materials, the visible began to arrive from the Invisible.

In my book *Galactic Shamanism*, I describe the three meditations/initiations that led up to the experience of the Blue Kachina Realm. In each of these revelatory experiences, I saw and understood deeply the principle of the Universal Law of Balance. It is a profound law of nature. It must be heeded and lived, for it cannot be altered. It is we that must attune to it.

This Law of Balance is the ancient symbol of such profound wisdom... the yin and yang in equal measure...lived. It is the masculine principle and the feminine principle in balance in all of nature. It is a cosmic principle. We must align with it.

This Law of Balance is the very Law of Love. Unity. The Undivided One.

At some point in history, man and woman defied that Principle and went into a belief in, and thus a sense of, separation. We are awakening out of that.

As I was uplifted into the Blue Kachina Realm, I realized I had been prepared all my life to enter into this Realm of Purity. It is a feminine realm of purity. The human mind cannot go there.

In this pristine realm, I witnessed ten luminous blue-white female kachinas in a circle. They faced inward. Before me was a radiant emanation. No features or details were revealed. Just pure and powerful cosmic energy. An experience of Stillness prevailed. Transcendence.

There were no human thoughts. They do not exist on this realm. I was simply a beholder of the beatific realm. A beholder of purity.

After this initiation experience, the cells of my body were open, sensitive like never before. I was open to the extreme. Feeling. There are many names attached to those of us that become ultra sensitive to Energies. The current of Life. But for me, it was simply taking in a bigger aerial view of what is in store for all of humanity in the recognition of the Vastness of who and what we are. And the opening to the collective enactment of the eternal.

The upliftment into this rarefied frequency catalyzed yet another form of creation for me.

It started this way. I began to create spaces, intuitively, that to me were holy spaces. I was doing this constantly all through my home. My Inner Life was birthing a conscious recognition of Life As Living Ceremony. I was ecstatic.

I also began to remember that as a youth, I had already begun to do this in many ways around the family home. I did it when no one was around. I did it quietly. No one seemed to notice what to me were "placements of beauty." I had no words for what I was doing. It made me feel wonderful. It was innocent. It was pure.

As I began to allow this deepened experience through me, after the "upliftment," I even began to call what I was doing by a name: Sacred Placement. Again, Life As Living Ceremony. I began to feel the energy created by the placement. I felt that the living forms were calling to me to be moved and shifted. I was ecstatic. It was living and it was real.

No longer did I care what others thought. What I was experiencing was deeply meaningful and it all had a powerful felt sense. It made me smile from deep within. I was being moved. I was being animated by the divine. And I was taking "no thought."

These sacred and holy spaces are, for me, a conducive environment to allow creation.

The small kachina sculptures began to arrive. I was aware these were borne of the Energy of the Blue Kachina Realm. Of course, one may simplify and call this Christ Presence.

Later, the small kachina sculptures were added to ceremonial gardens. They were reflections of our ever moving, changing, living space of life. They were mirrors of Life living as our very Being. As we accept. As we open. As we allow.

Each small kachina sculpture and each ceremonial Kachina Garden was different, new, fresh. Never to be repeated again. Like life that is in the moment of now. Inspired by the Source...alone. The Eternal.

I had the distinct awareness of moving beyond the set rituals and prescribed patterns of ceremony of traditions.

The Kachina Ceremonial Gardens

The gardens are sacred reflections. They reflect Life As Living Ceremony. They reflect back to us that which is simple, flowing, organic, and natural. They reflect life beyond humanity's dream of duality and drama. They reflect the every present moment that we call Life.

These Kachina sculptures and gardens are a call. They are a call inward. To the Oneness. The Stillness. The Direct Knowing.

These Kachina sculptures and gardens are a living prayer. They speak with no words. They reveal the Formless as form.

These sculptures are an ever present invitation. They invite us each to that sacred enactment that is ours. They invite us to our perfect expression. They invite us to remember that we are all stars on this stage called life. They invite us to enact.

Enact our truth. Enact our very self that is the Self.

Thus each of us discovers our life as a Sacred Enactment of Being. And it is holy.

I will make a brief mention of the cactus and other natural symbols in the ceremonial kachina gardens, for the sculptures were a big part of my life for close to a decade.

Once the gardens were being created, I turned much of my dining room into a cactus garden, with many types of cactus. I choose very small ones, so they would fit easily into the small gardens. I even learned to mix cactus soil.

During daily walks in nature, I began to gather natural objects. Feathers, stones, bones, sticks, dried plants. These beautiful natural objects, as well as candles, found their way into the gardens.

Reflected in these gardens was natural life as a living ceremony...a life close to plant, animal, and mineral kingdoms and also close to the sky, sun, and even the starry nights. A life that is one with the very Web of Life.

Included in each garden was one or two handmade kachina figures, either standing or sitting in awareness of Infinity or dancing as the One with all. Idealed here is The Garden. The original garden.

Creating these figures and the gardens was an exhalted experience. It is a distilling and refining of one's life. Joy arises.

It is as child's play, where the symbolism transcends that which is mental. In an instant, one is a part of a transcendent landscape. This mirror, in art form, may serve as a door to higher consciousness.

This mirror reveals the marriage of earth and sky. A holy wedding of Mother Earth and Father Sky. Undivided HE and SHE.

It is a meditation of the Eternal. The single Principle is felt.

Soul Glyphs as Sculpture

These small kachina sculptures, I call Altar Art. I gave them that name partly because they are small and delicate and are the perfect size for a small home altar. The main reason that I called them Altar Art was because they were art form, rather than words, that were pointing directly to the experience of the sacred in each of us.

I have spoken in other books about how I turned the pregnancy and birth of my second daughter into a nine-month ceremony that resulted in a conscious, painless forty-five-minute home birth. That birth and the ephemeral Soul Sounds that came through me at that time were the catalysts for Soul Sounds and Movements that continued to come to me. They simply were there and arose spontaneously. I did not see others doing them, so I kept it all to myself for a long time.

I discovered that while allowing myself to do these movements and sounds that I felt joy arising and I felt free. I often had very deep insights. And I often had solutions to challenges arise, as well. I could see that beliefs about "how to be in society" were melting away. The beliefs were no long my masters. I could feel that the love in my heart was beginning to lead the way.

Sounds and Signings of the Soul. This is what I called these arising sounds and movements. I allow the Sounds and Signings of the Soul daily, not really as a discipline or a practice, but rather from an arising inspiration. They help me feel centered and aligned with the Presence of the Divine.

I began doing one-half-day workshops called Sounds and Signings of the Soul. The ones present could do any of the following: Sounds, Silence, Signings, Stillness. Each person is invited to align with the Infinite and feel which of these arise and to allow. There is no checking to see what one is being "told" to do. There is no right or wrong. One begins to learn via feeling and knowing. It is a powerful way to come into clear intuition and/or direct knowing. Ones are amazed at the clarity that may emerge.

There is a powerful connection between the Sounds and Signings of the Soul and the ceremonial kachina sculpture.

As these movements and sounds run through me as an illumined river, I find certain body positions that feel deeply moving. I find that these positions are different for other people.

So when a powerful position of my body is experienced, I can just stop moving and hold the position. I can feel the energy pour through. I call these positions of the body, Soul Glyphs. (It is much like the birth experience I mentioned above, because my inner being positions my body like a cosmic runway for an easy birth...another version of a soul glyph.)

The positioning of the body is a configuration of the body. The person holding that configuration can feel the inner Presence and often there is awareness of qualities of the divine coming through powerfully.

The position of the body may have an inner purpose or meaning for the person with that particular alignment. It often is an experience that is not easy to put into words. It is an experience prior to words. It is an experience of that which is Invisible. The Unmanifest.

These positions of the body are sacred postures, holy gestures. Soul glyphs. So the body actually becomes a "pictograph" of sorts allowing the holy current to increase. That current of light is a carrier of unconditioned love, higher intelligence, and the very substance of the abundant creation. The position creates the experience of a heightened current. That current allows one to feel on a cellular level the reverence of life.

Many of those experienced soul movements and positions began to find their way into the ceremonial sculpture.

The kachina sculptures represent the Timeless. They are like frozen movements in time. They are the ancient Temple Dancing brought into sculpture form. They are signaling the Infinite...in form. Formless As form. The sculpture reflects our True Nature as Pure Awareness.

The sculpture is infused with soul, that it might emanate. That it might be a carrier of the Essence world. The sculpture may reveal "outer expression of Inner Essence."

Artists may unveil that Essence, that Emptiness, that Stillness that has no end. Through art forms, that Essence which seems so hidden may be unveiled to emanate and become the known.

It is noted that on many images in this book, the faces include an open mouth. This represents the Soul Sounding. Another way to describe

Soul Sounding would be to say, singing sounds of the soul that come forth from the heart. It is singing songs of the soul and voicing sounds that feel connected to the very Christ.

And it is noted, as well, that other than a mouth, that the sculptures are faceless. They represent...Everywoman and Everyman. They are Universal.

Sounds and Signings of the Soul may be catalysts. They may be used as a way to move us beyond the belief in and sense of separation that bring fear and all of its offspring. The Sounds and Signings of the Soul issue forth from the heart and from the Soul. All else does begin to fall away.

The sculpture in this body of work is a visual meditation...a prayer in form. It invites living from this level of higher Consciousness.

The sculpture is a reminder that we are to attune to this primal force, the Energy of the Infinite, and allow our own perfect and True Life to come forth.

Then...it is...that we experience the Unity, the Oneness, as Star-Stone Ones.

Then...it is...that we have leaped from reading about it to claiming it. To living it.

The formless as form. One. Essence As Life. The Unmanifest as manifest as our very life.

Gift of Ceremony

I awake in the night. I see three words, illumined, starting near the ceiling. The letters are all vertical. My mind is empty. I witness. I acknowledge. I open to know.

These three words, Gift of Ceremony, came as an unexpected vision in the night decades ago. It had an immense effect on me. I wanted to understand its import in my life. And because I know that the personal life and the Impersonal Life is the One Life, I wanted to know the import in our lives.

I came to realize that Gift of Ceremony is something we all carry. It is beyond prescribed ritual and ceremony. It is free, moving, fresh. Spontaneous. It is the light moving through all of life. It is that Life. It is the current of the universe. And Gift of Ceremony is our innate and unconditioned response to this Life. True Life. It ever abides. It ever awaits our notice.

It is the Energy of Infinity. Raw, primal, primordial. Virgin. It is the I Am Awareness with no interferences. No distortions. It knows no duality. Sense of separation from it is not real.

This Energy of Source awaits. It awaits our opening. It awaits our allowing.

Because we are unique souls with individual expressions of the Infinite Love, we always may allow the great mystery to reveal itself in the present moment.

This sacred ceremony is Life lived in higher Consciousness. Higher frequency.

For me, it was borne of inner odysseys into the "once upon a non-time." This sacred Timeless Realm of Now is ever here.

We may sit on the edge of paradox and share the unity of Invisible AS visible and formless come as form. The Unmanifest...manifest.

When Life is thus realized as "the mystical (union with God) AS the practical," one is living Life As Living Ceremony. It is then that Gift of Ceremony is understood. Each moment is seen as exalted.

With each of us, Gift of Ceremony will present in its own way. The joy of our unique expressions will grow and is growing around the globe. Appreciation is uplifting lives everywhere.

One of the ways that Gift of Ceremony arrived in my life was/is as sculpture. Each piece is infused with soul Essence. Each piece is offered to viewers to interpret and/or experience according to one's own experiences and Consciousness. Each piece is allowed to have its own sacred voice and reflect and mirror what one is experiencing and/or what one would like to experience.

"Allow one's Self to be danced by the Infinite, for we are that Living Ceremony, here now."

Sacred Enactments of Ancient Remembering

During my deeper glimpses into the Oneness, the Unity, the Infinity that Already IS, I began to access from more depth for the living of my day to day life.

The deepening and expanding times are immense gifts and reveal Essence in new and profound ways. And I soon learned that I had to learn how to live, on a daily basis, from the higher state of Consciousness. I immediately began to learn more about the beliefs, opinions, and reactions that were ready to jump into action in my life. I immediately learned that I must be vigilant and abide in the deeper place of the heart, regardless of the appearances in the "outer world." I had to discover what things in the world would serve as temptations to me to go into the sense of separation. Duality. I had to dedicate my life to this "inner world" to be able to dissolve these habits of human being.

As we attune deeply, the ongoing moments of Ancient Remembering of Oneness keep us on a sacred path. The Unmanifest as manifest is worthy of contemplation and meditation. Much may be revealed to each of us.

I began to share expressions of these Essence rememberings through many forms. Drawing, painting, sculpting, dancing, sounding, and writing. Calls began to come to me as spiritual educator. So the form of Soul Sessions, retreats, workshops, and consultations ensued, as well.

For eight years I performed Sacred Enactments of Ancient Remembering. They were multi-media, multi-dimensional enactments using narration, soul sounds, soul dance, art showings, and music. Shadow dancing was included as the light engineer set the lighting to include shadows of dancing on the screen. I set out to reveal more of the Essence world I was experiencing.

I realized that we all may be living this remembering of who we are. We all may allow our true nature to shine through and brighten the world of form.

When the inner glimpses and rememberings began to be expressed as sculpture, around 1987-1988, it continued for almost a decade. It is sheer joy of creating freely. Ask any child playing in the primal mud if they are having fun.

In this way sculpting became another way for me to Enact the Eternal.

That is the way before us all.

Insights about Life as Living Illumined Ceremony

After my near death experience in a car collision in 1971, I began to see the light body emanations of living things. Some would call it an aura. Or a quantum field of light.

Once an experience, such as this, is taken in and assimilated, one is shifted forever. One realizes that all is a sacred life as a living and illumined ceremony.

God...dancing as the living light...in and as all forms.... Formless and form...One...without separation...

The actual experience of the near-death experience did unmask me. I unmasked from the belief that I am a human body and mind. Underneath that mask was a light body. A soul body. Joy. And pure awareness.

During the near death encounter, I experienced my life, past, present, and future as One Life. The ceremony of Life. I experienced this all through the eyes of the Soul. Beliefs, opinions, judgments do not even exist in this elevated state of Consciousness. There was nothing to release or dissolve or remove. Nothing.

I saw everything through the eyes of an exalted joy.

For me, a new life began.

No longer was there a demarcation between mundane and super mundane. All was ecstatic. It had no end.

Then comes the realization that we all may open to these holy currents. To the Light of God. Then life as living and illumined ceremony ensues.

*And, yes, on this plane of existence we have challenges, both our own and ones in the world. But they are all seen in a different light. No longer are they formidable blocks. They become that which deepens and strengthens us when we see them as part of the human belief systems. They are not reality.

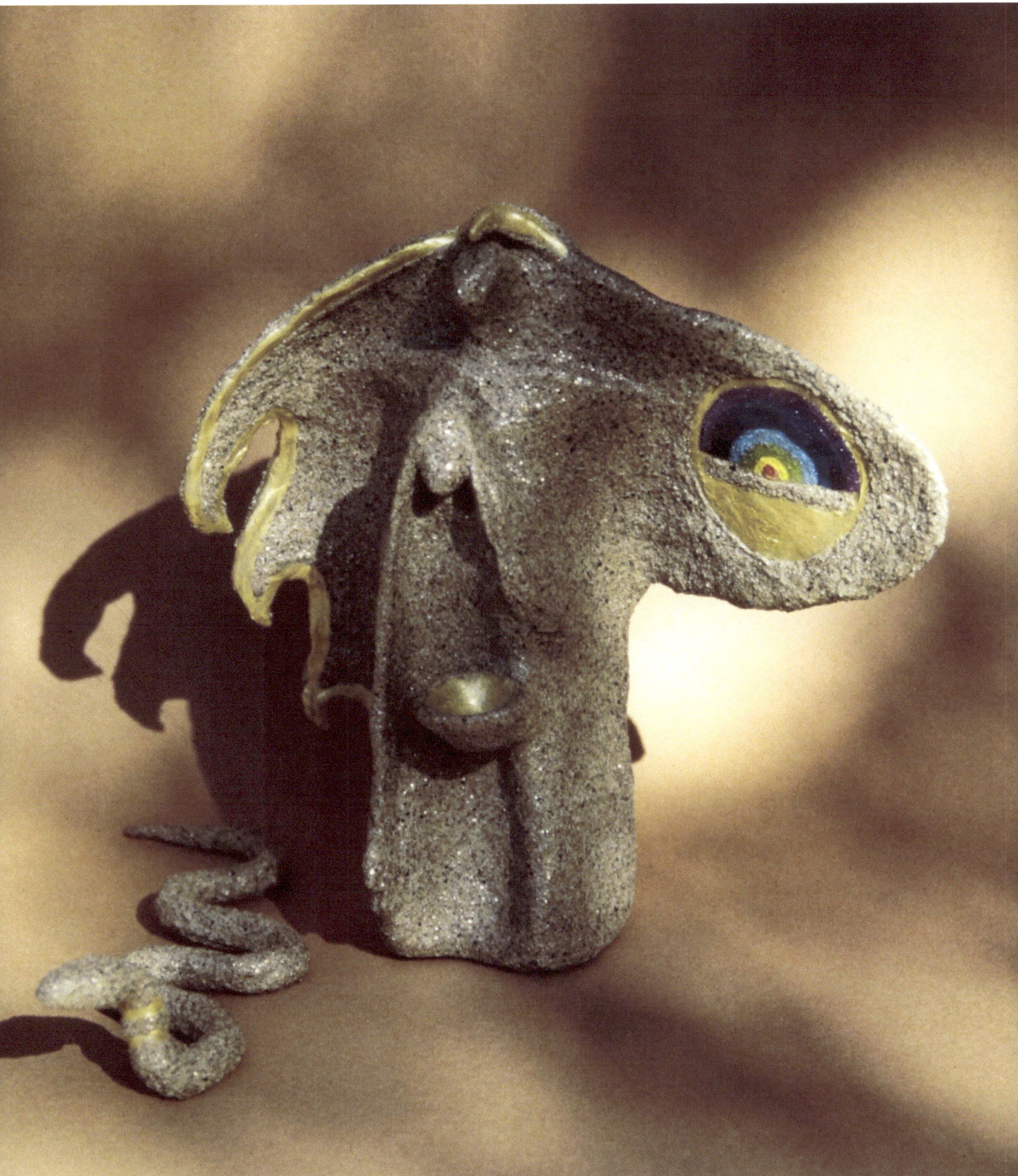

Part 2:

Phases

First Phase:
Robed Figures

The Two...Remembering

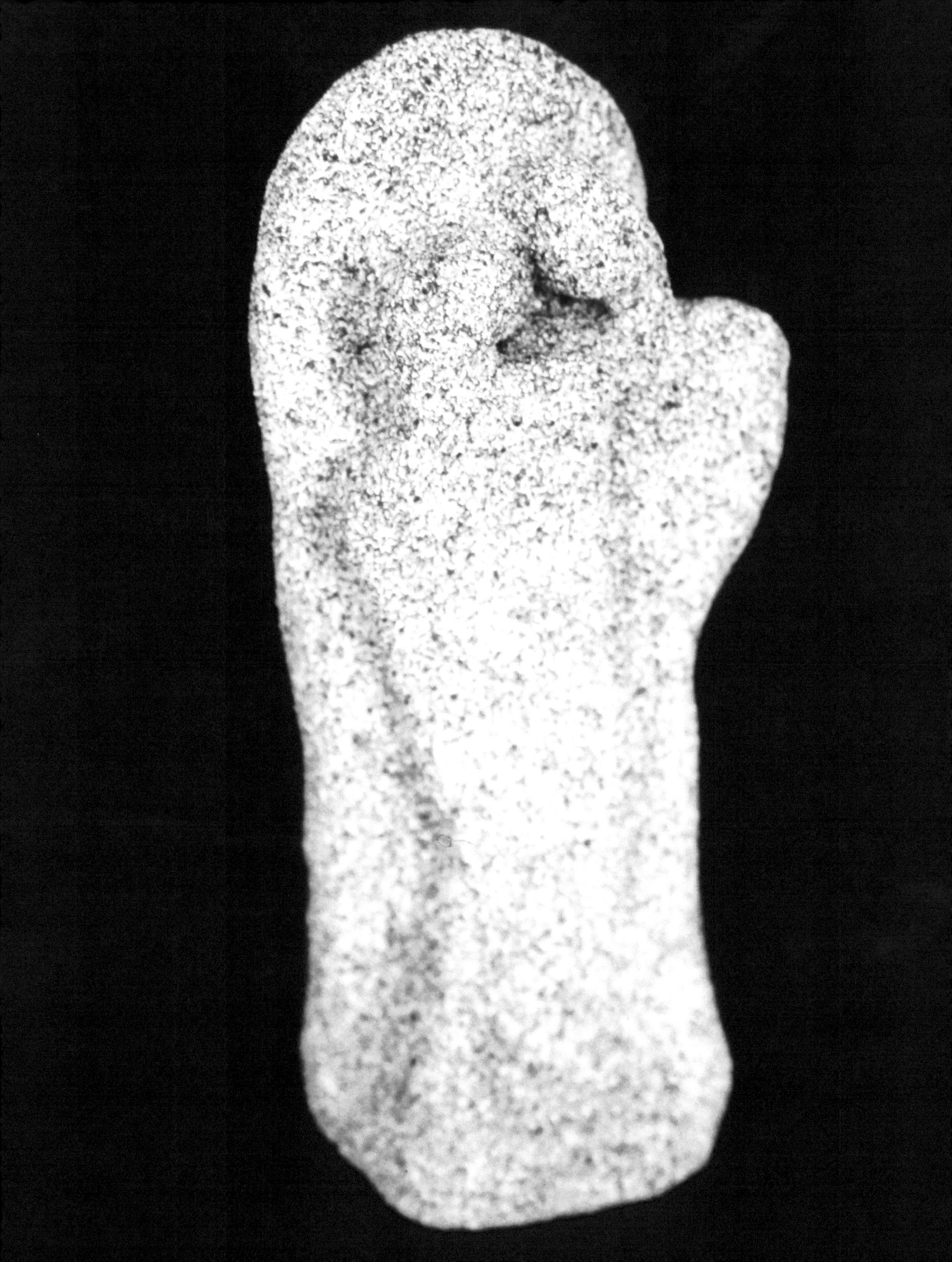

Robed-SHE…bearing the gift

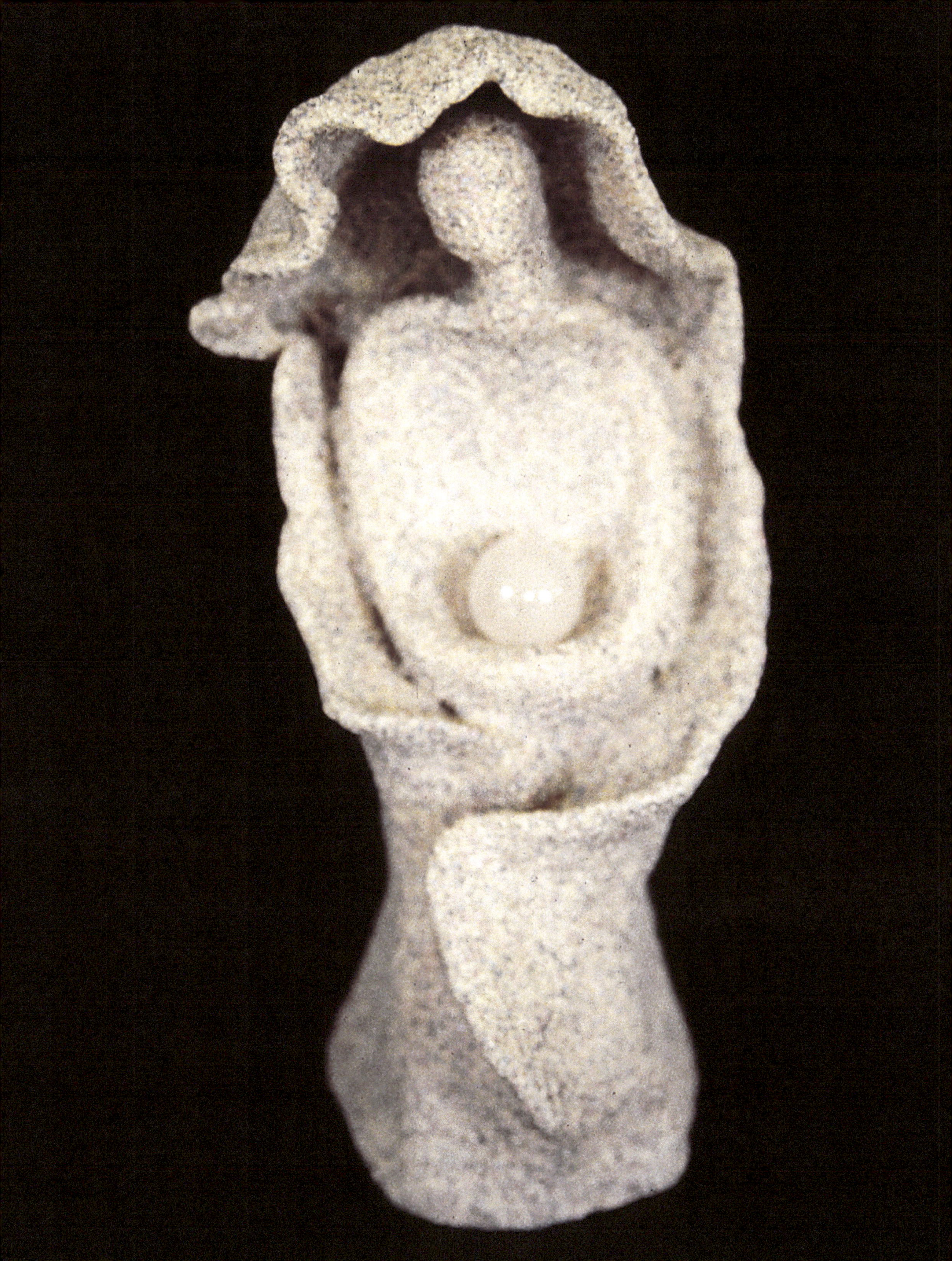

Bonding Ceremony of Light

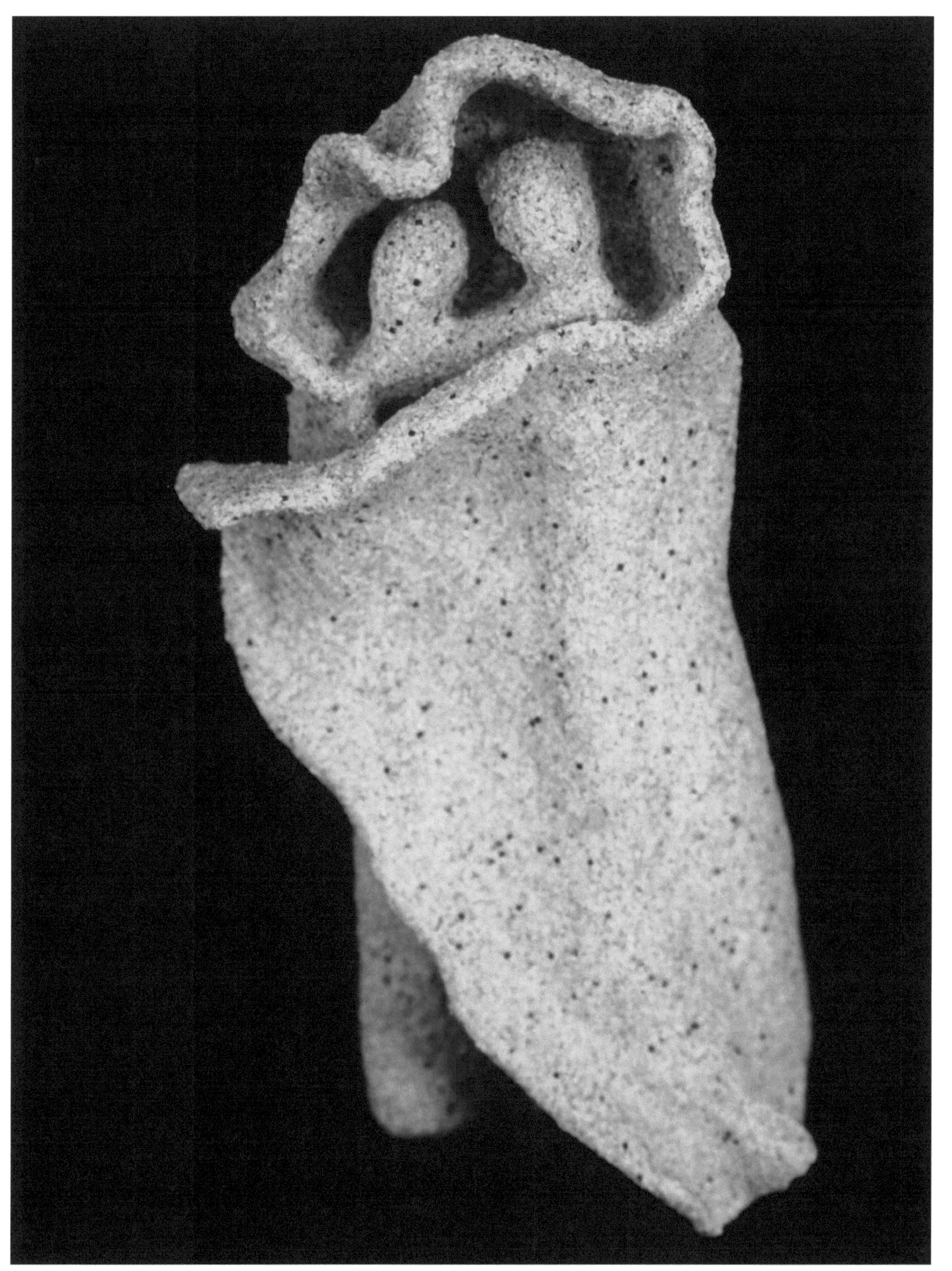

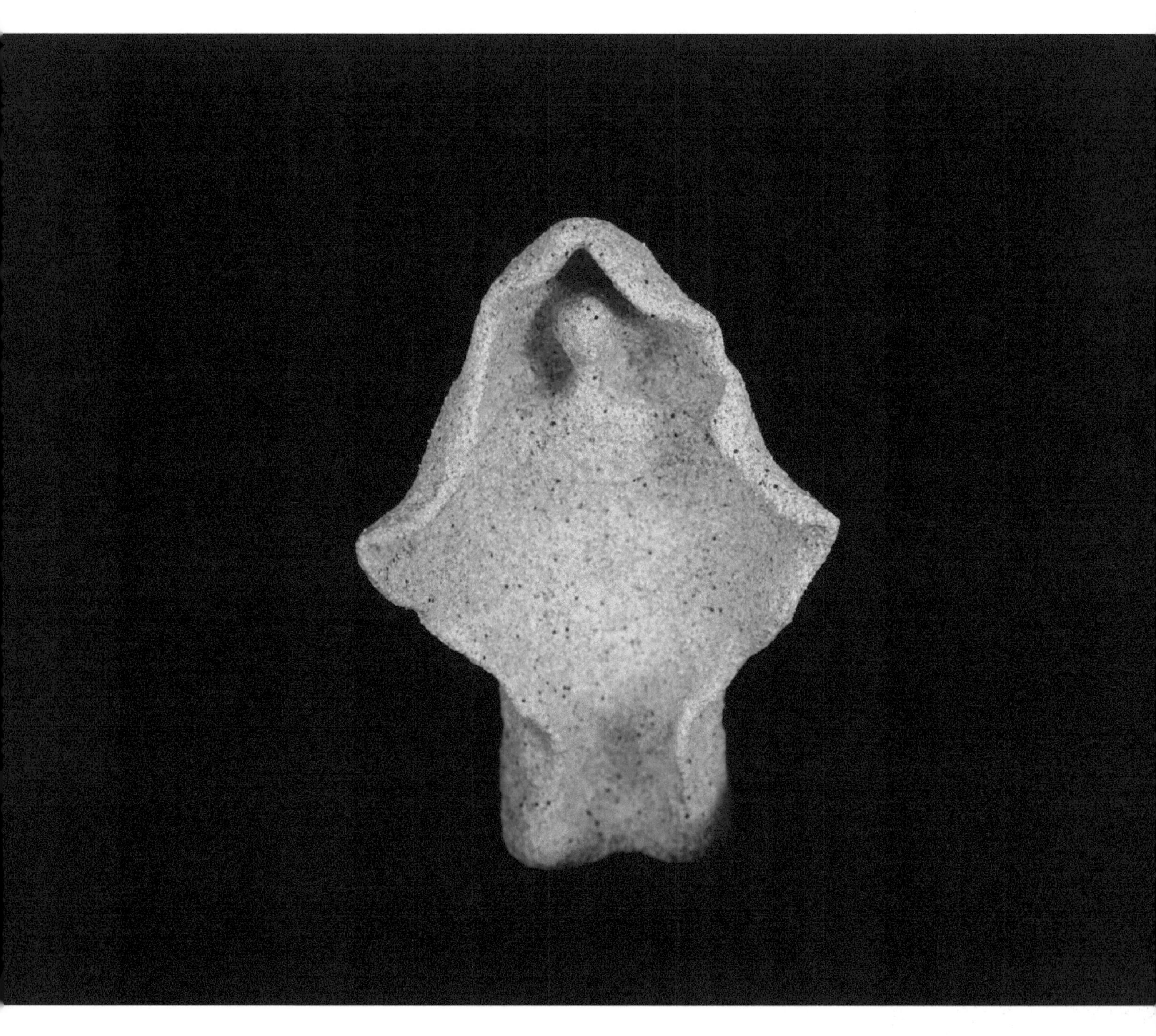

Robed in Light-SHE

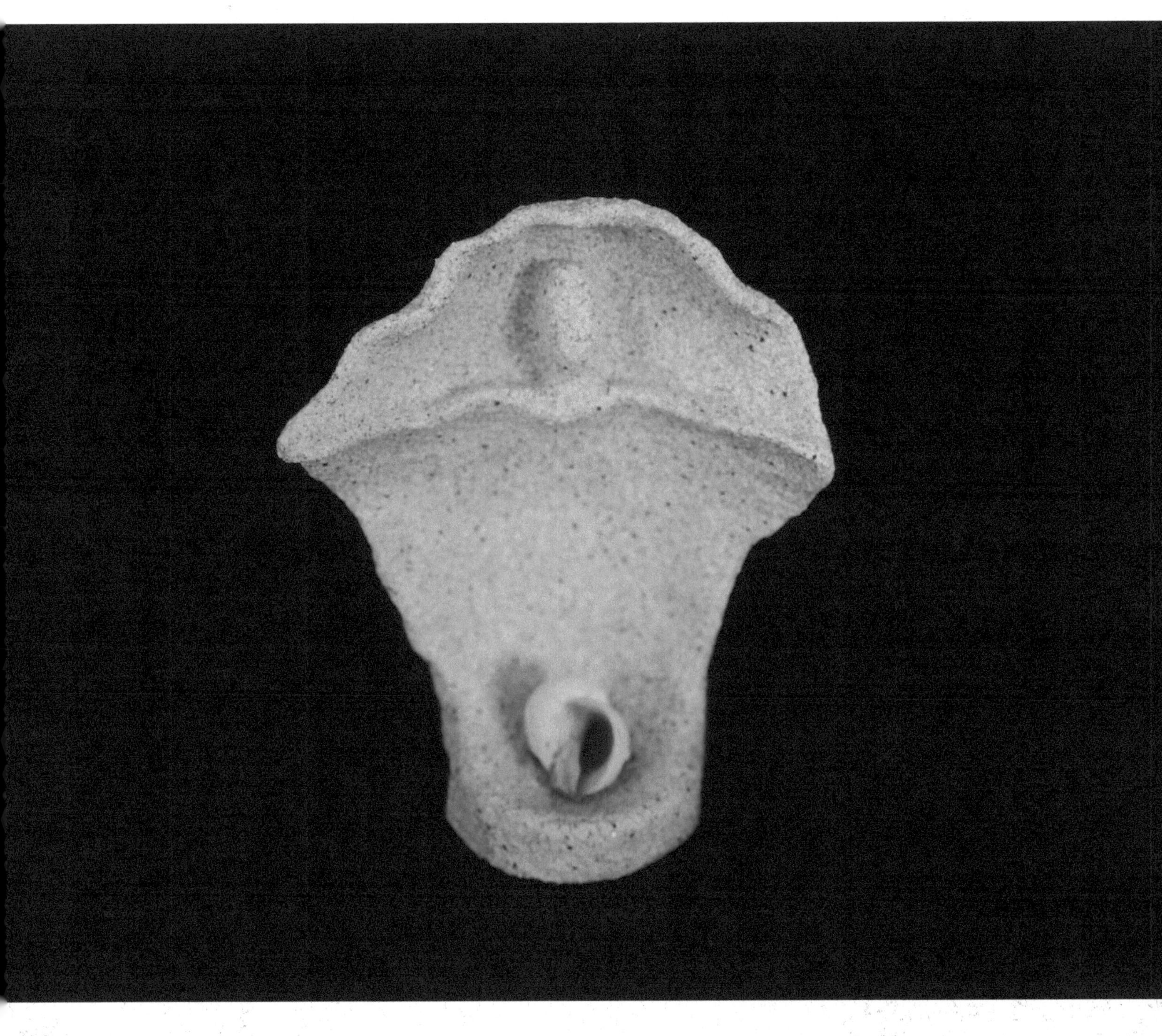

Robed-SHE...with the offering

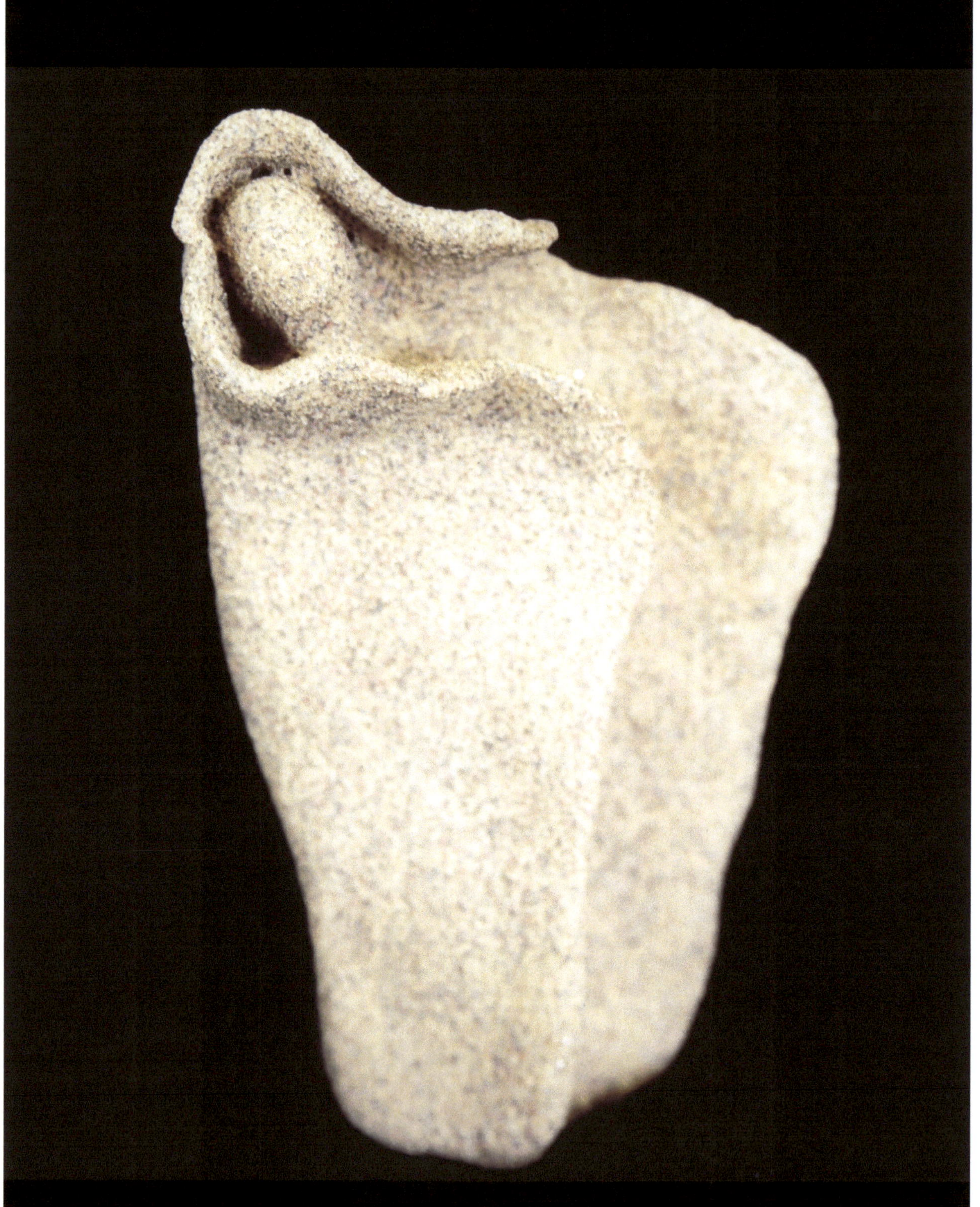

Robed-SHE...of the wind...

The sculptures in this art book are each from very different inspirations. Some came from actual experiences in sacred and spontaneous ceremony. Some from deeply felt experiences in nature. There are ones that came from the experiences of soul movement and gestures. Entire body glyphs would arrive and be felt in my body. Others were inspired by the Infinite, with no ideas or preconceived image.

This particular sculpture was one of the many that was inspired by Spirit that lives as all of Nature.

In the mid eighties into the nineties, I awoke most mornings at pre-dawn and dawn. I went outside standing naked in the morning air. That was part of my inner practice. I was gifting myself with the experience of feeling transparent. I opened to Spirit, to holy presence via the breeze, wind, snow and rain. I stood and made of myself a transparency that I might feel the wind in, around and through my being. The experience is one of exaltation. Sensitivity grows.

There are many wind experience sculptures in the book. In this sculpture, it is absolute simplicity. The figure and the robe revealing the wind through the figure.

Any of these sculptures may be used as a simple meditation. It may be used as a portal into the essence space of the Infinite.

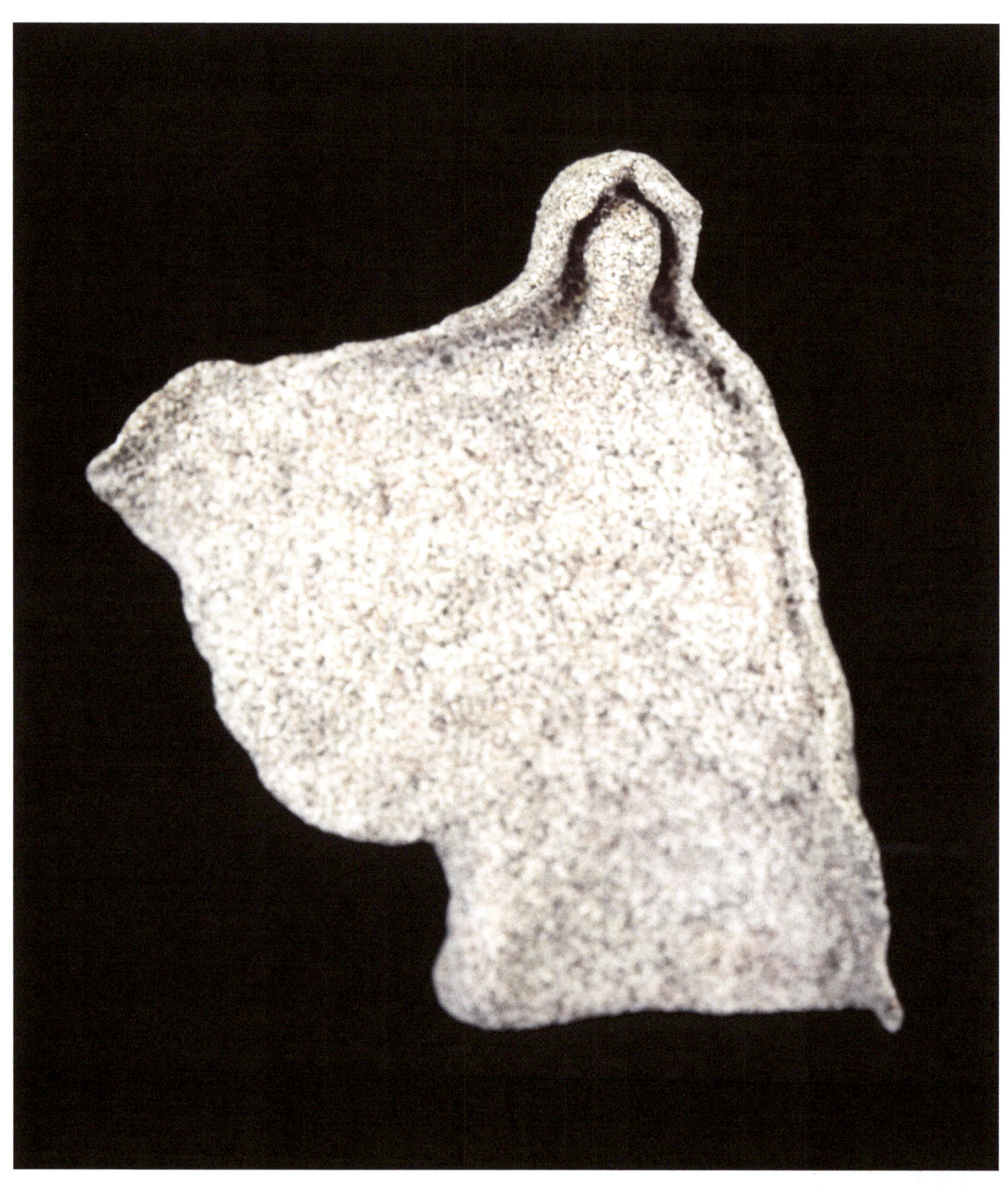

I AM Creation's Dance

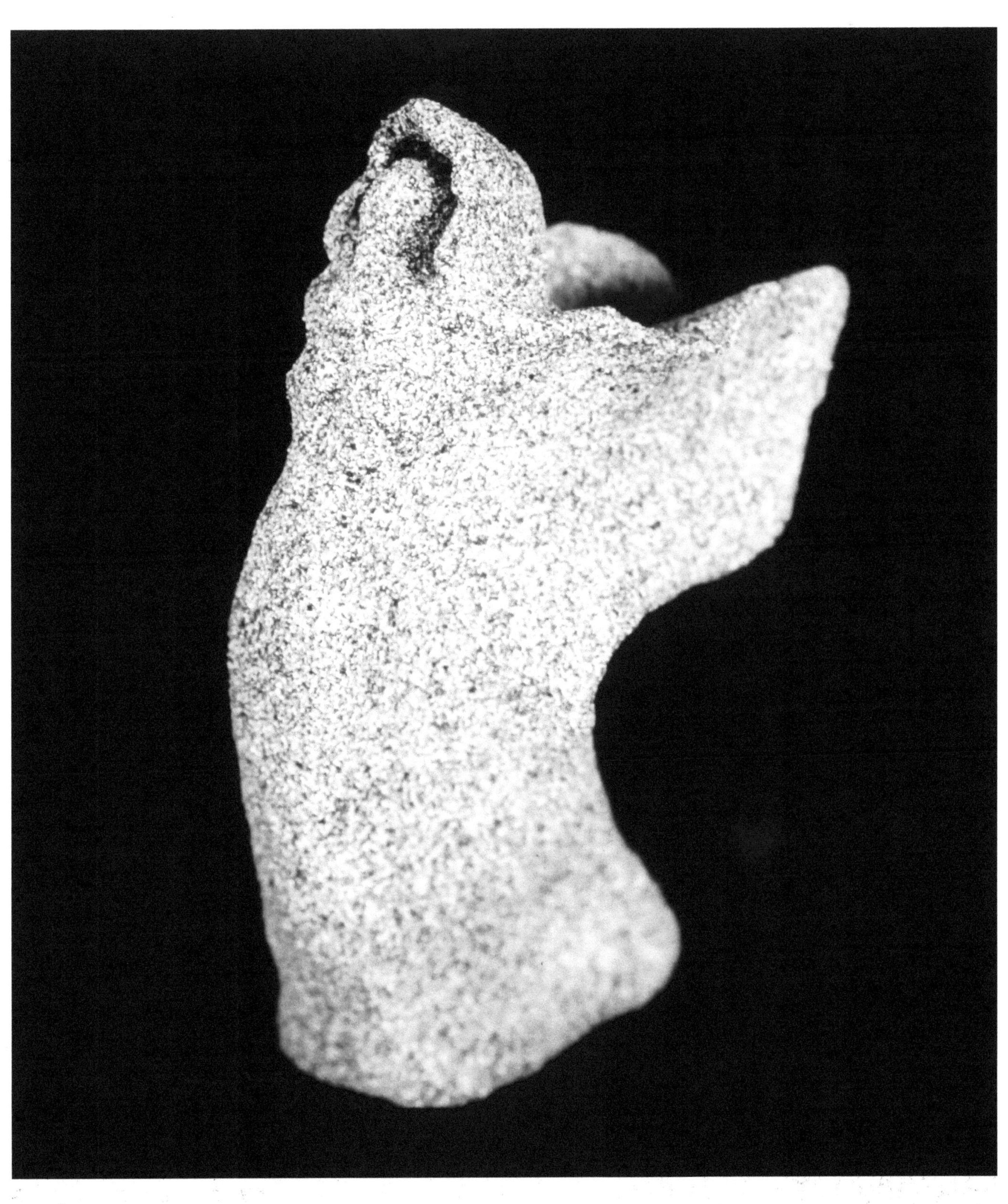

Robed-SHE...of the Winged Ones

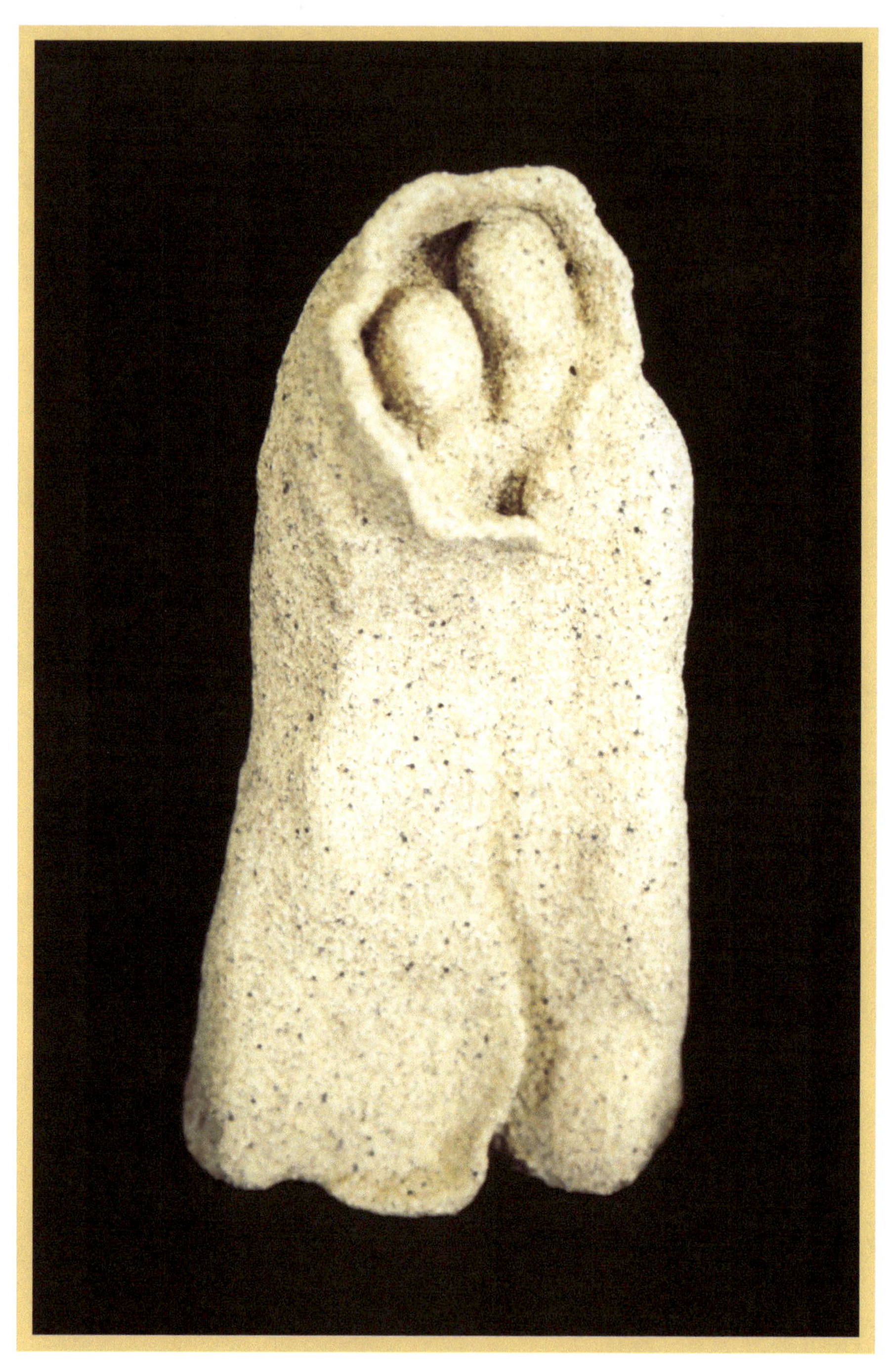

Bonding Ceremony of HE and SHE

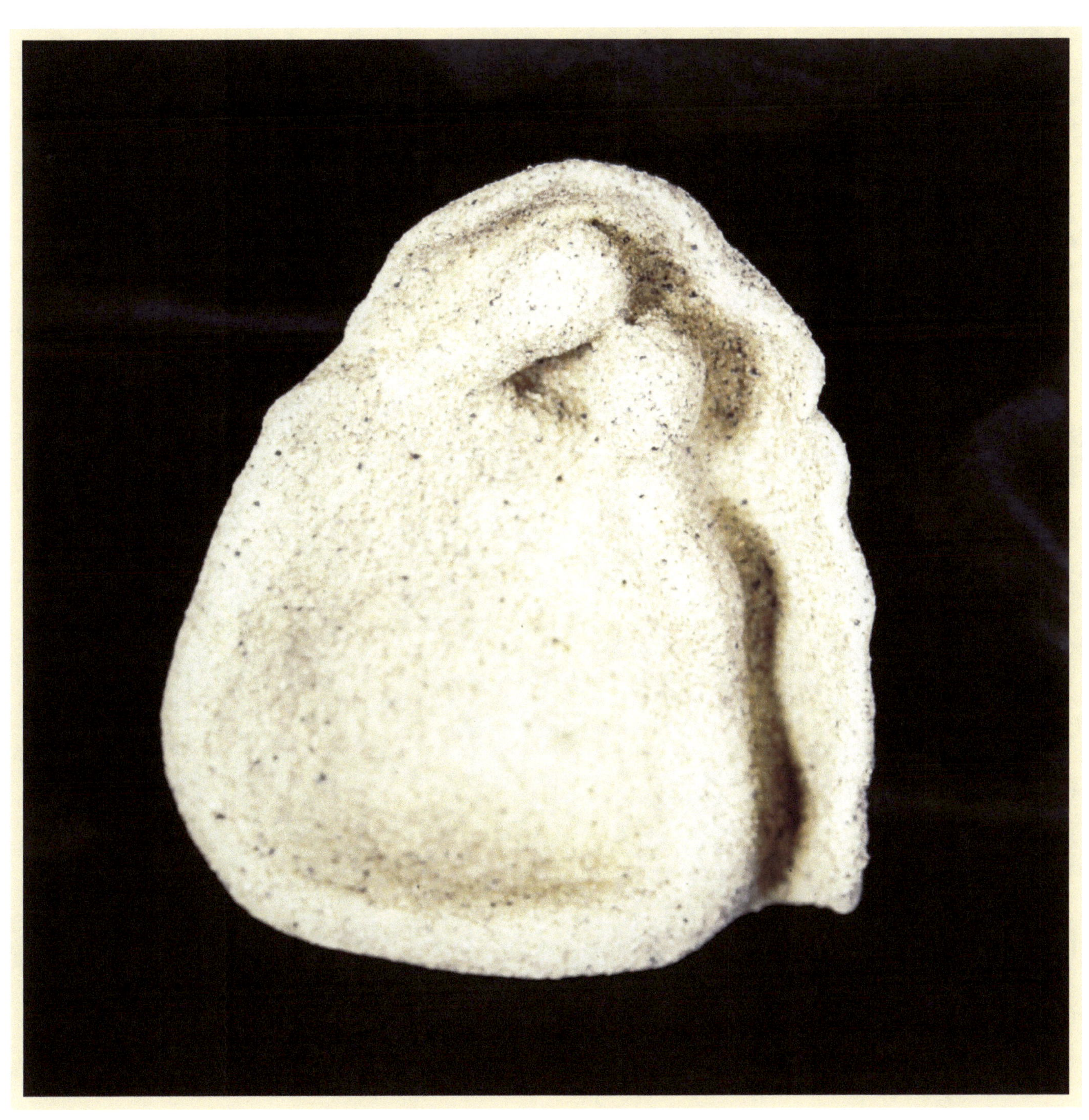

The Robed Union

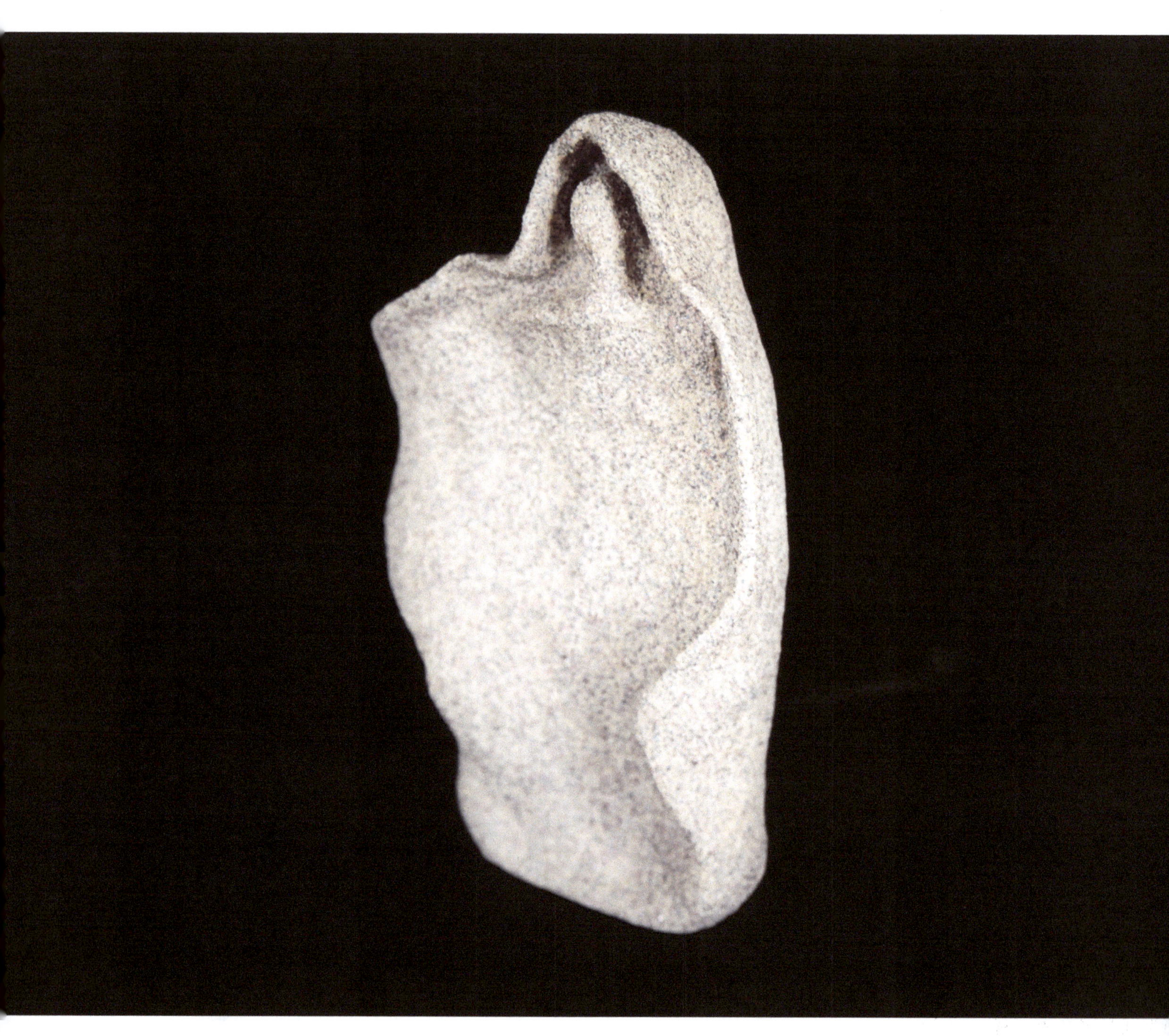

Robed One

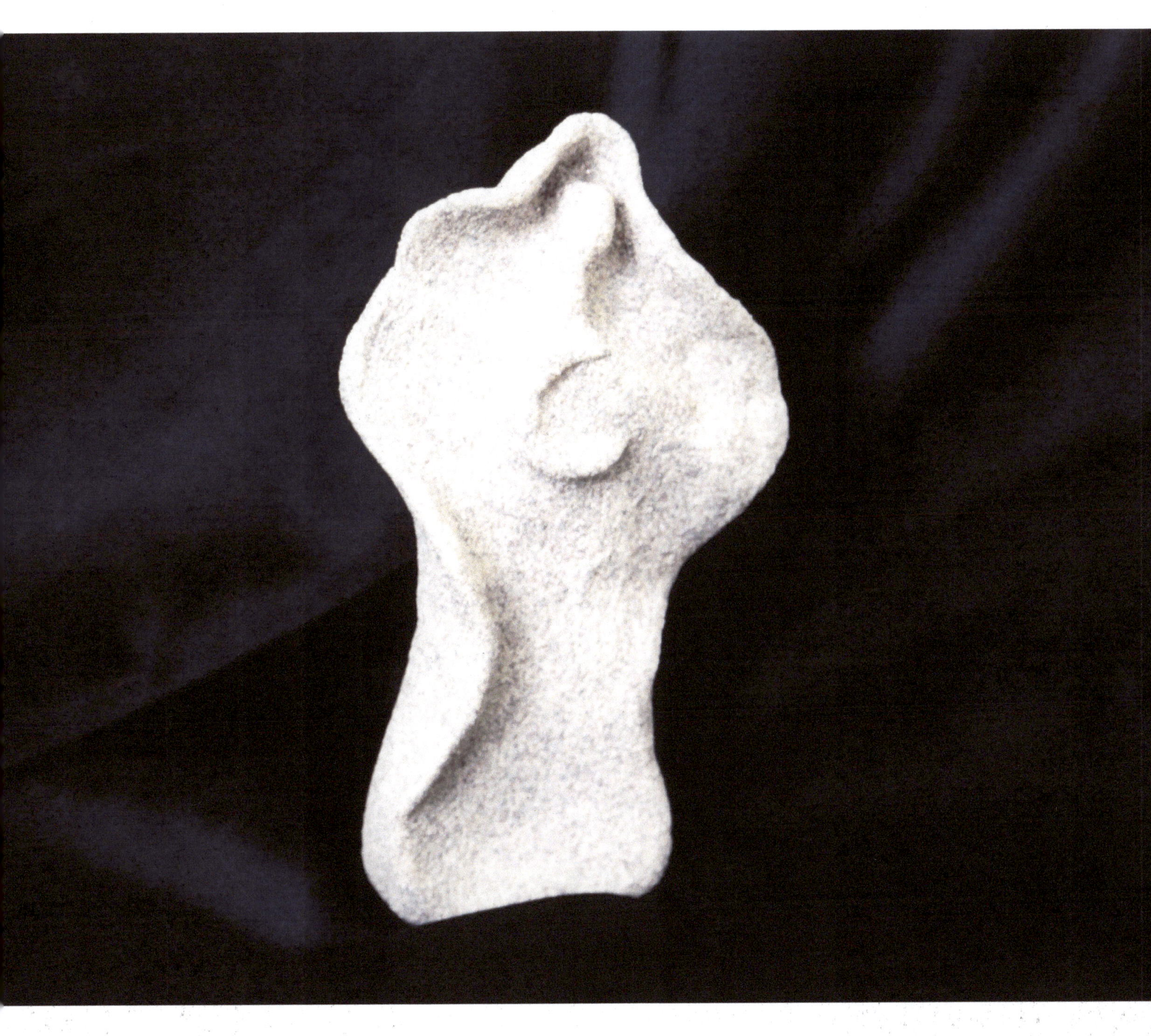

with glad heart...
I am the dancer of the moon...

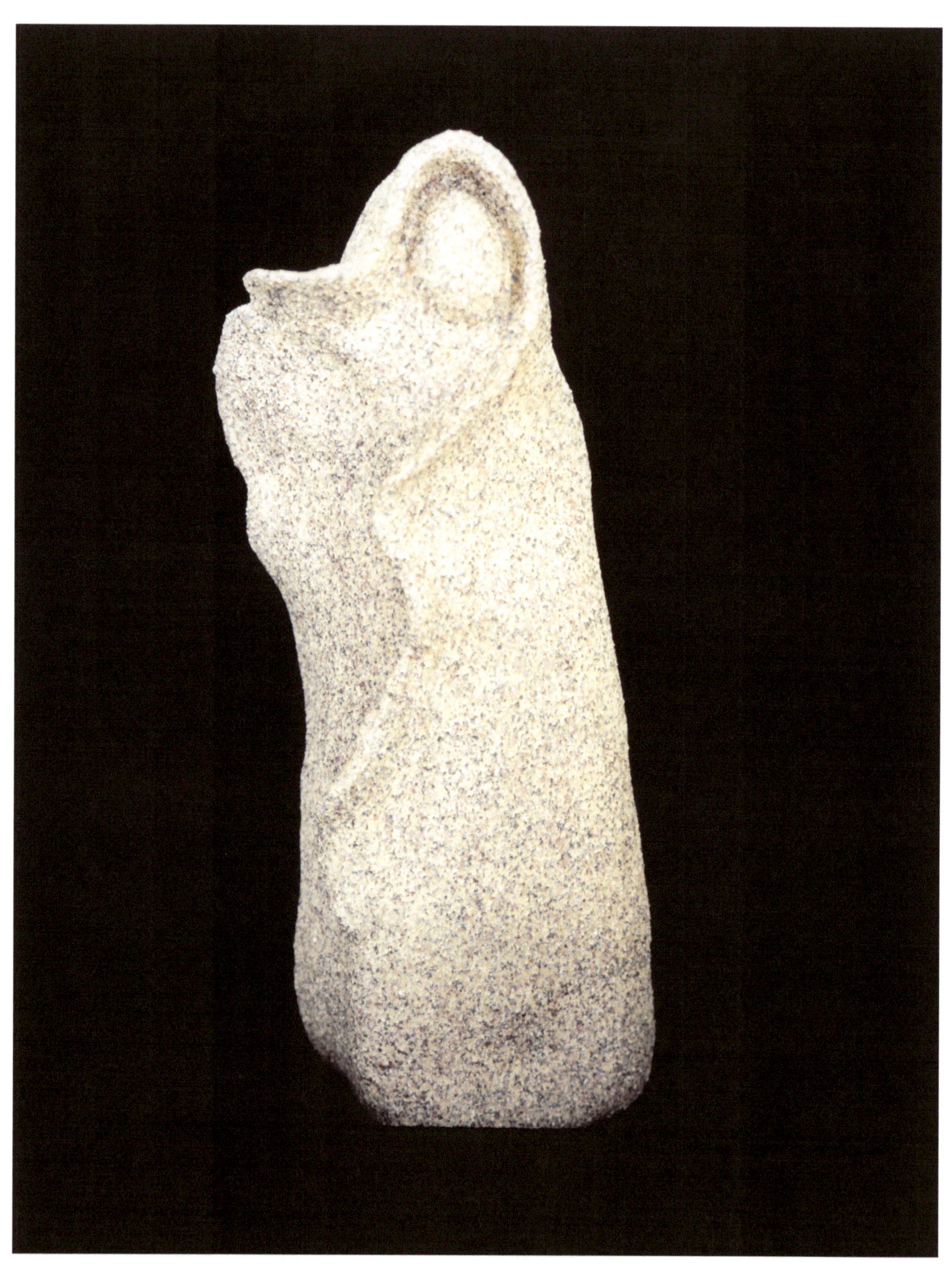

Robed in Light-SHE

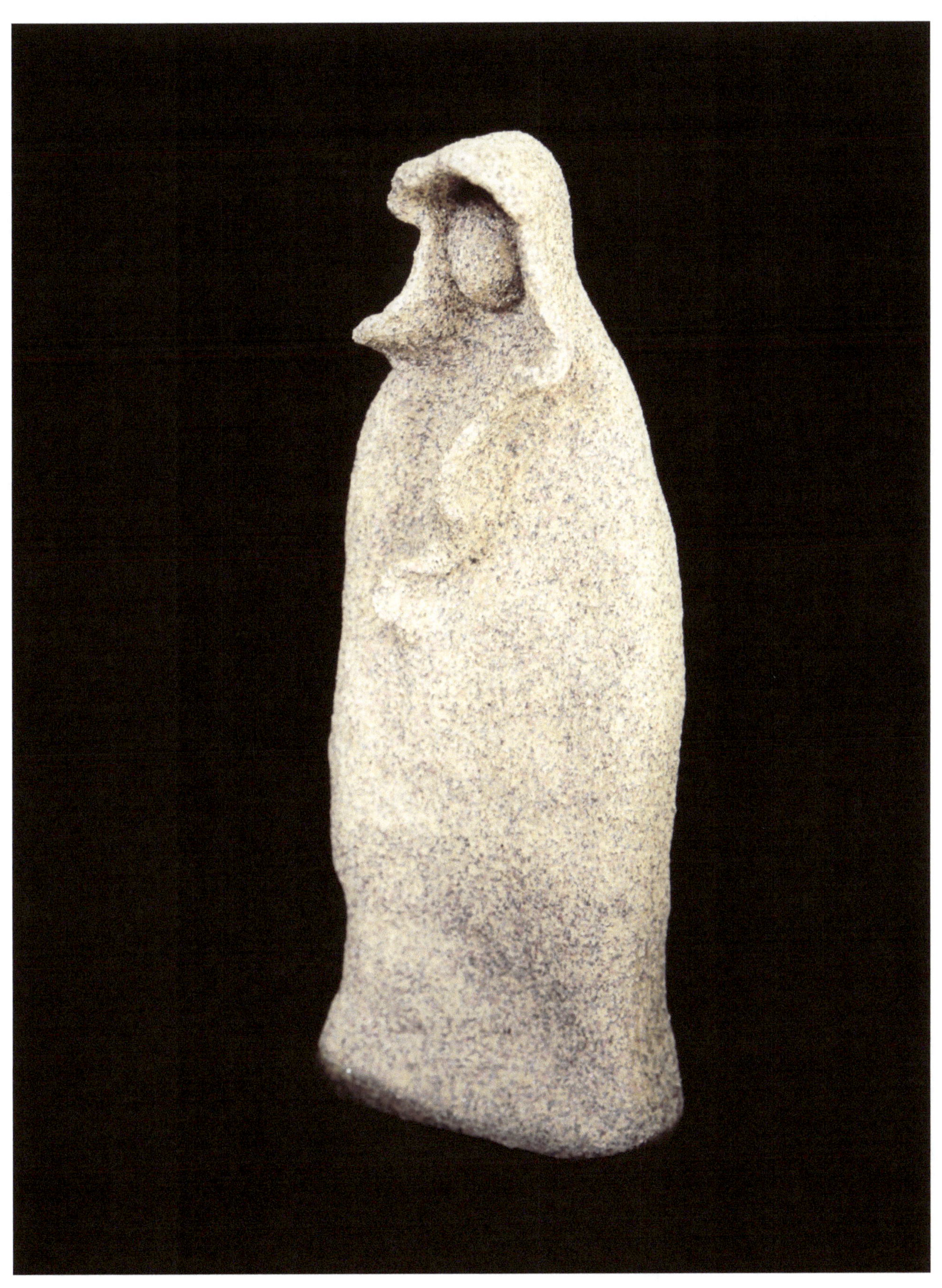

Keeper of the Vision

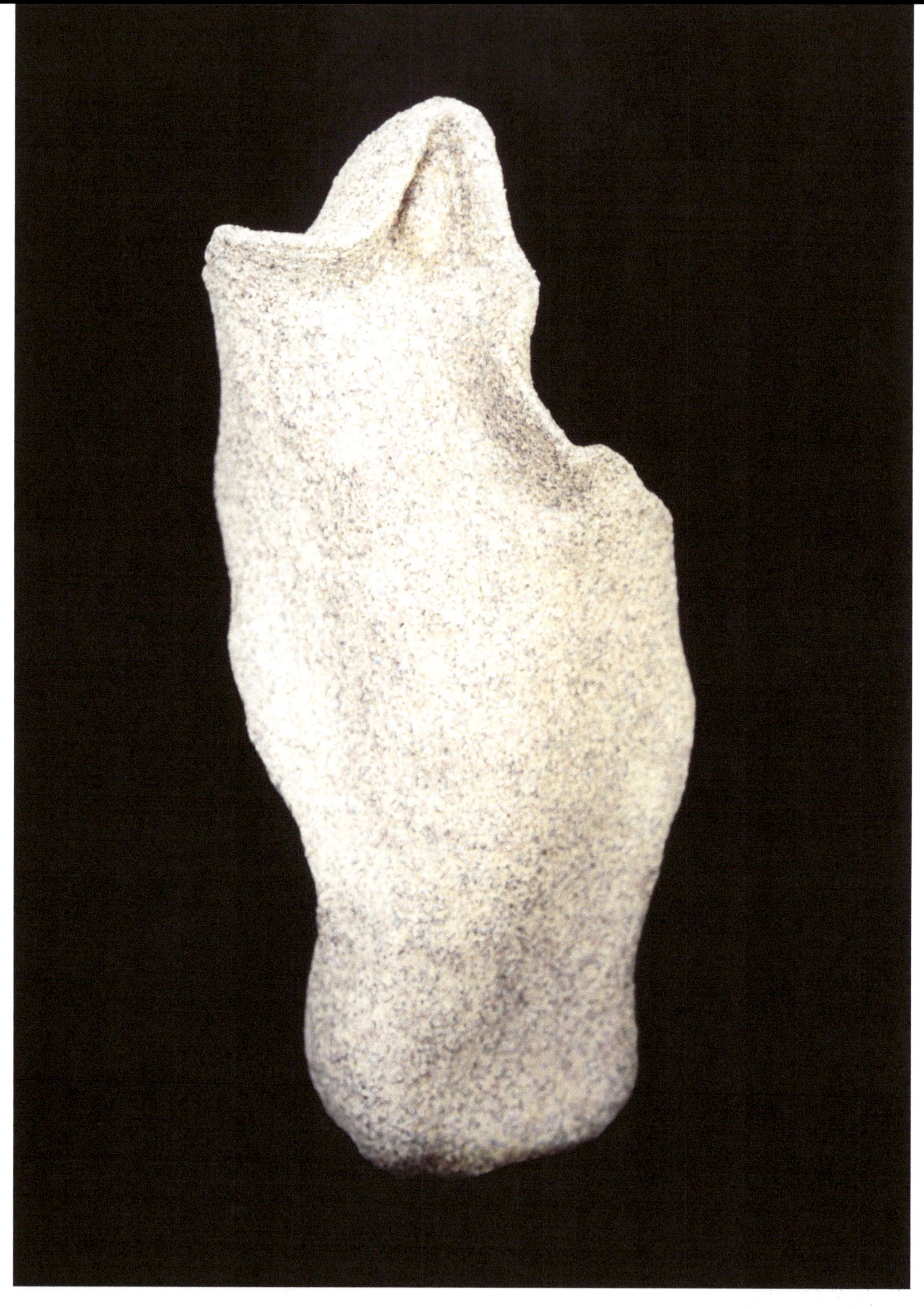

Keeper of the Dance

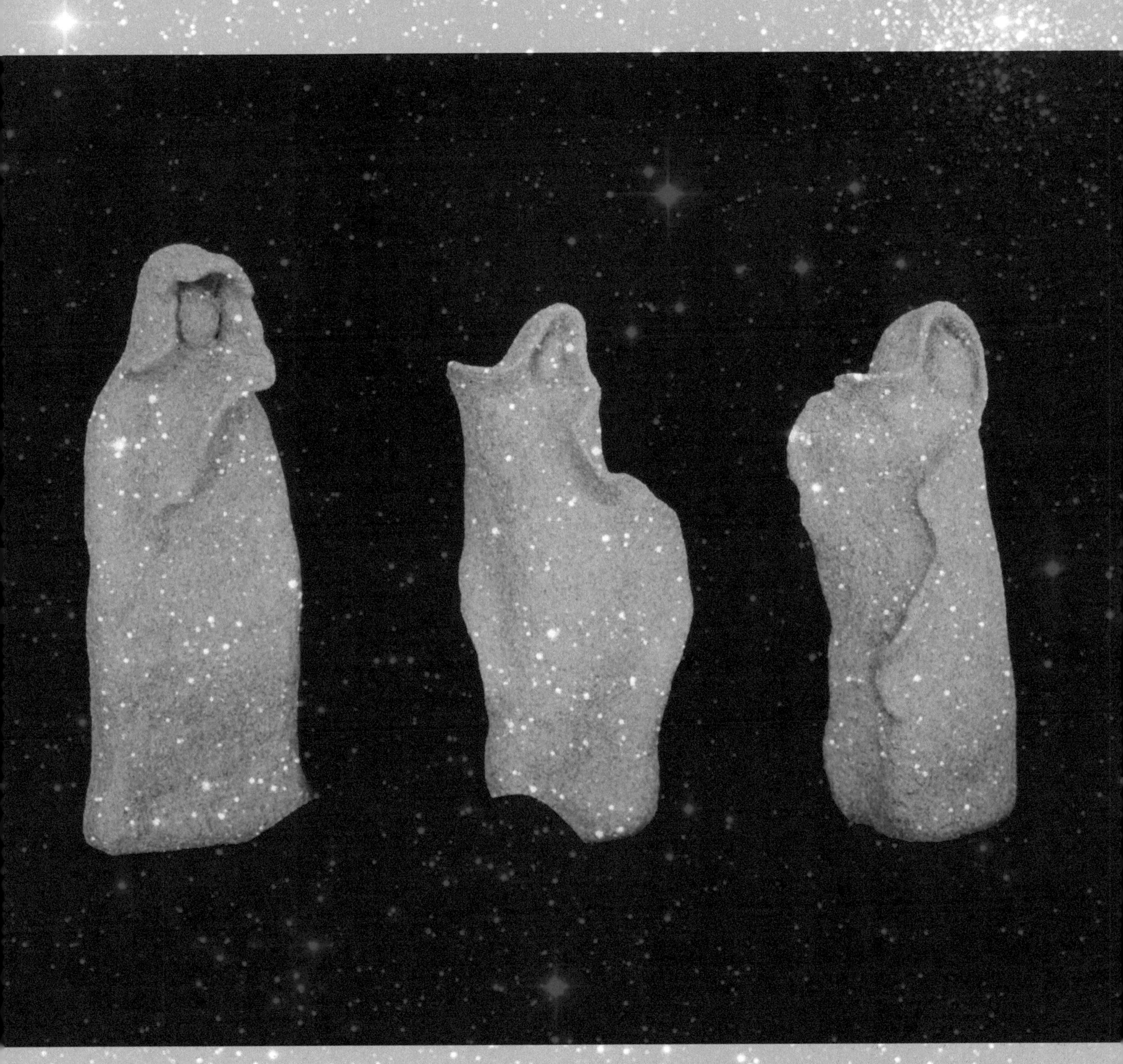

Robed Ones

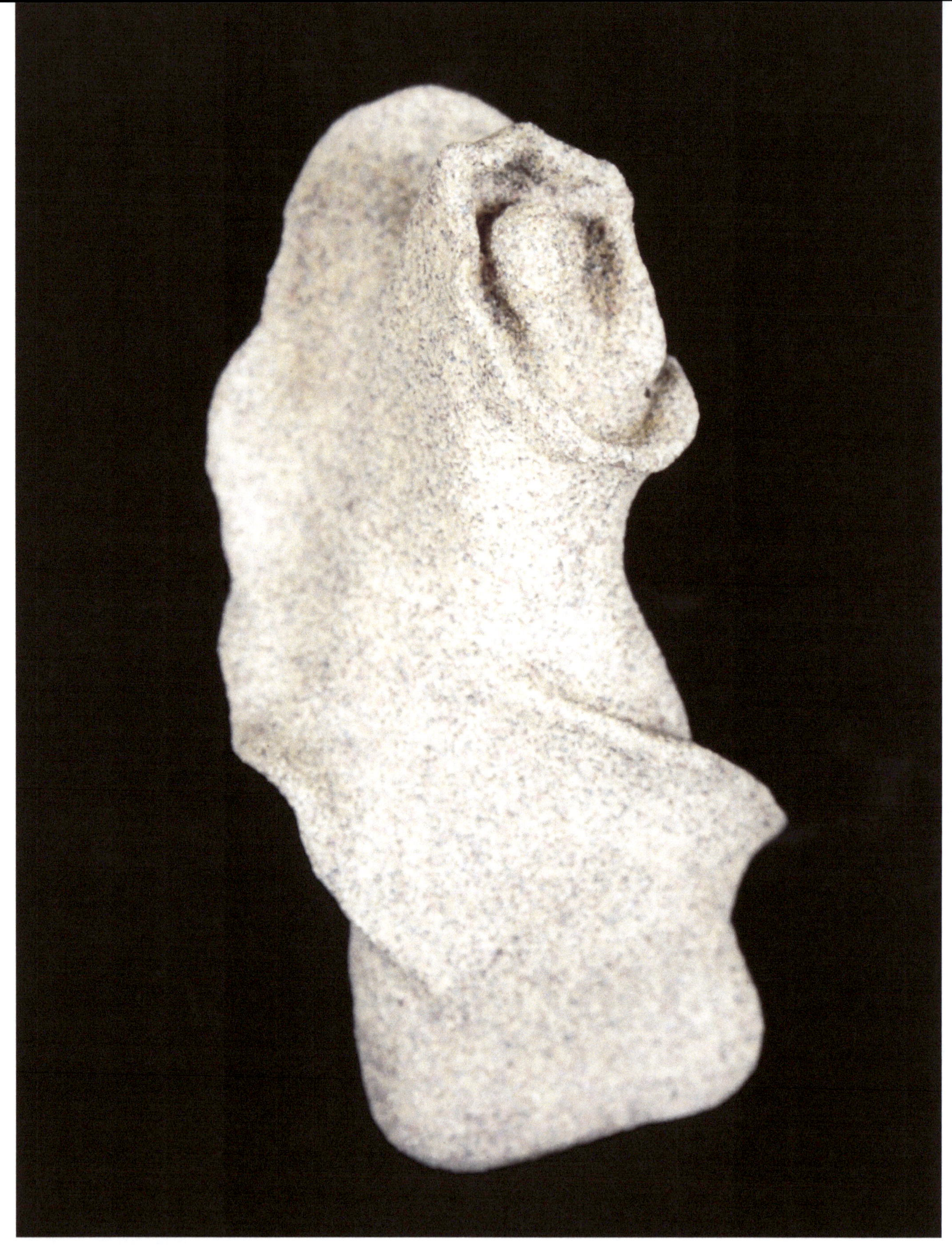

Robed-SHE...with the veils...

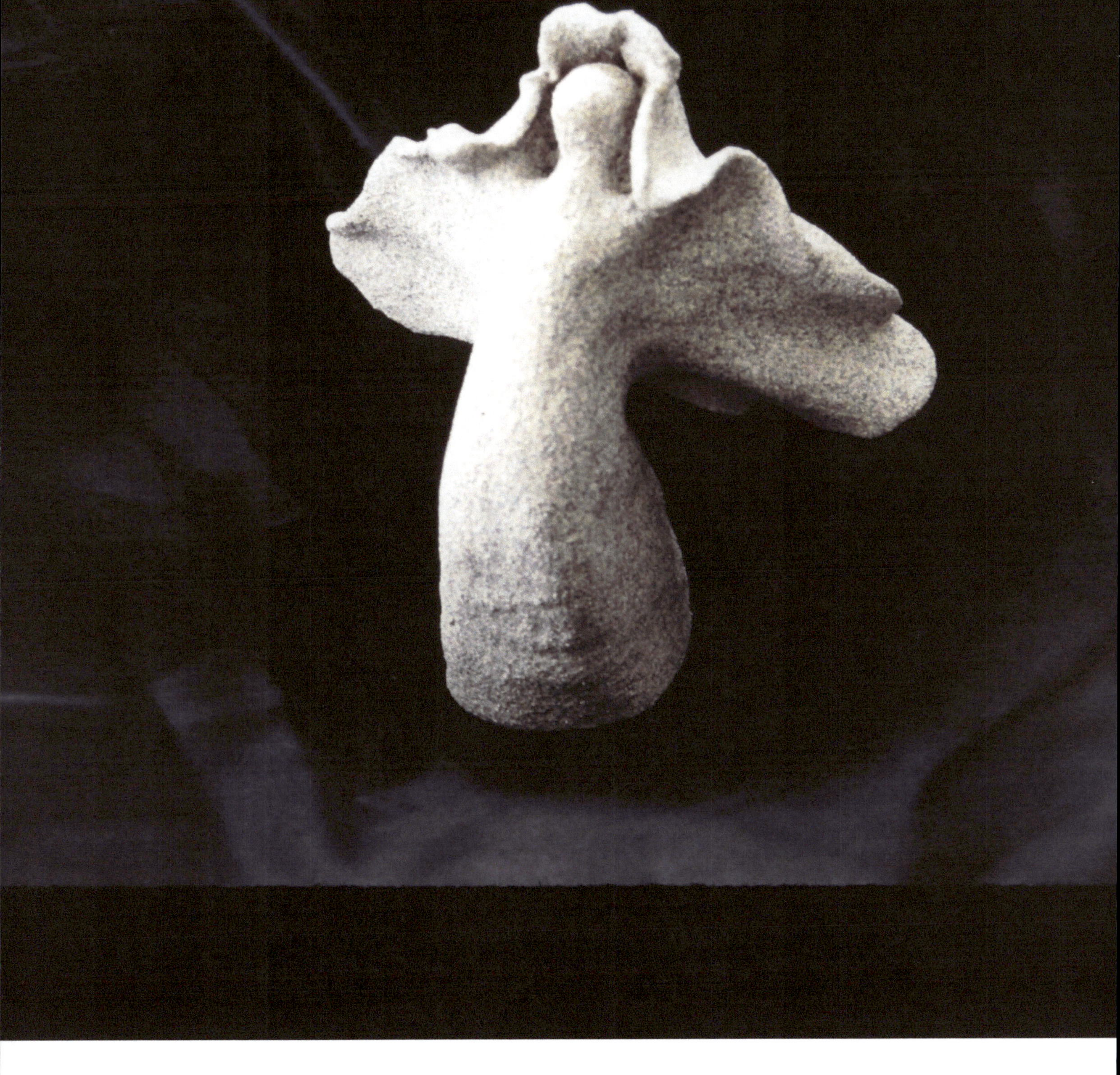

Robed-SHE...in flight

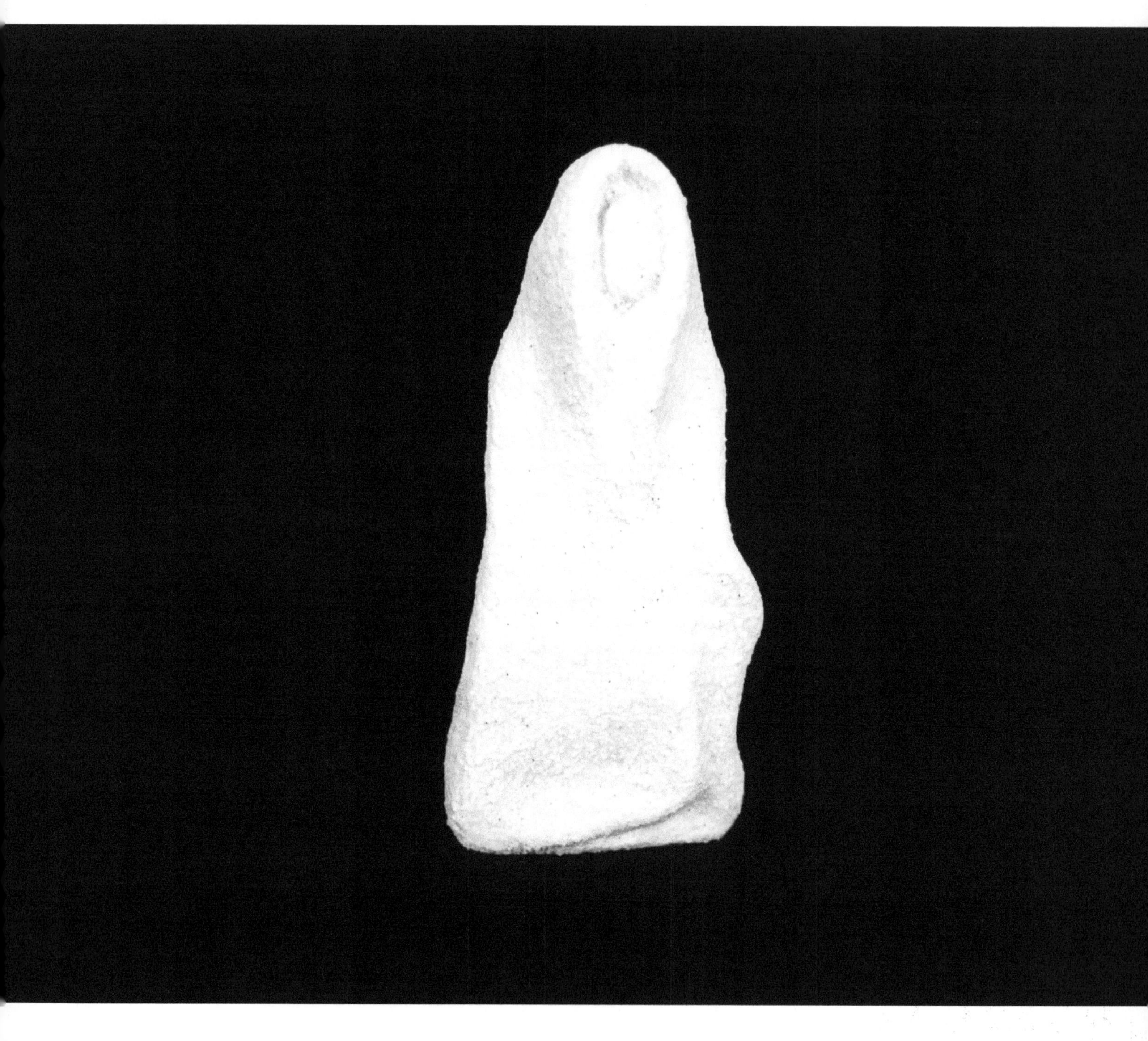

Robed One of the Ancient Sounds

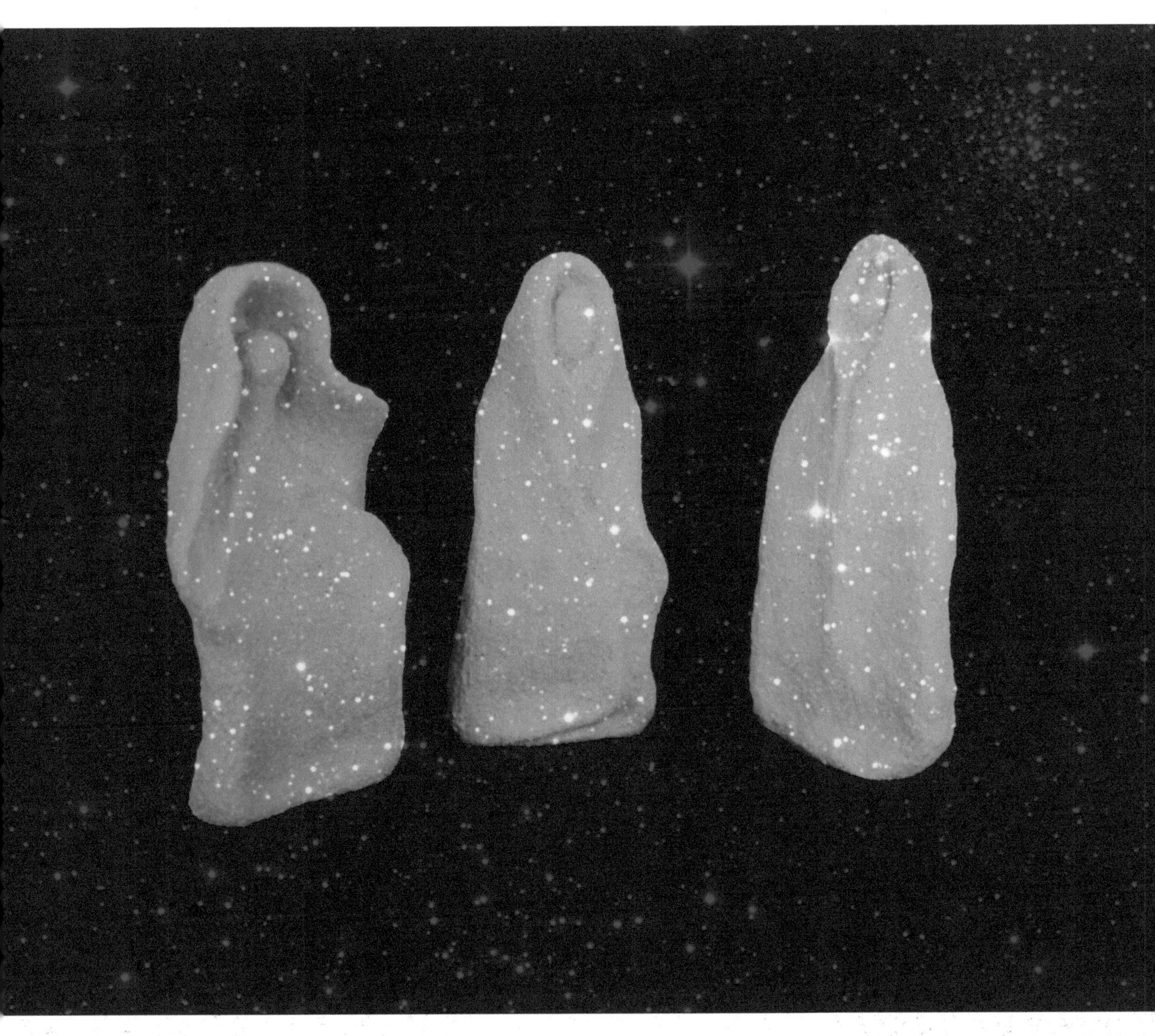

Robed Ones of the Ancient Sounds

Robed Ceremony

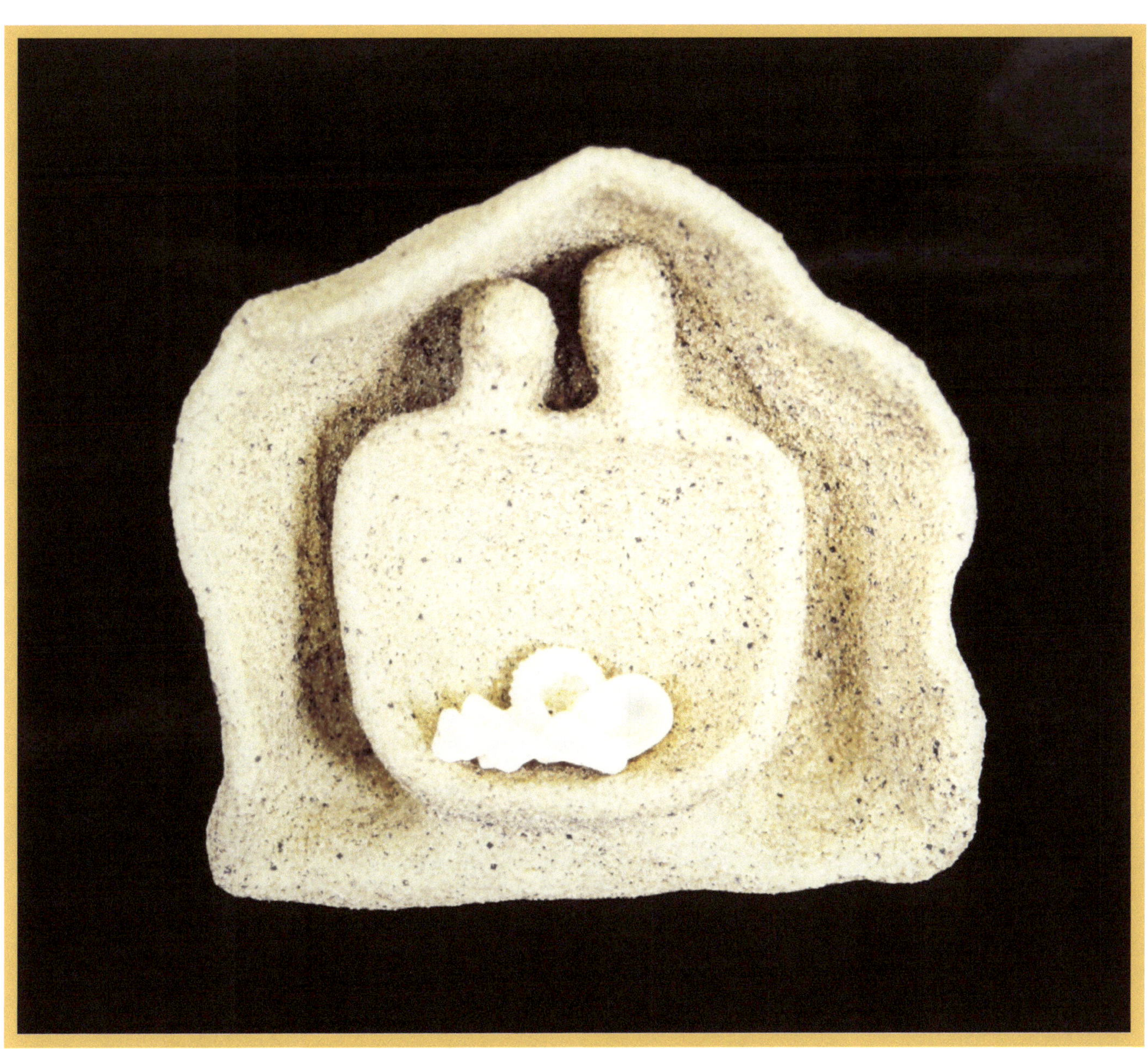

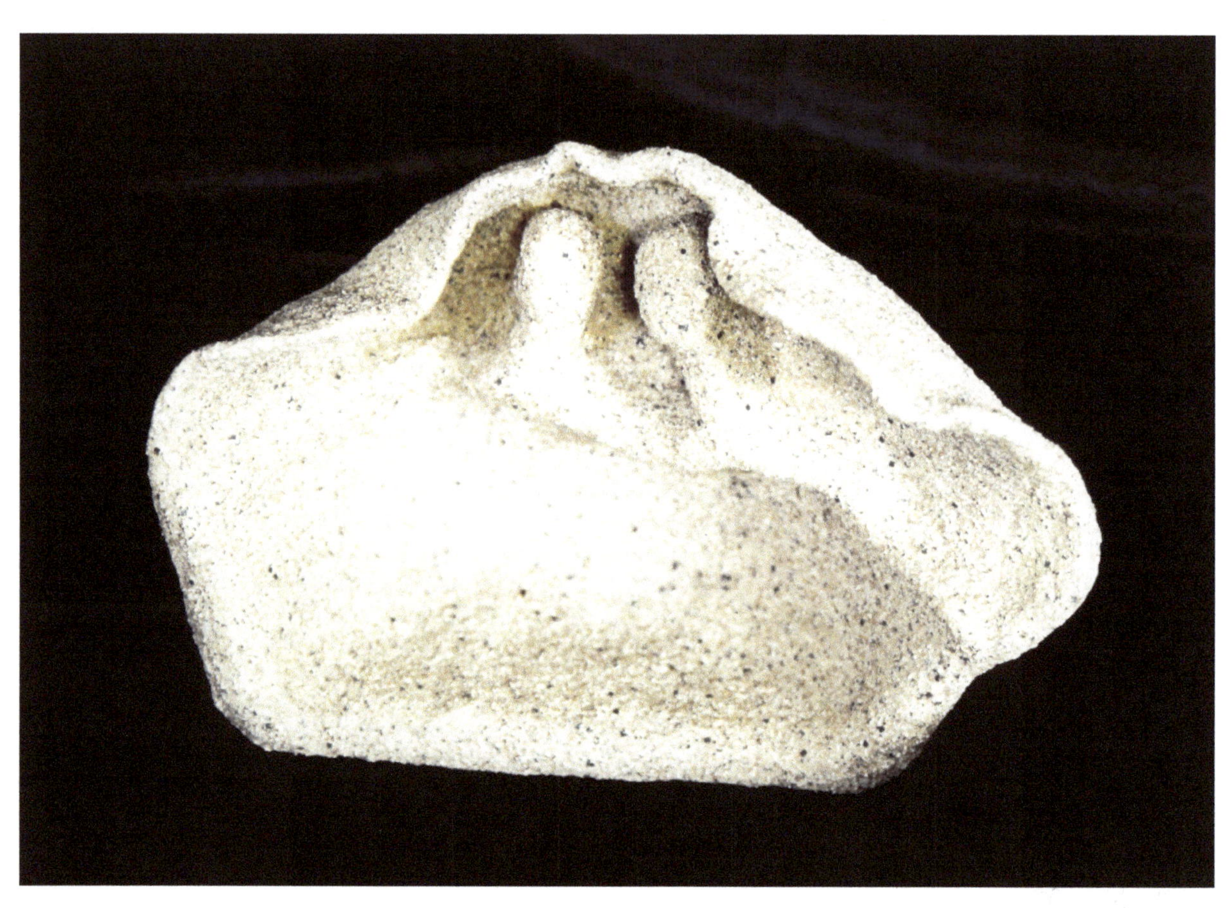

HE and SHE...Remembering...

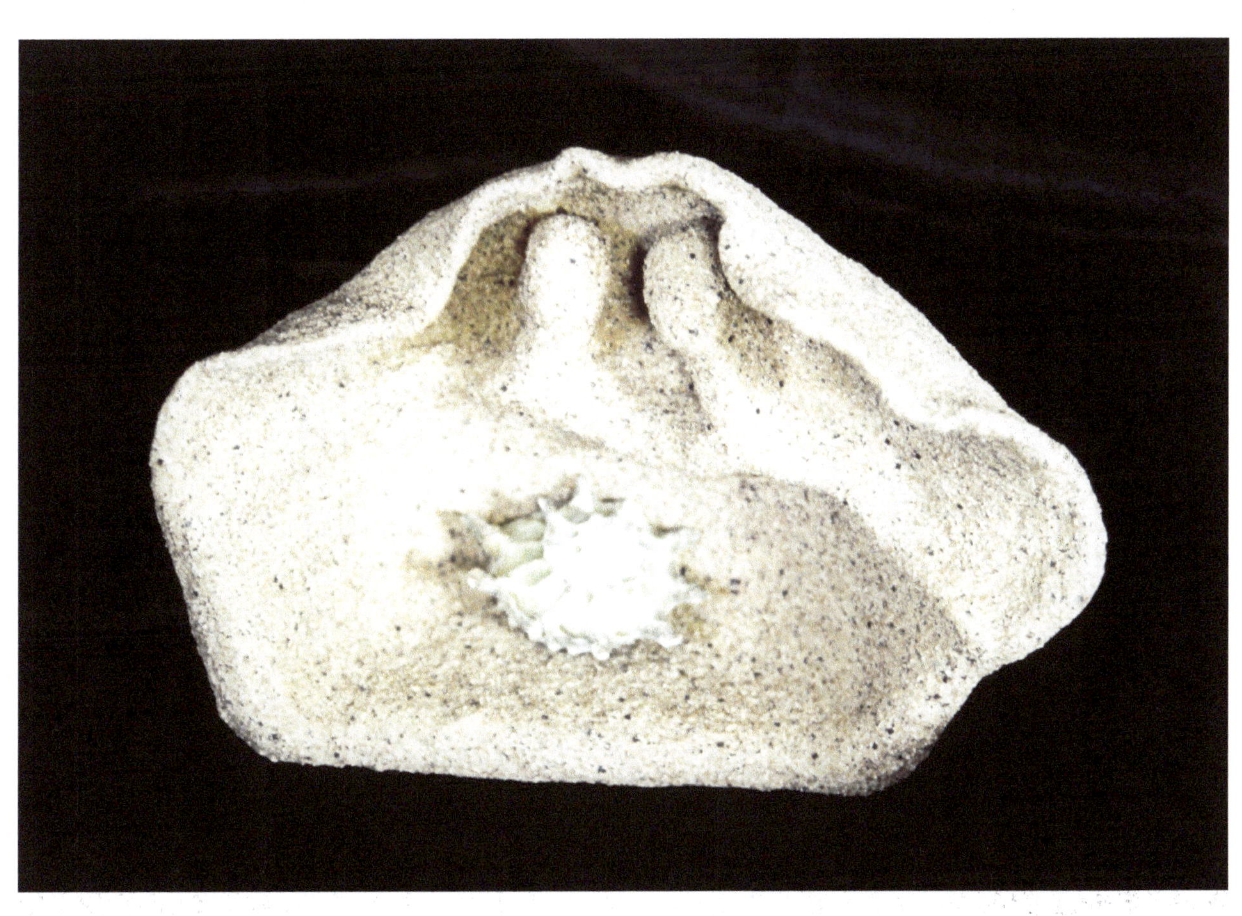

HE and SHE…Remembering…

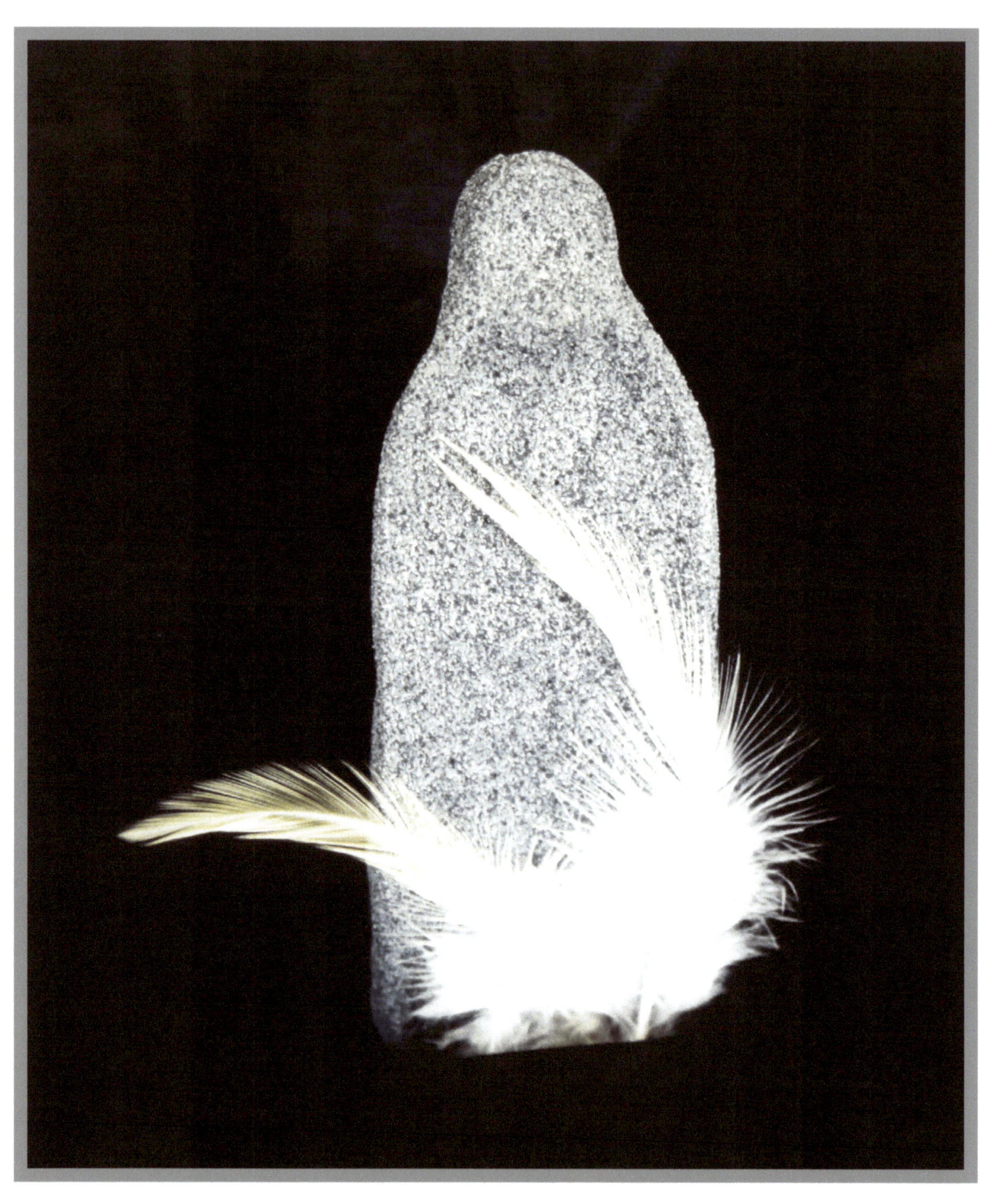

Robed-HE...of the Sacred Door

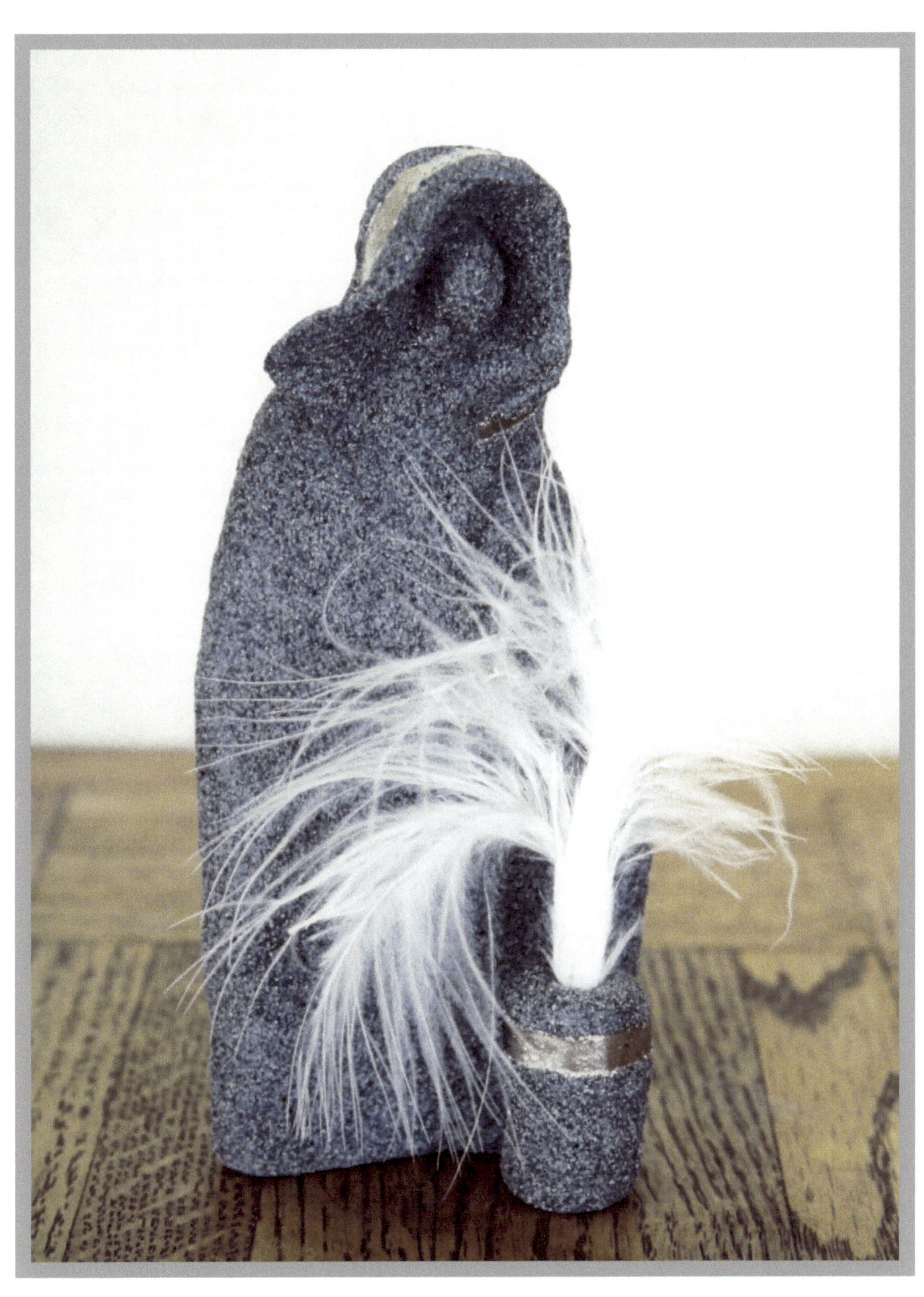

Robed...and waiting

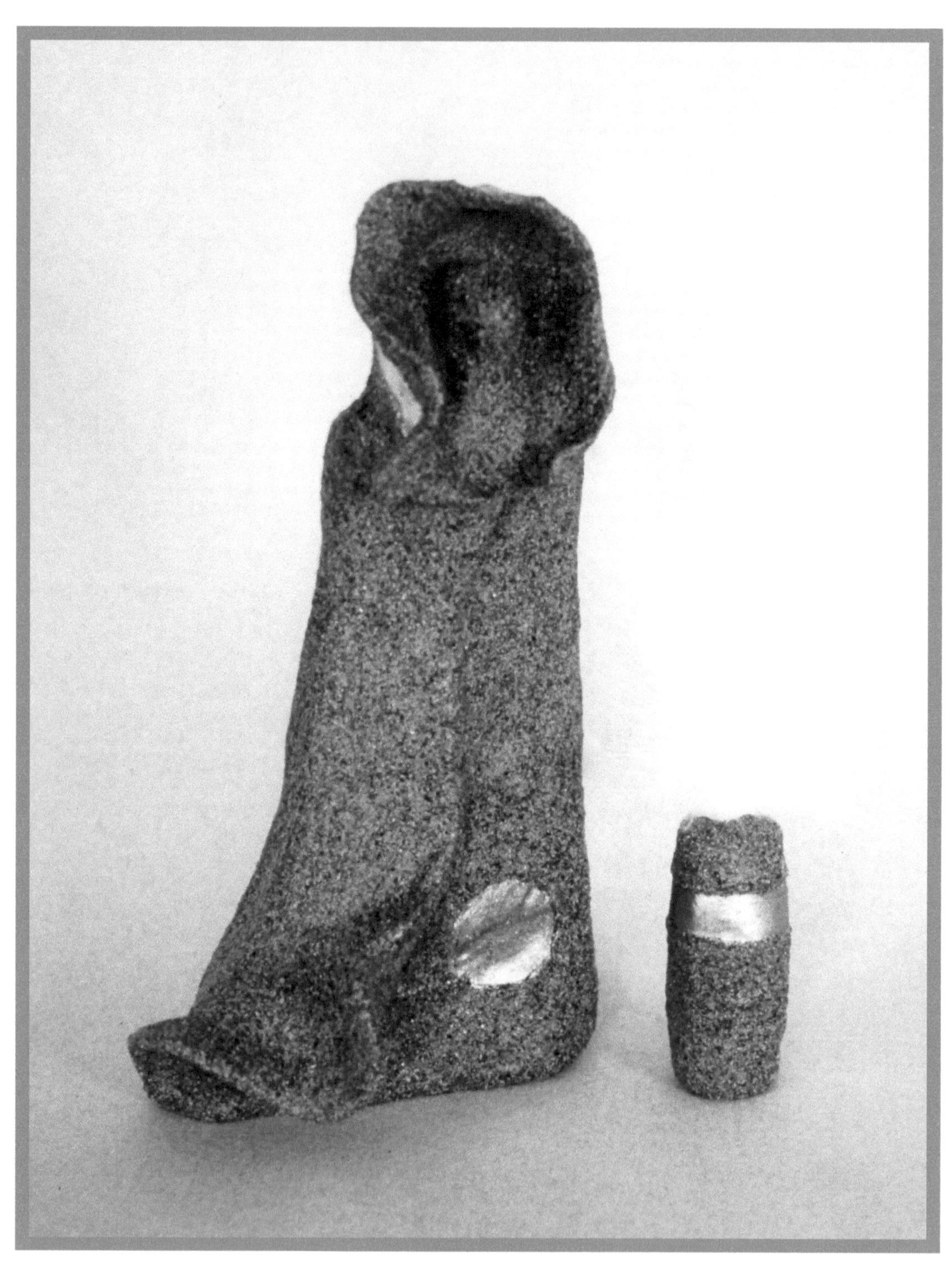

Robed one...and the full moon...

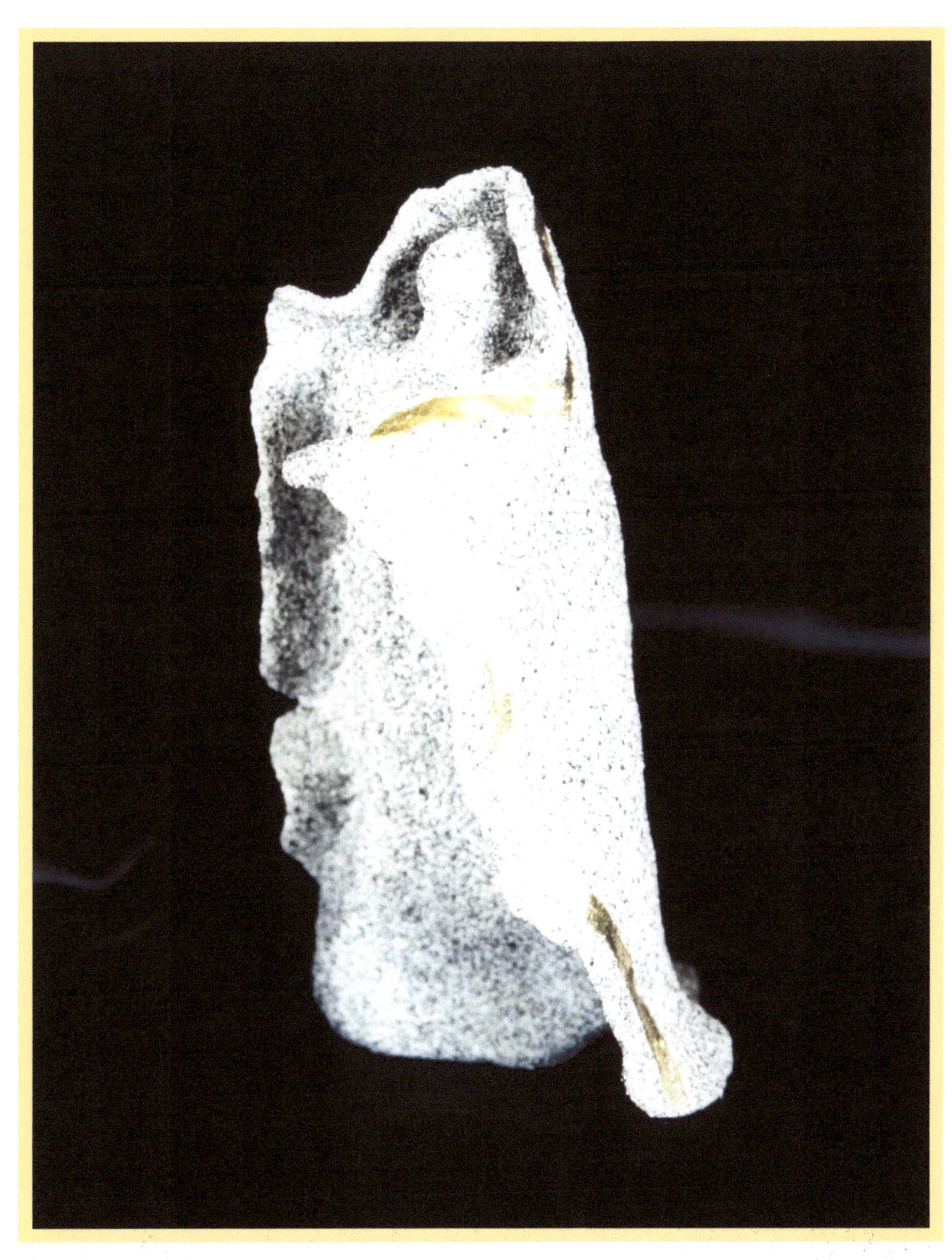

SHE…it is…Dancing in the Light

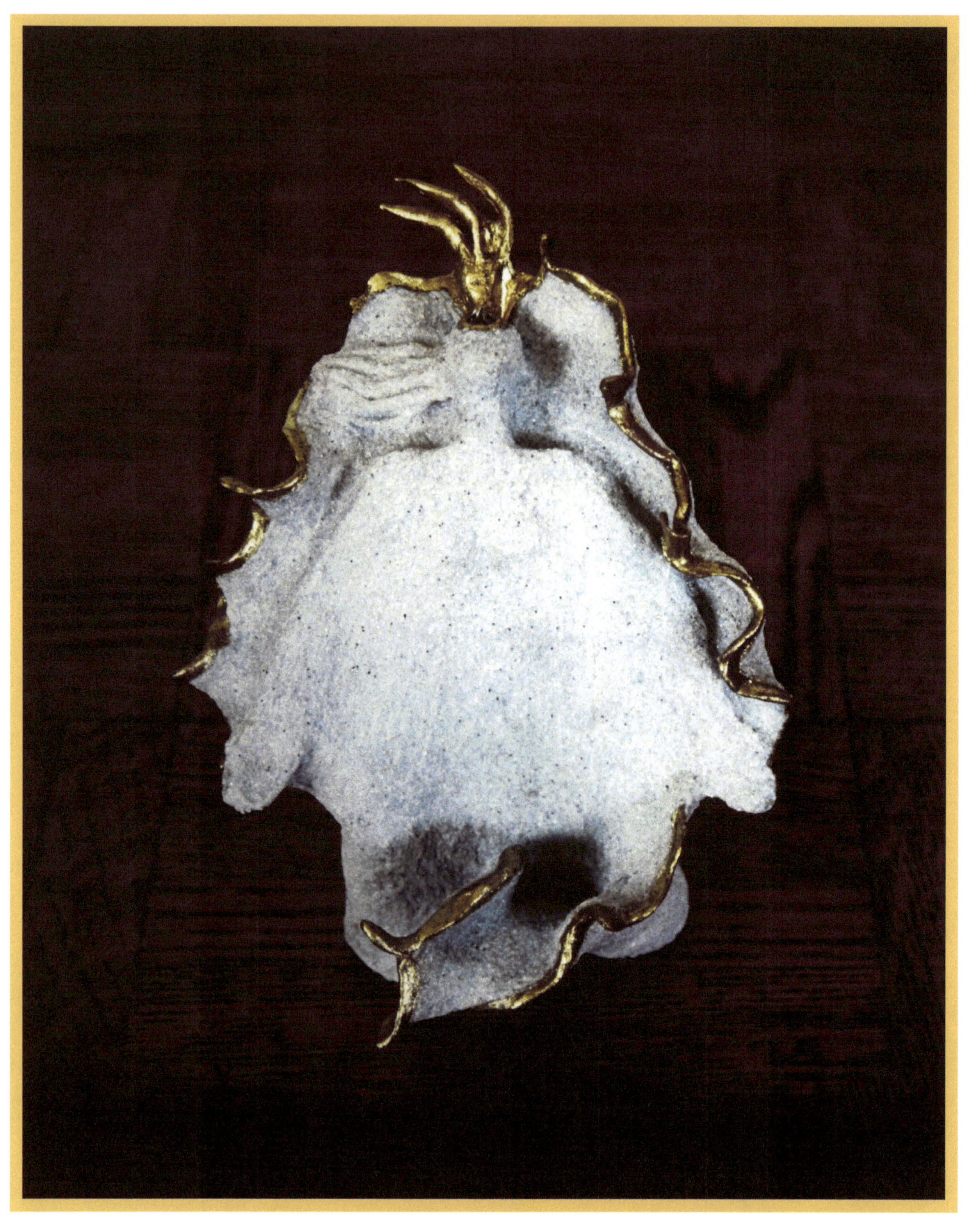

SHE...who dances in the fire...and as a million stars

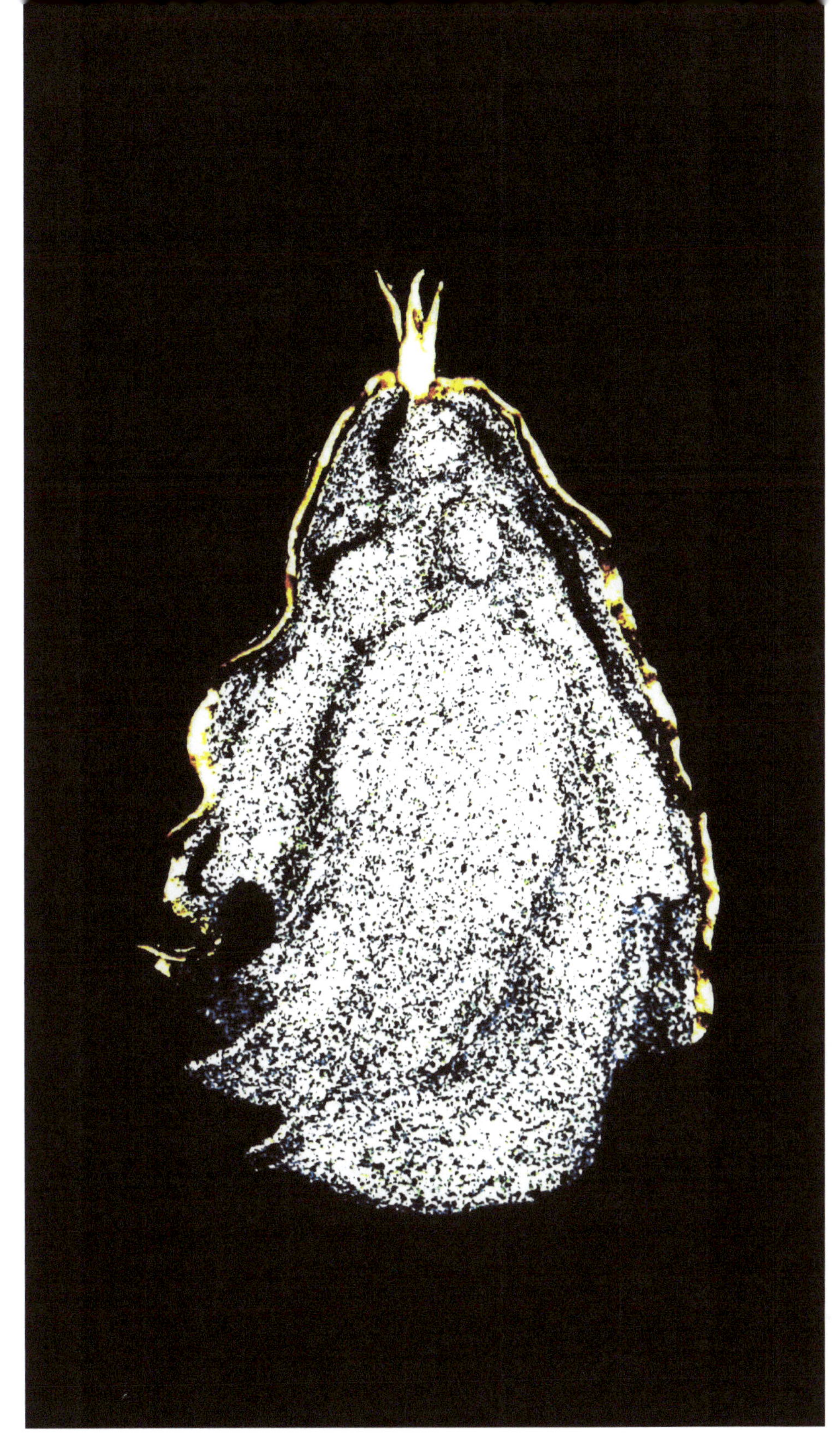

Robed Union of HE and SHE

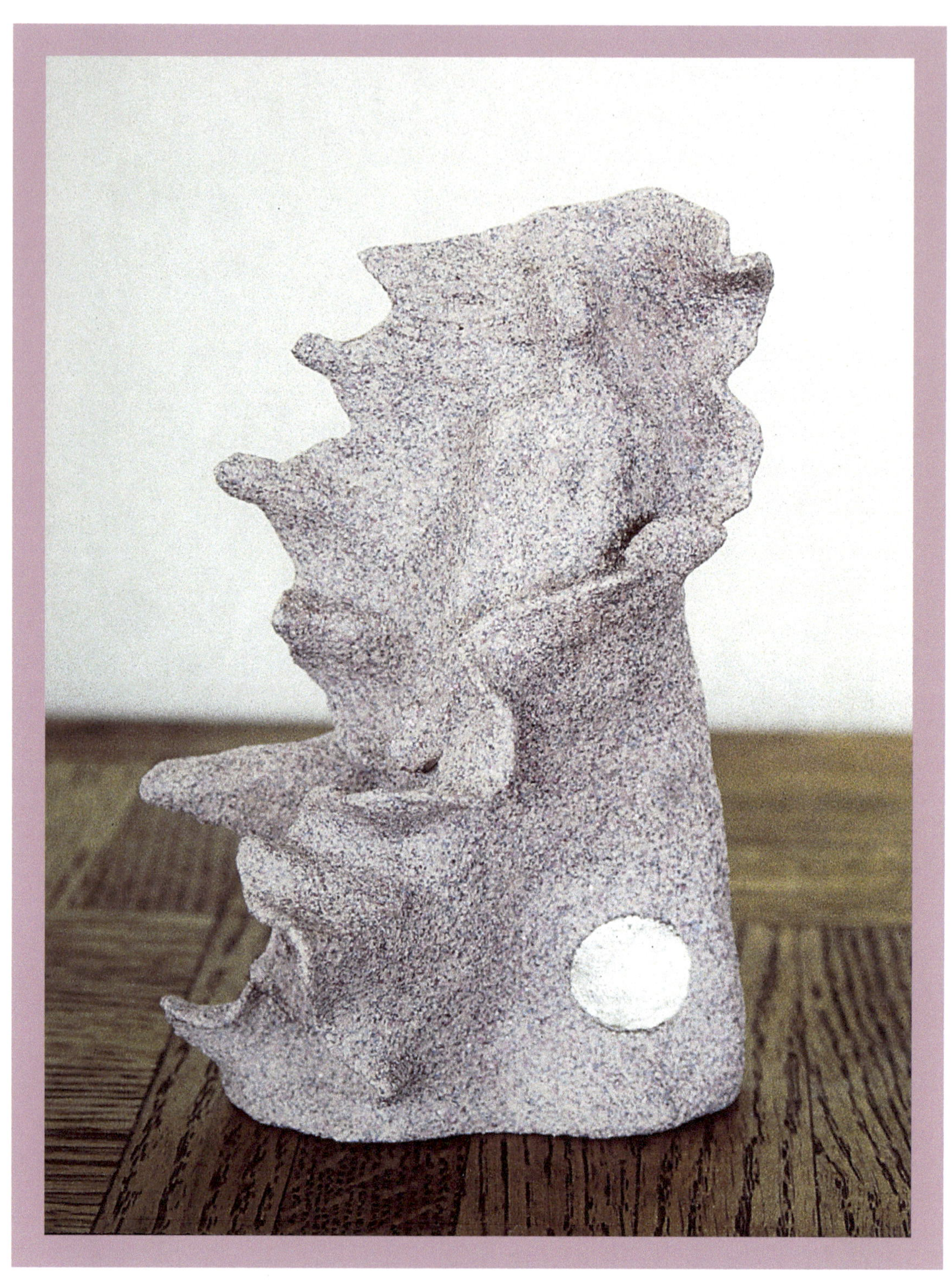

SHE…the wind…and the rising moon

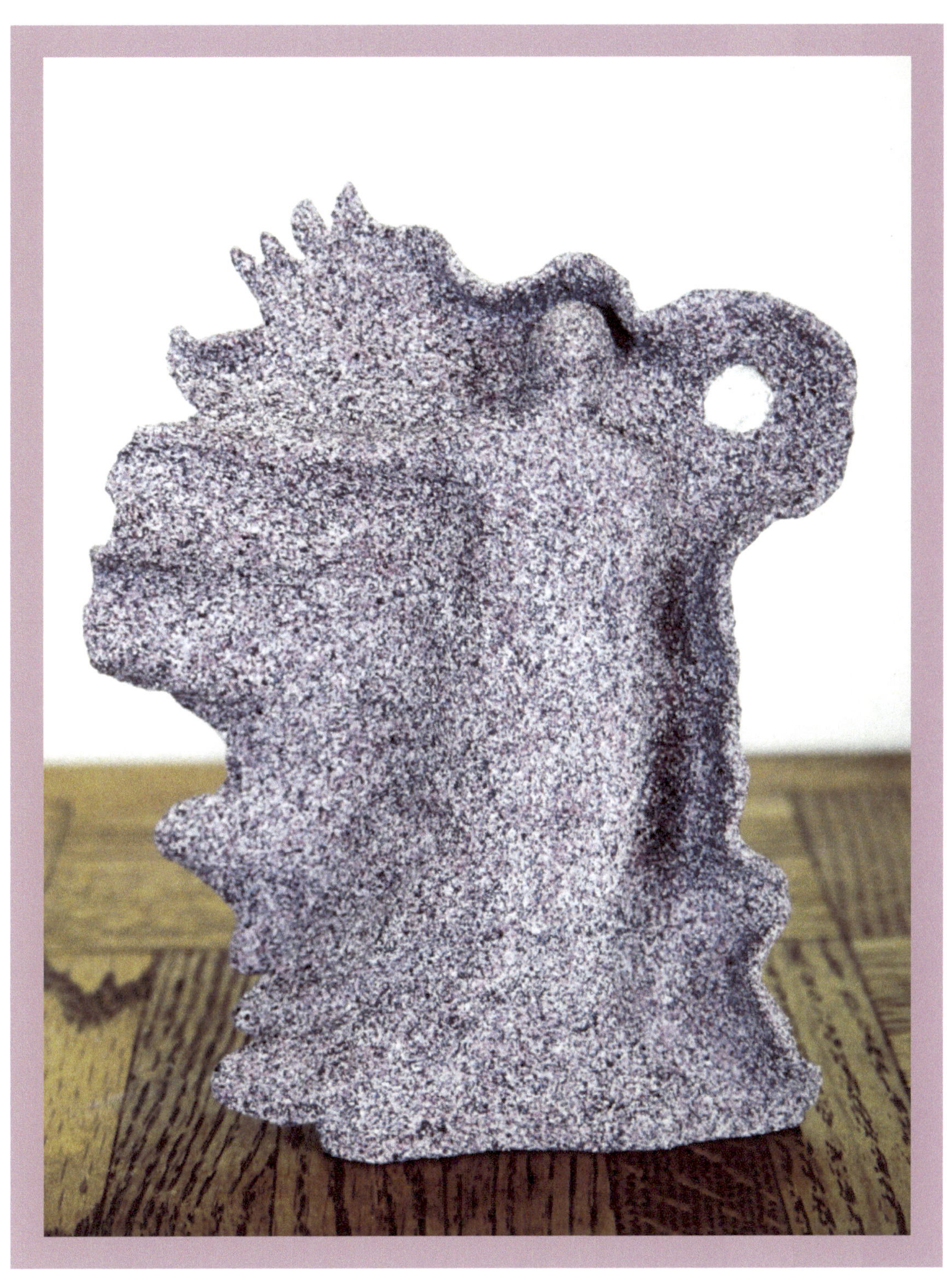

SHE…who comes as the wind…

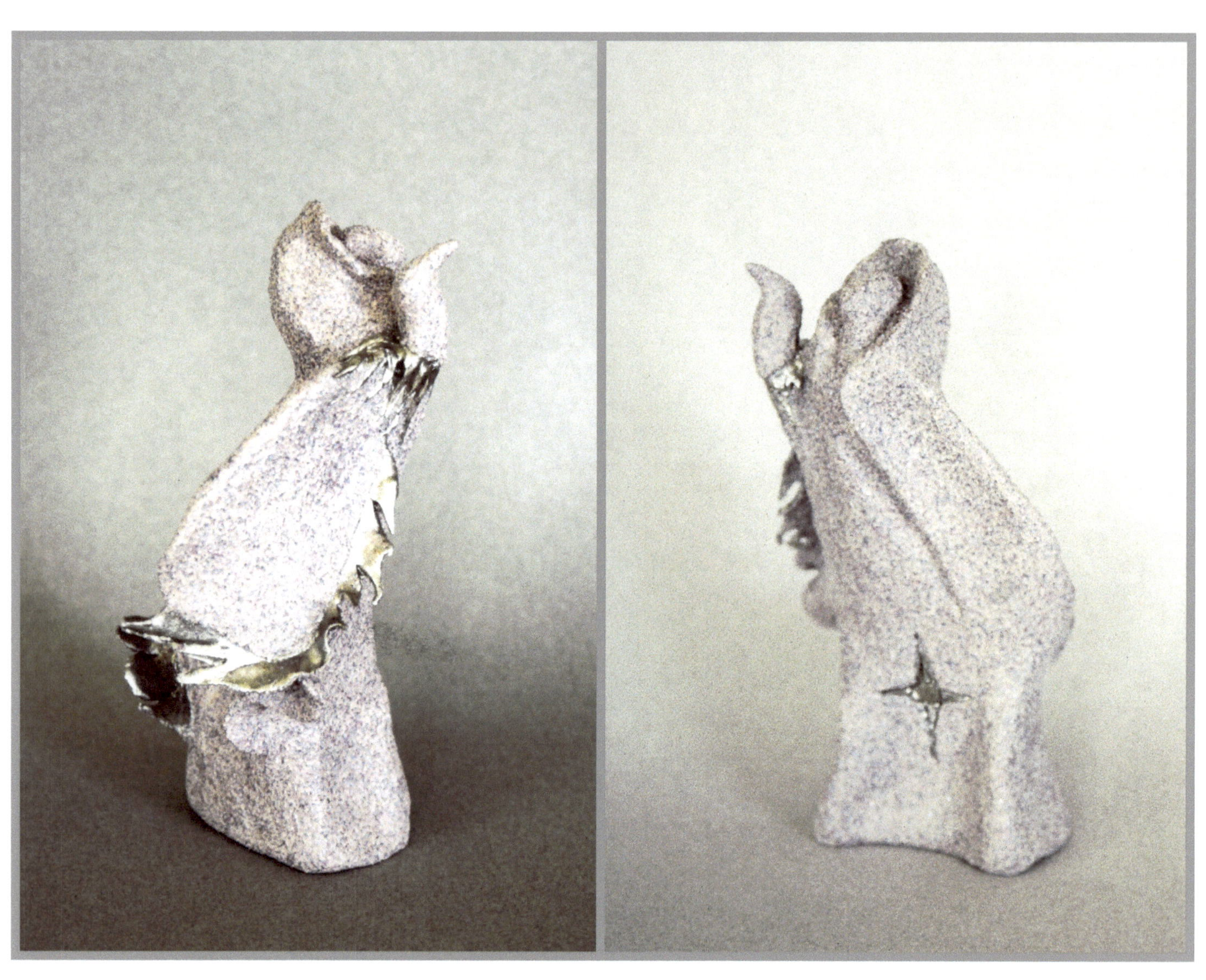

Bird-SHE and the farthest star...

The formless One comes in form. We are informed. We are defined by the Infinite, as we open and allow. This is the Self as the self. The One Self. Individual, unique, seemingly separate...and the One... simultaneously.

In this sculpture is seen the inner attunement revealed through awareness of wings taking flight into the vastness of space.

The sculpture is an awareness. It is a portal, an opening into the vastness of our Being.

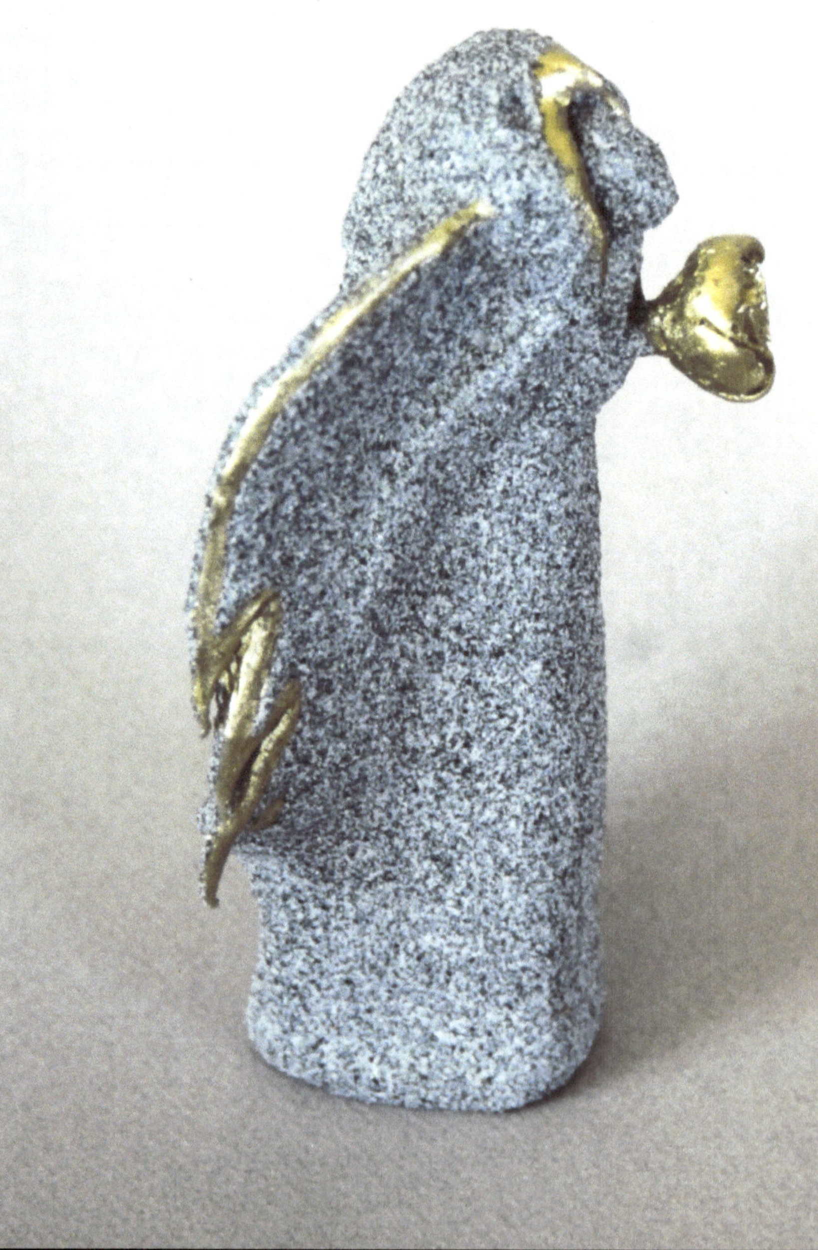

owl-woman...and the golden lotus...

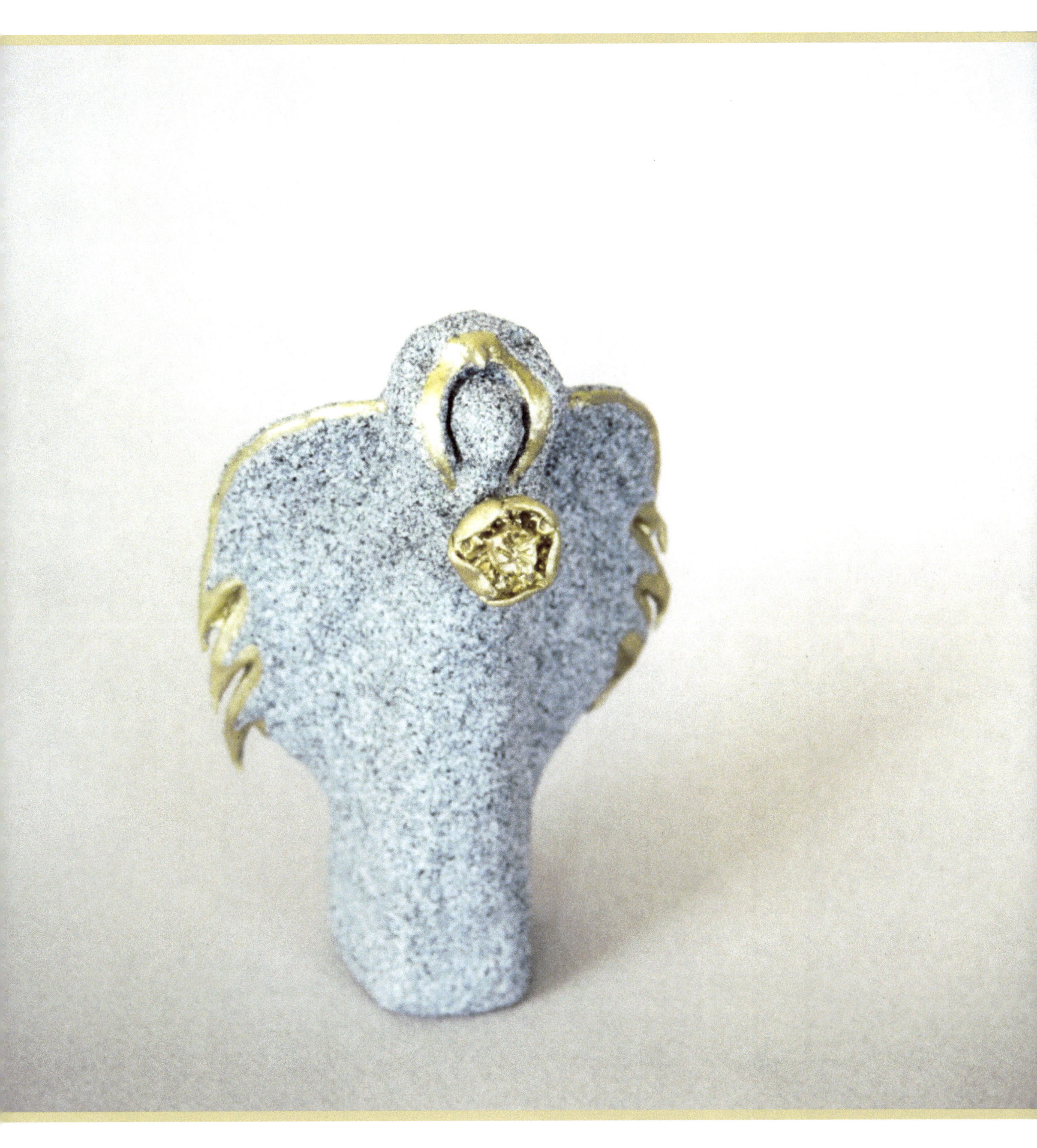

owl-woman...and the golden lotus...

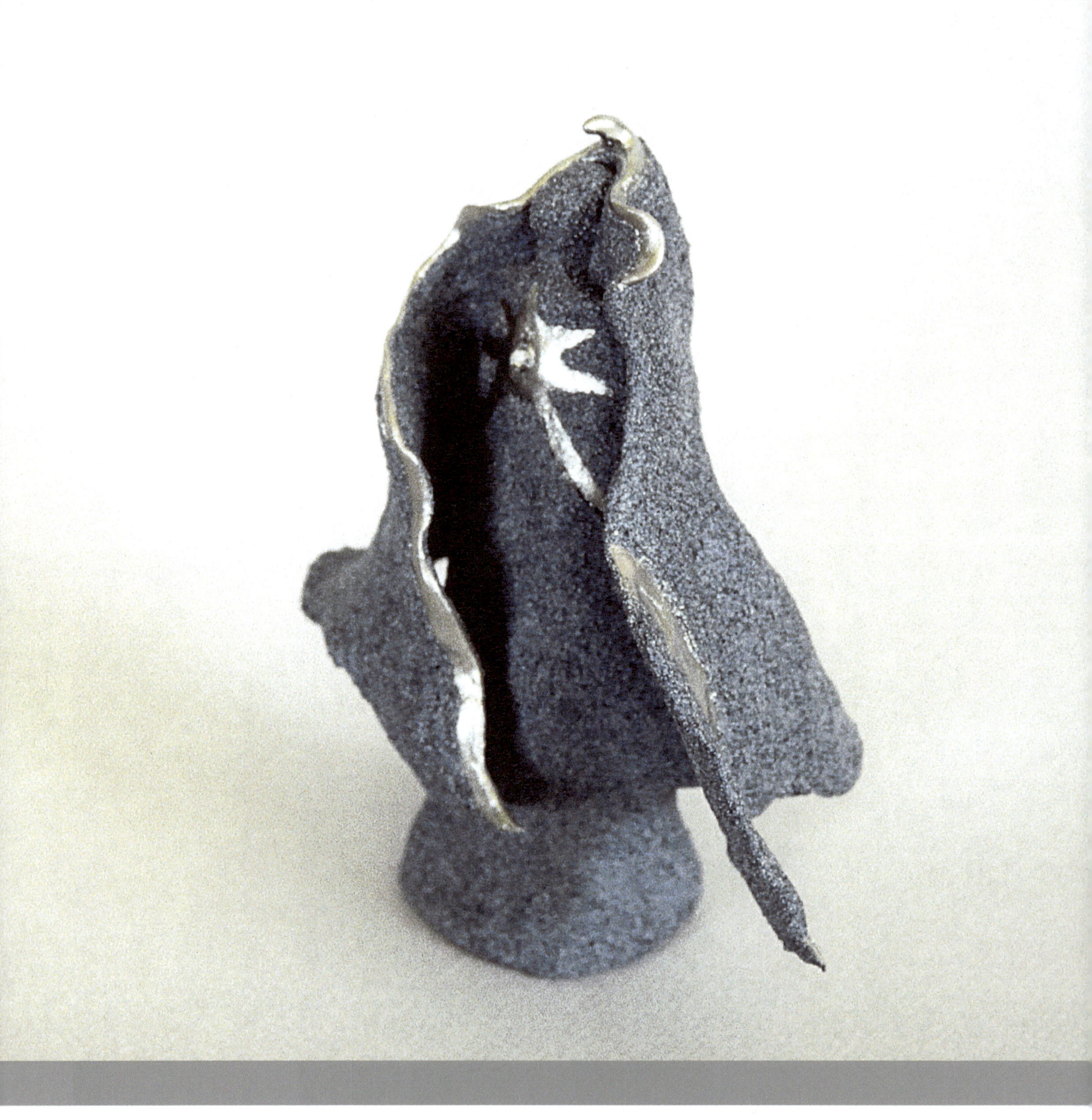

Monk-HE...in heart's flight...

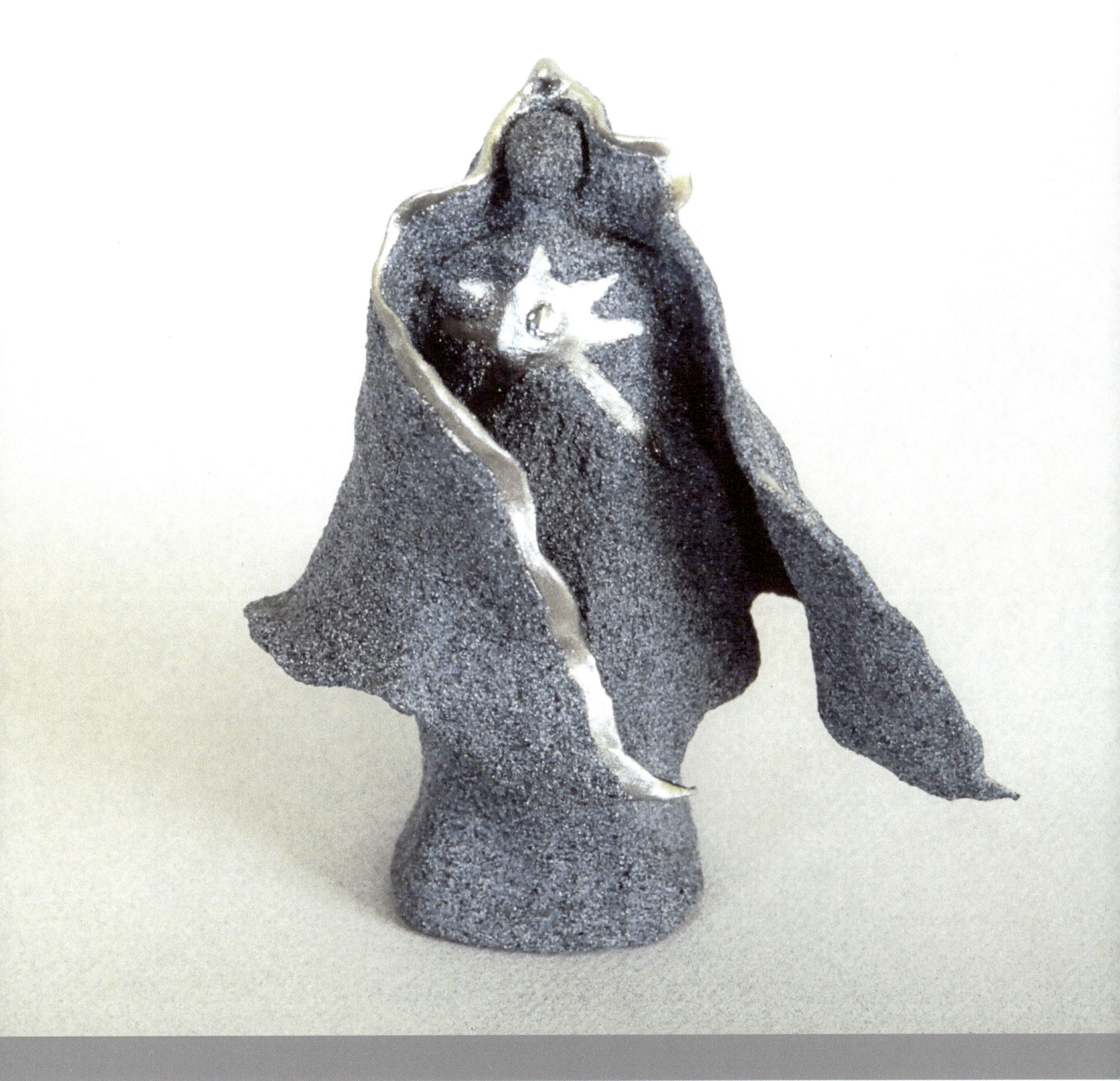

Monk-HE…in heart's flight…

SHE...of the wind-swept birds...

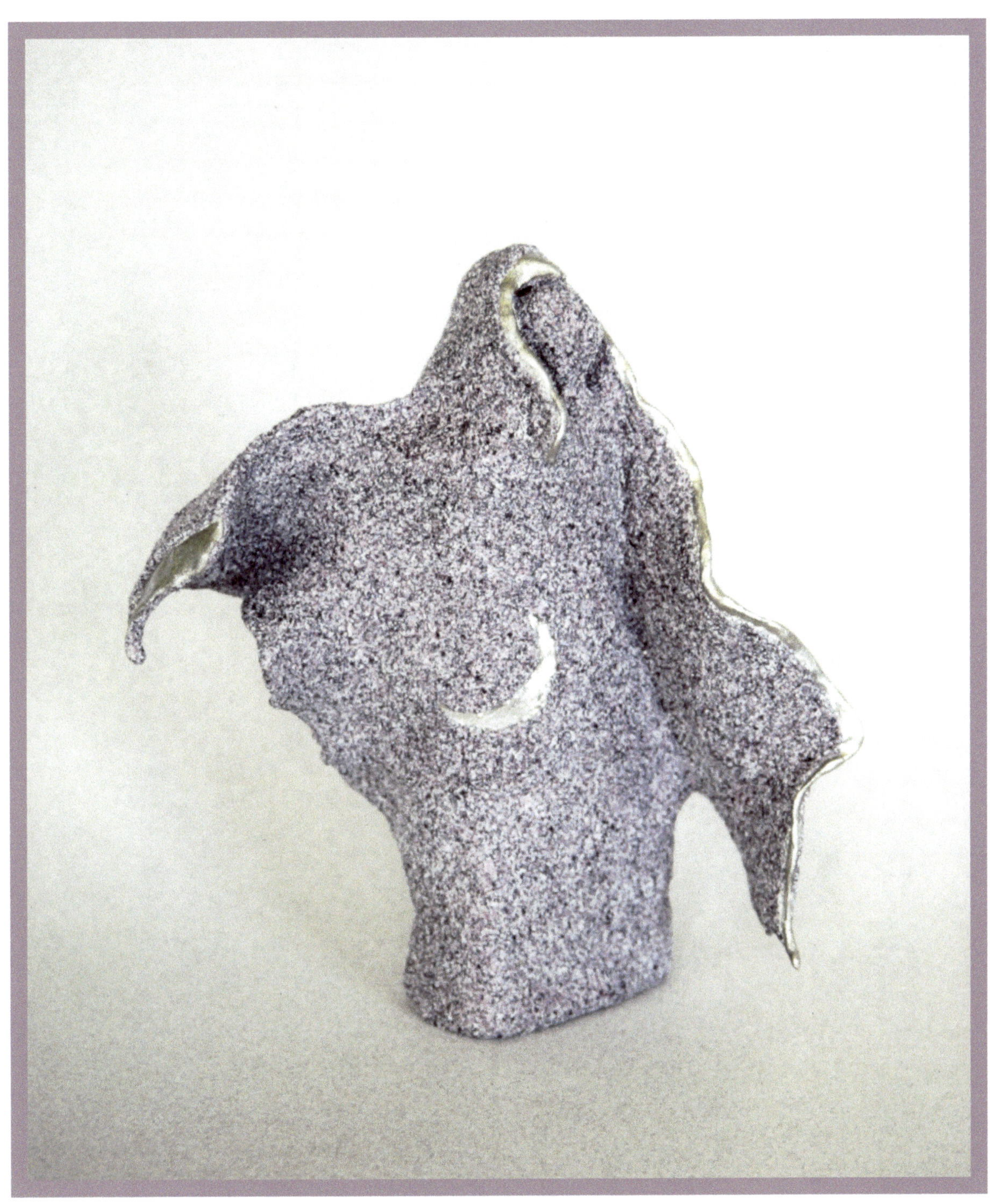

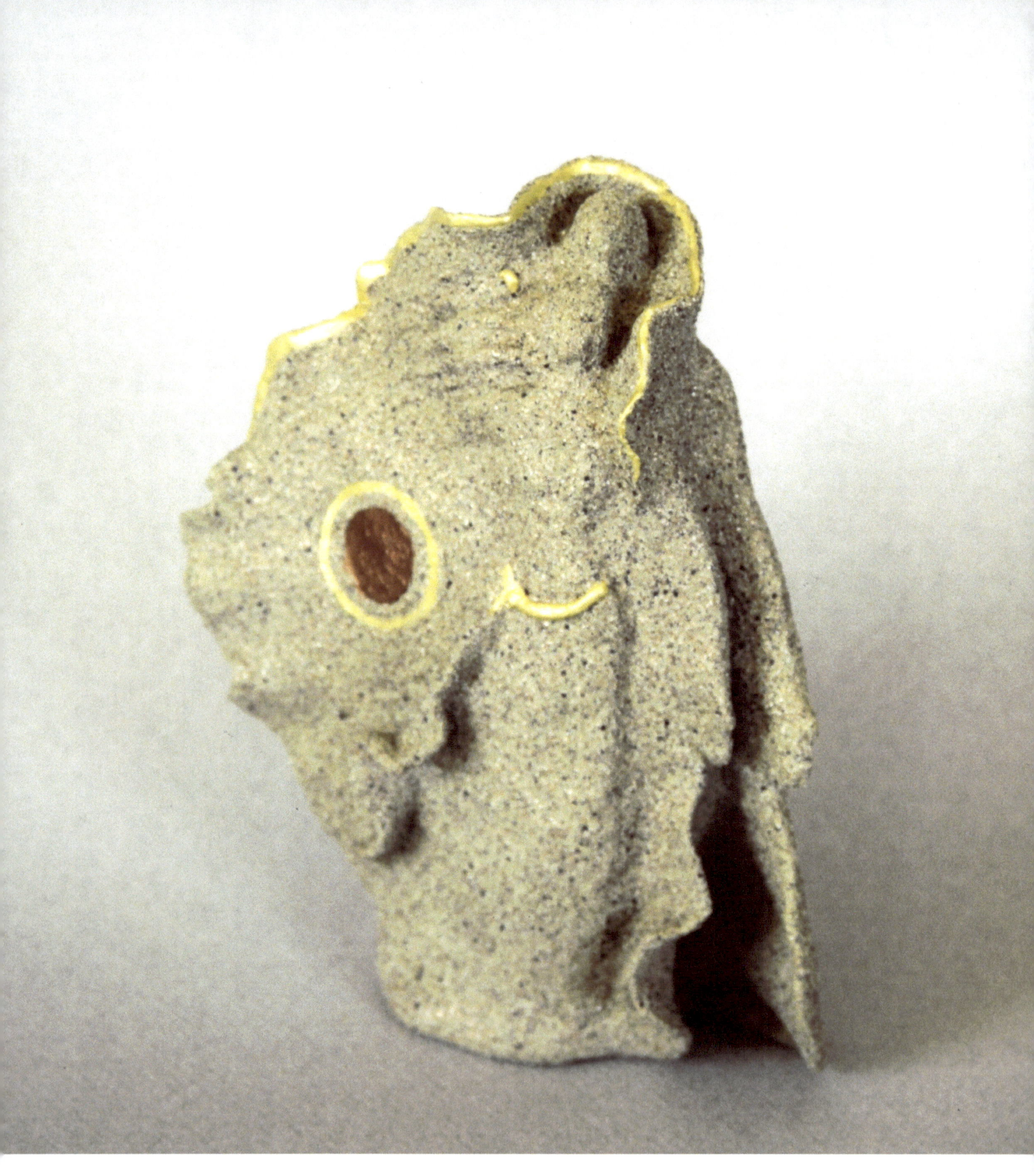

Together...they are the sun...

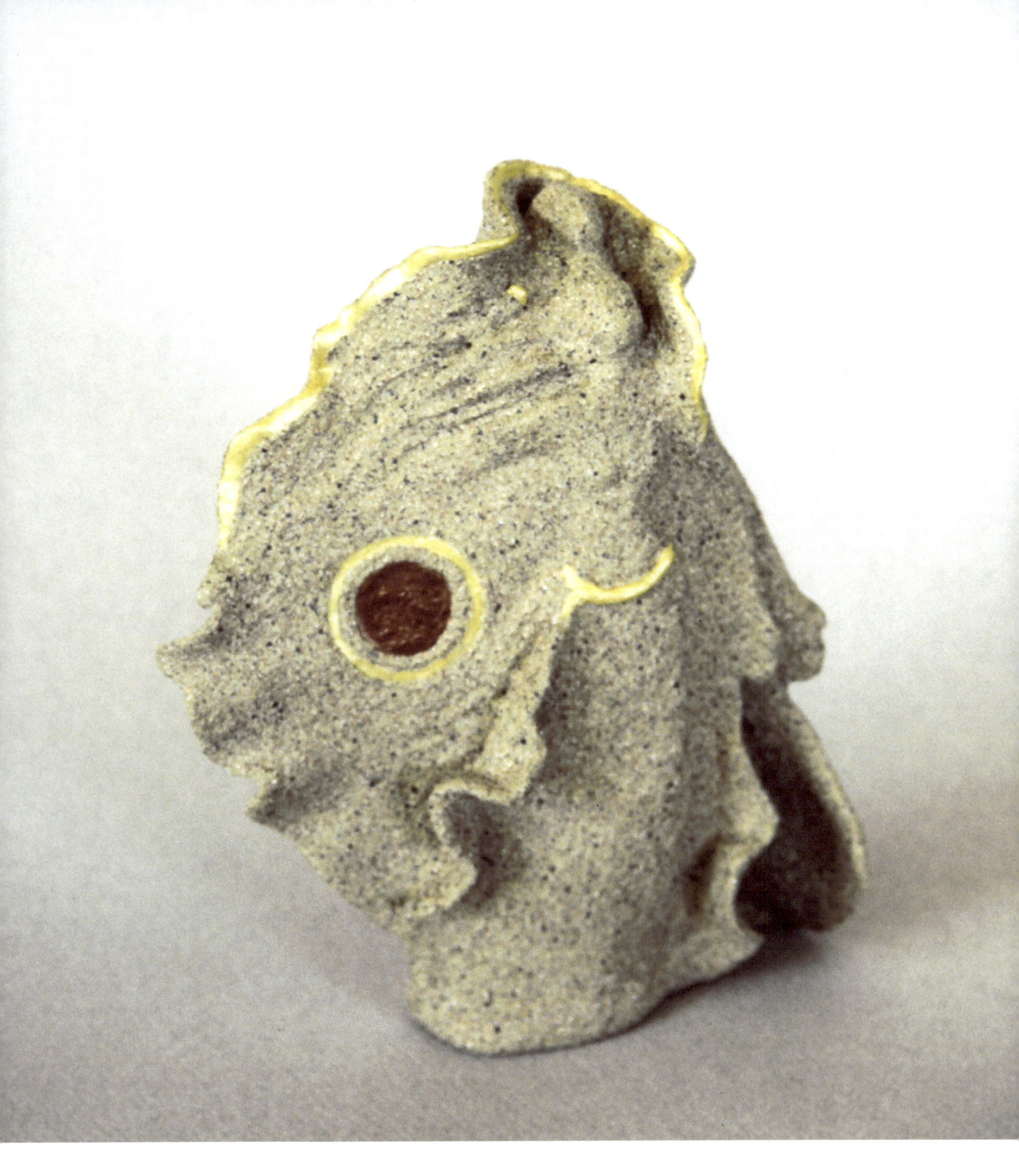

Together…they are the sun…

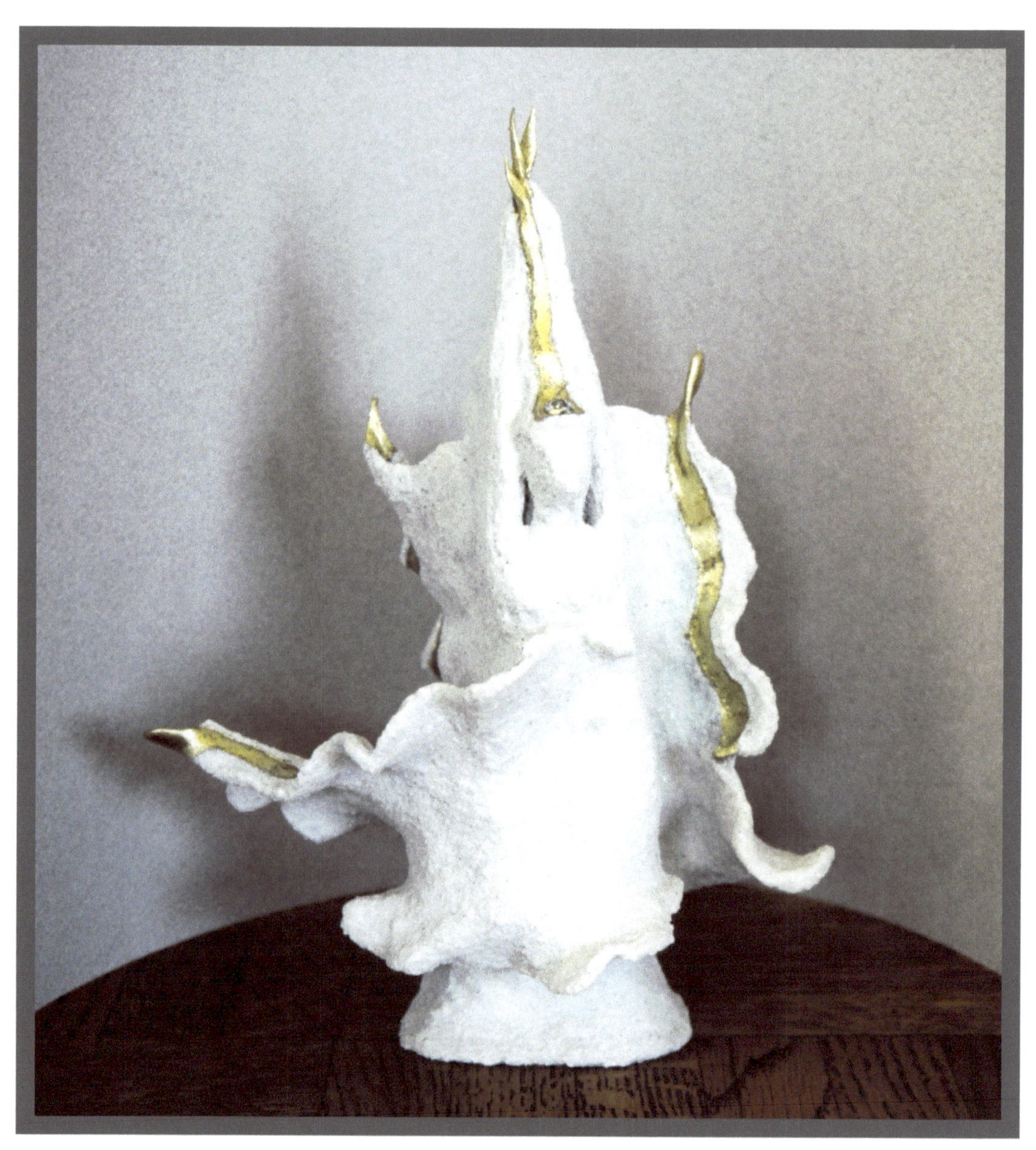

SHE...comes...as the wind...

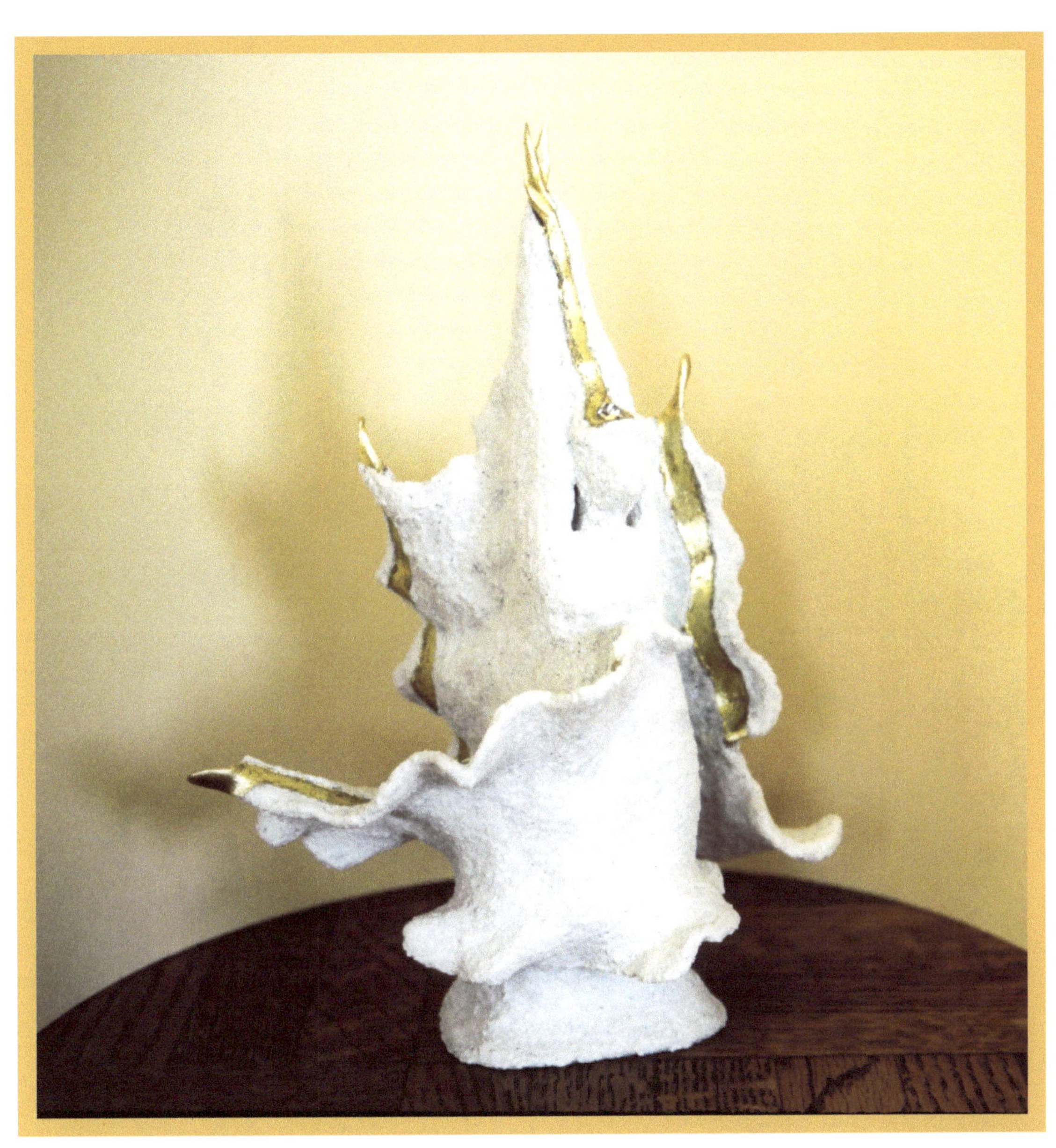

SHE...comes...as the wind...

Wind-SHE...and the Rising Sun

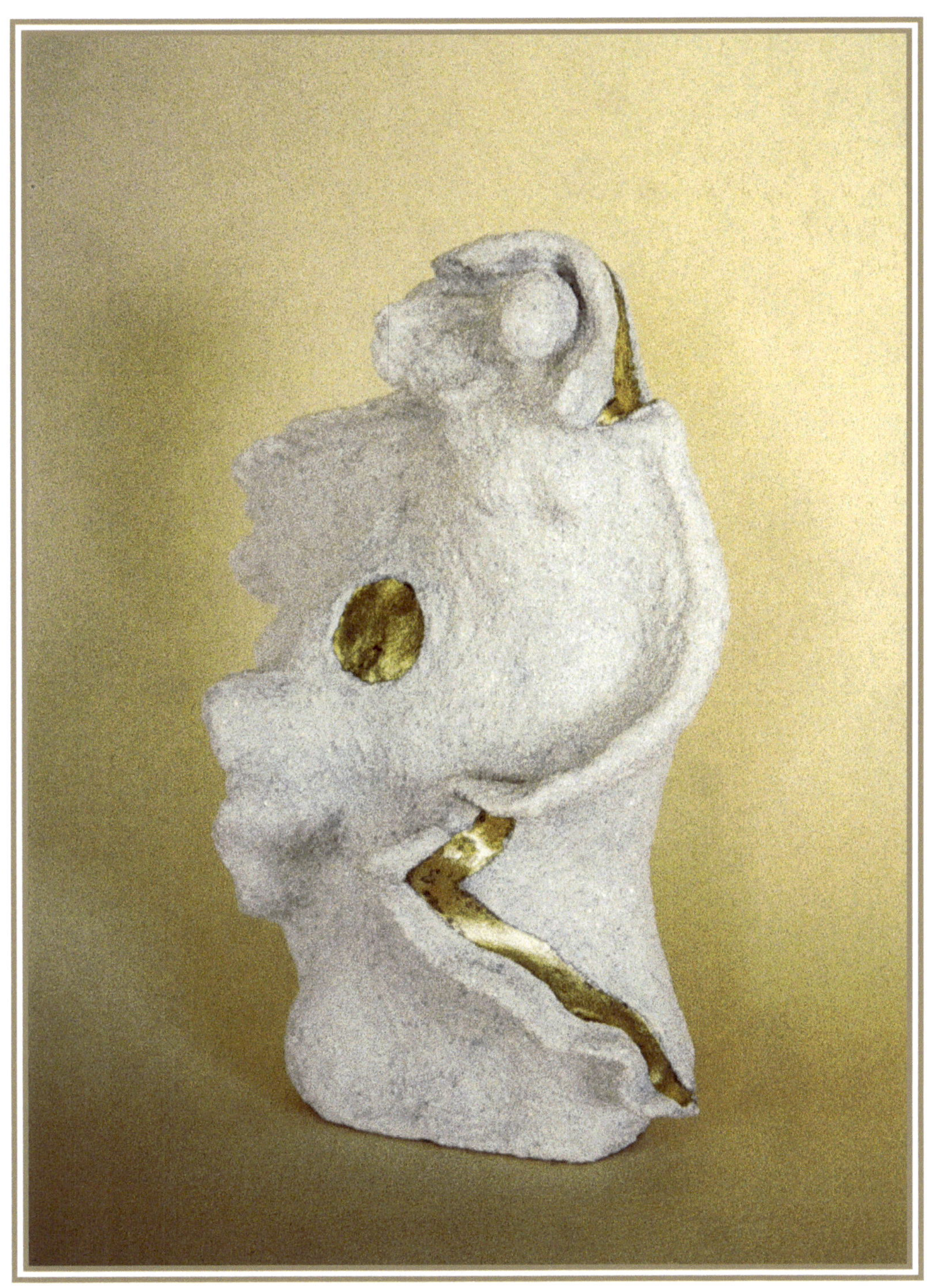

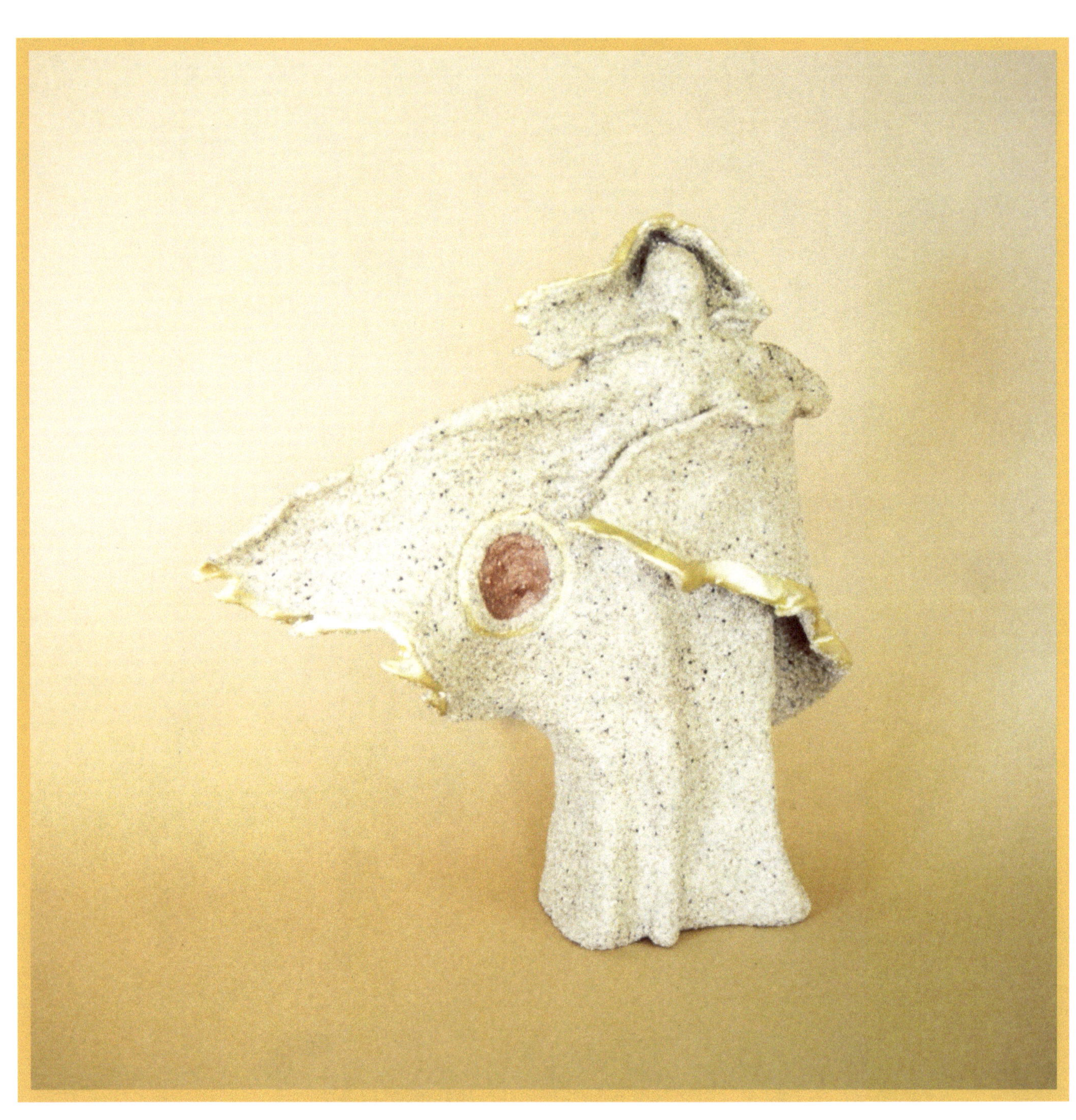

Bird-SHE...and the desert's dawn

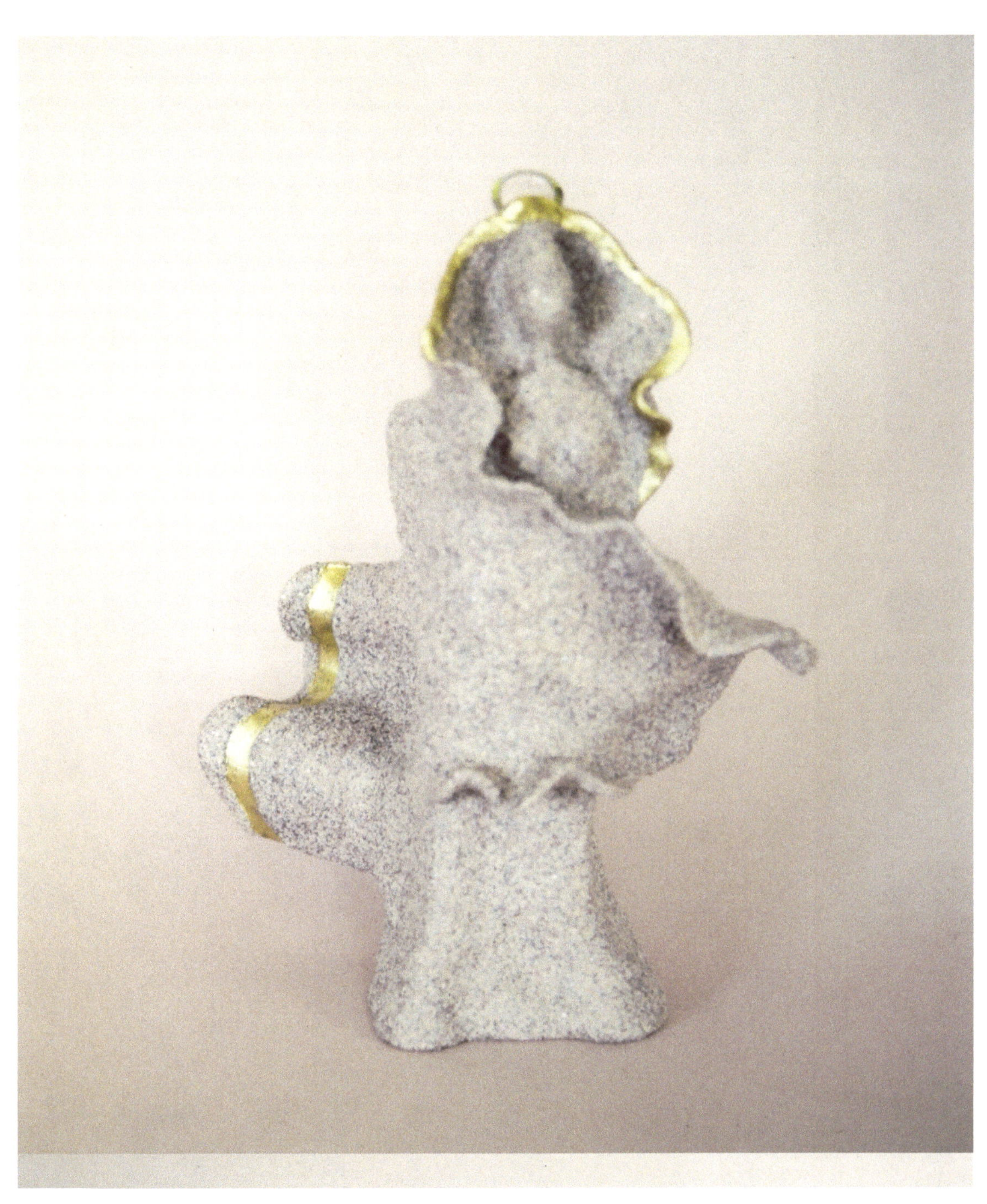

Queen of the world-SHE

SHE…comes…as the very bird in the sky

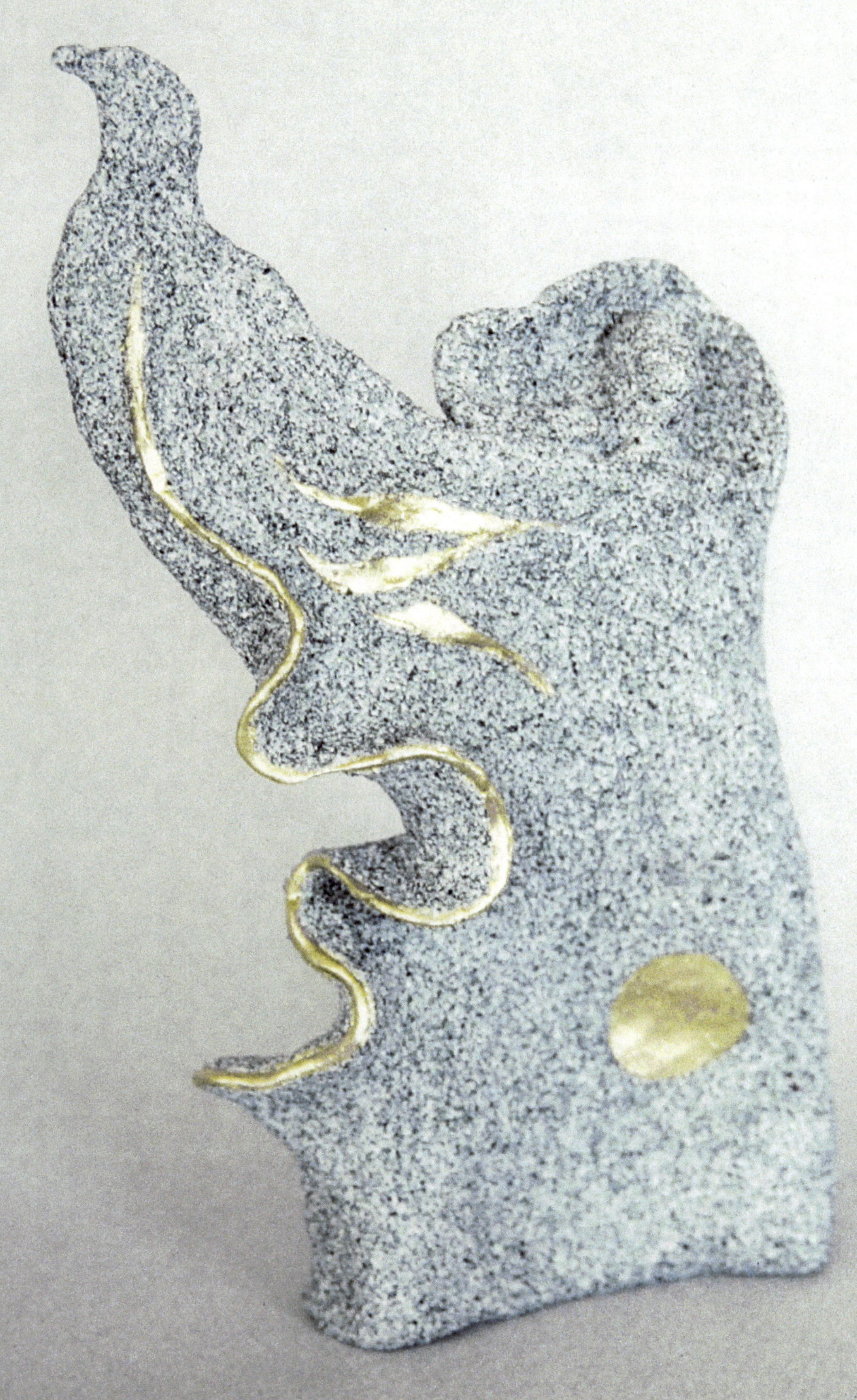

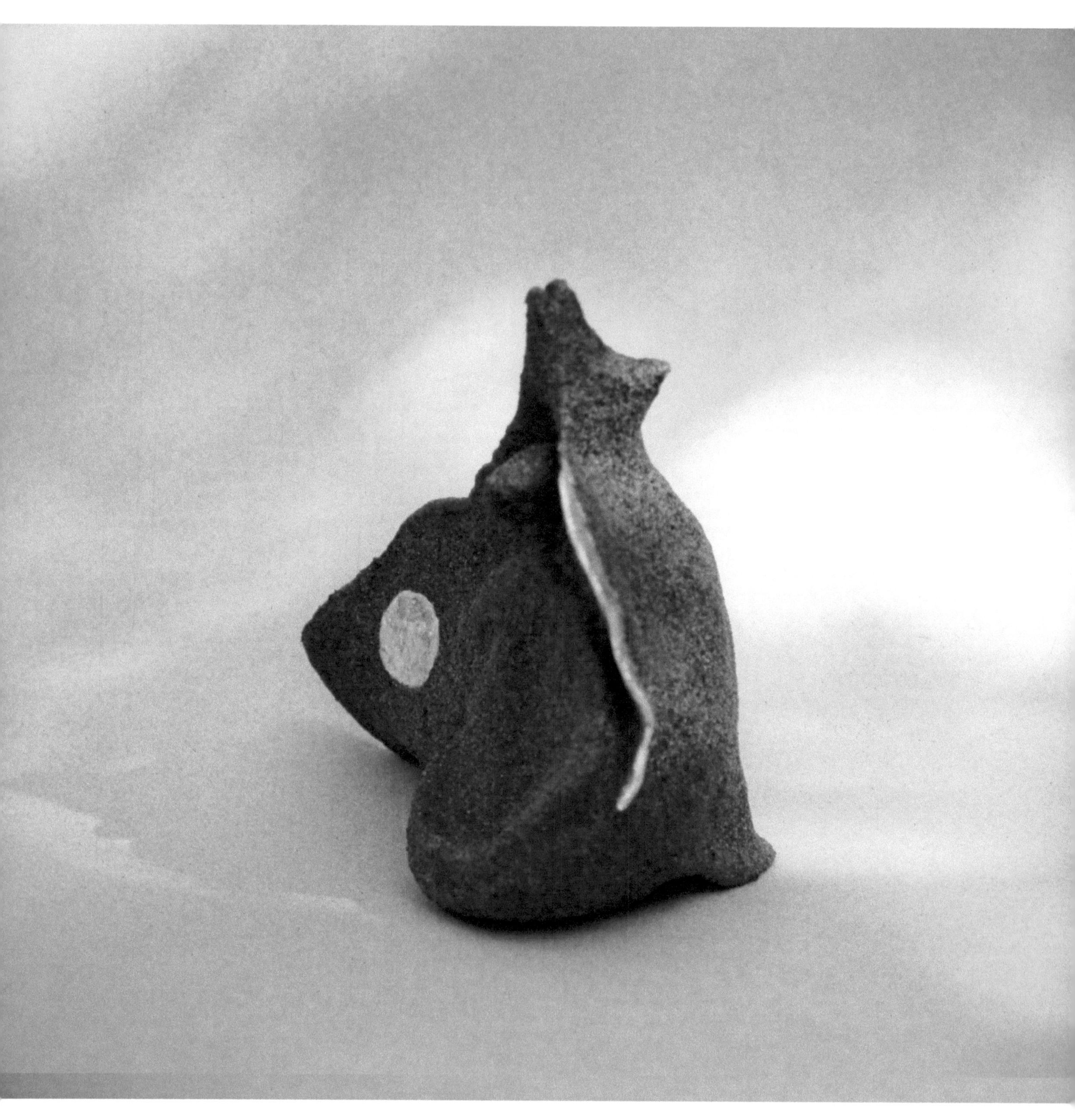

Wolf-SHE

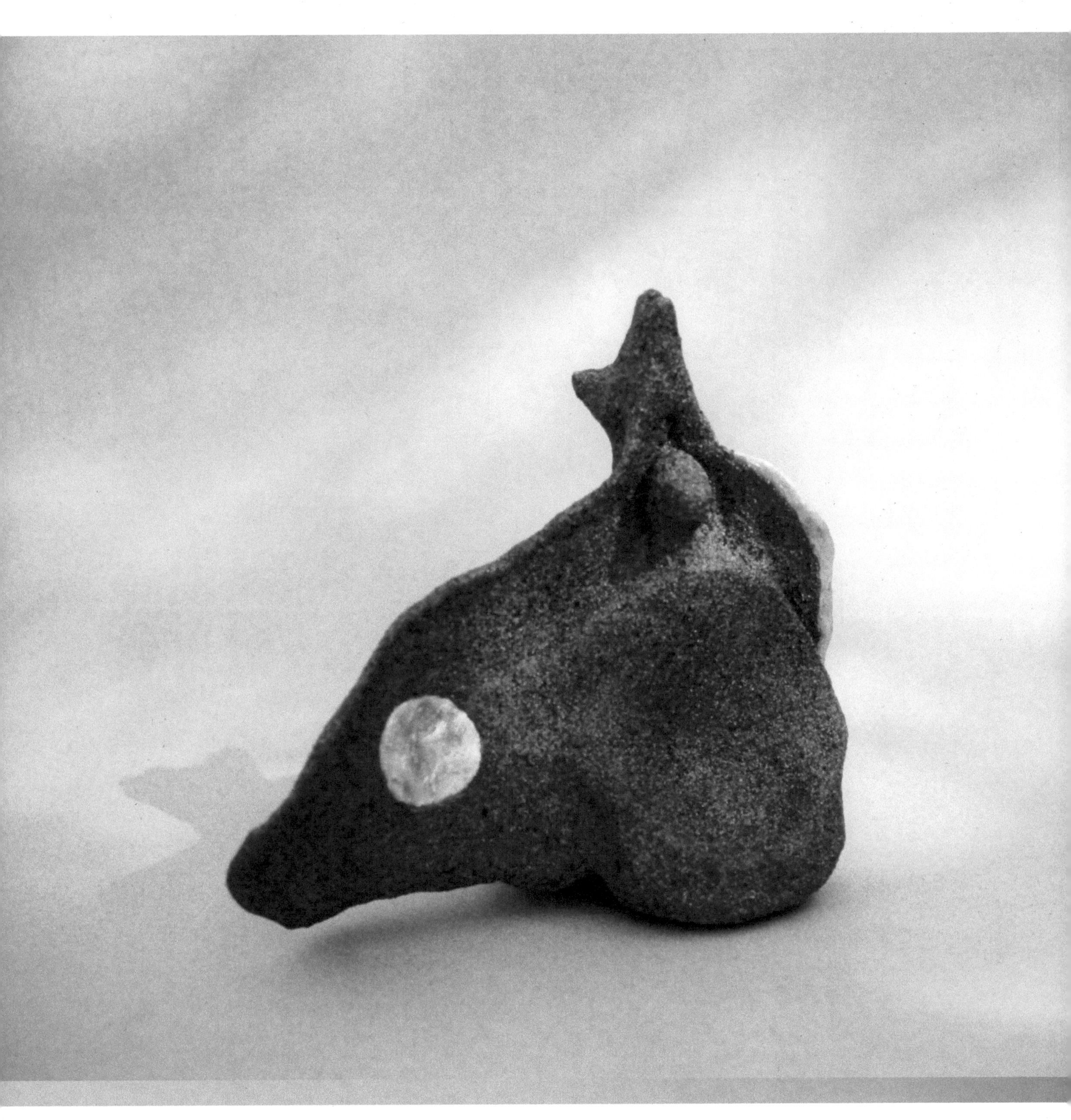

Wolf-SHE

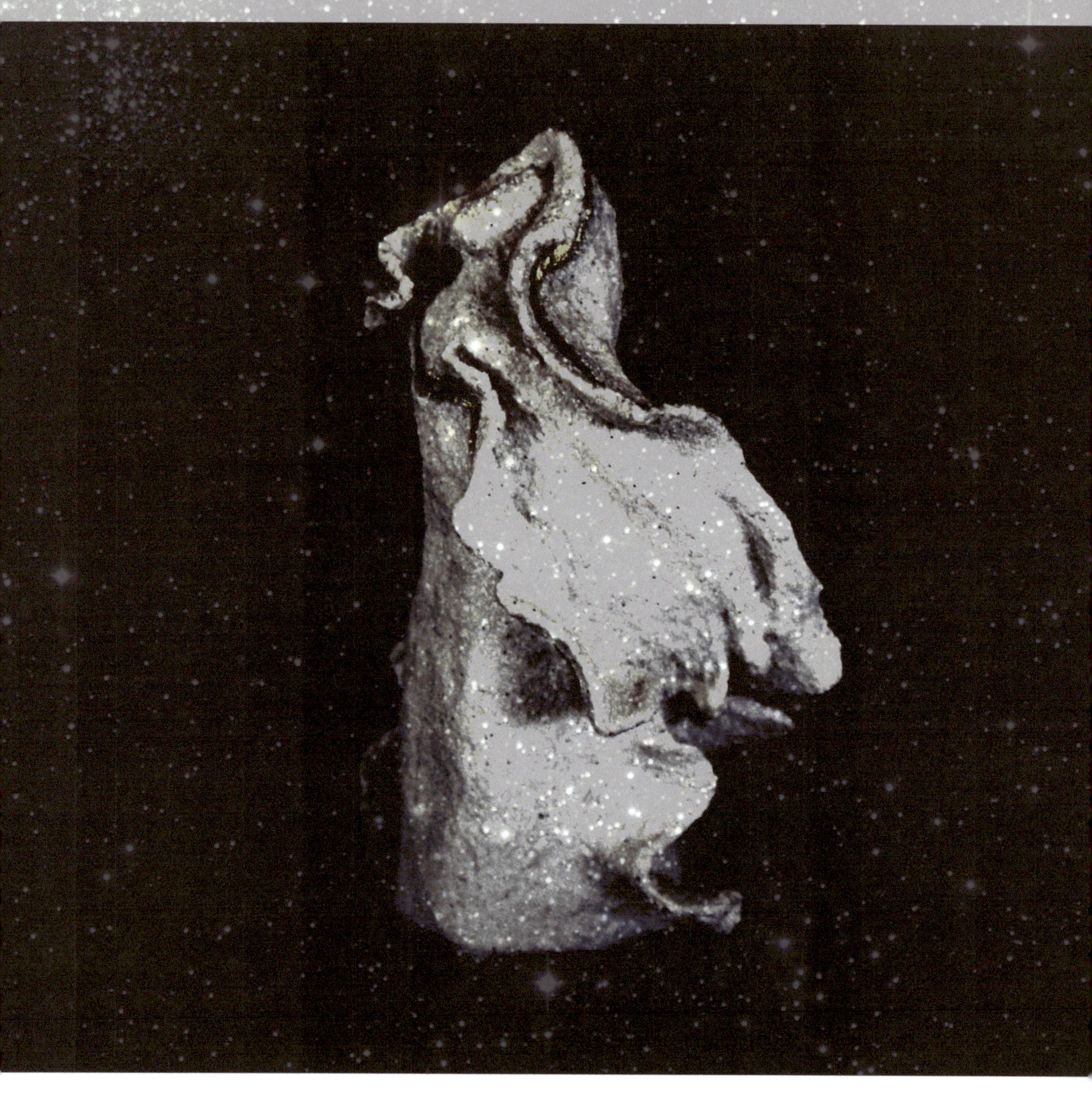

Robed-SHE...of the Alabaster Marriage

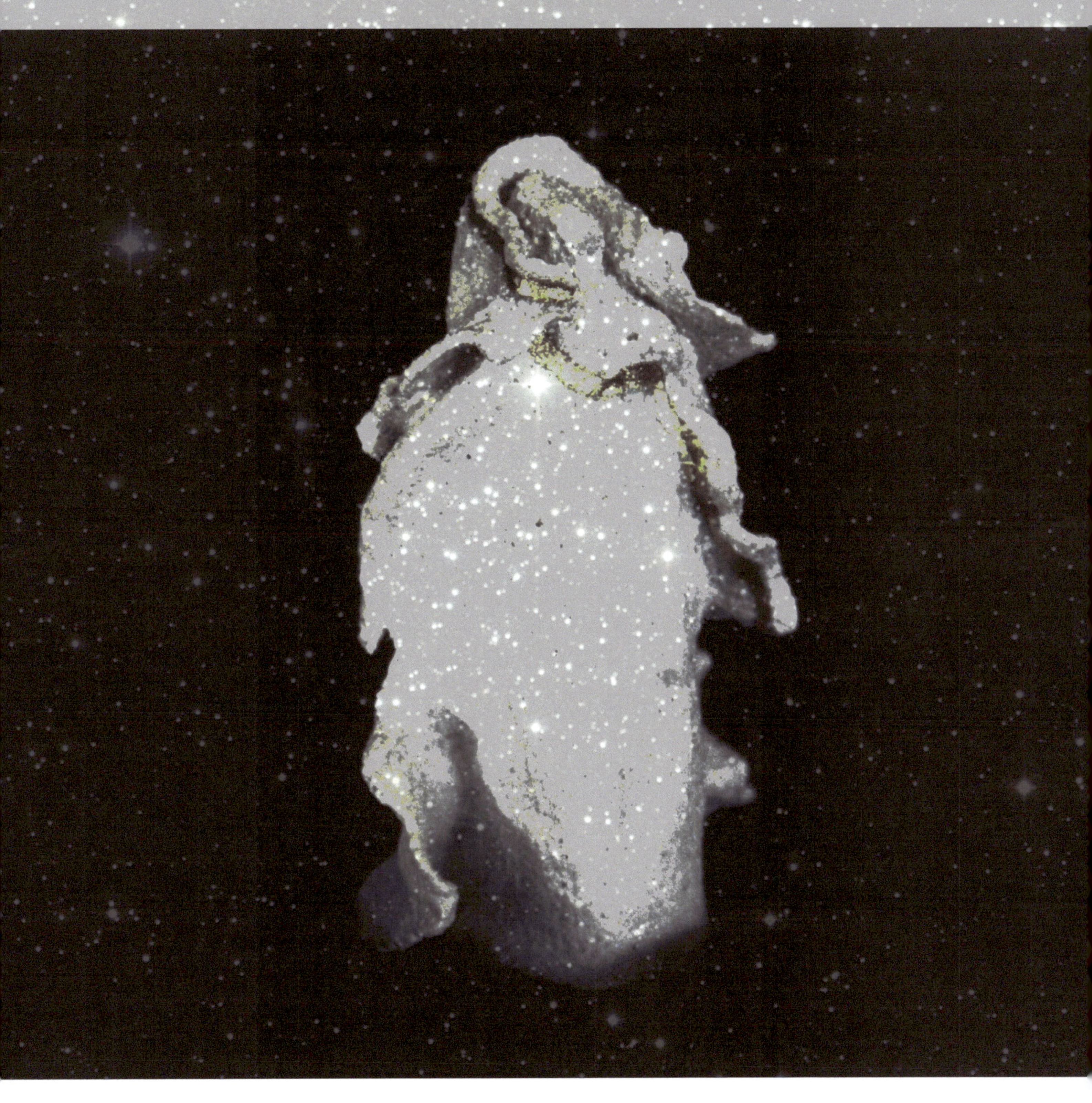

Robed-SHE...of the Alabaster Marriage

SHE…it is…who Beholds her Kingdom

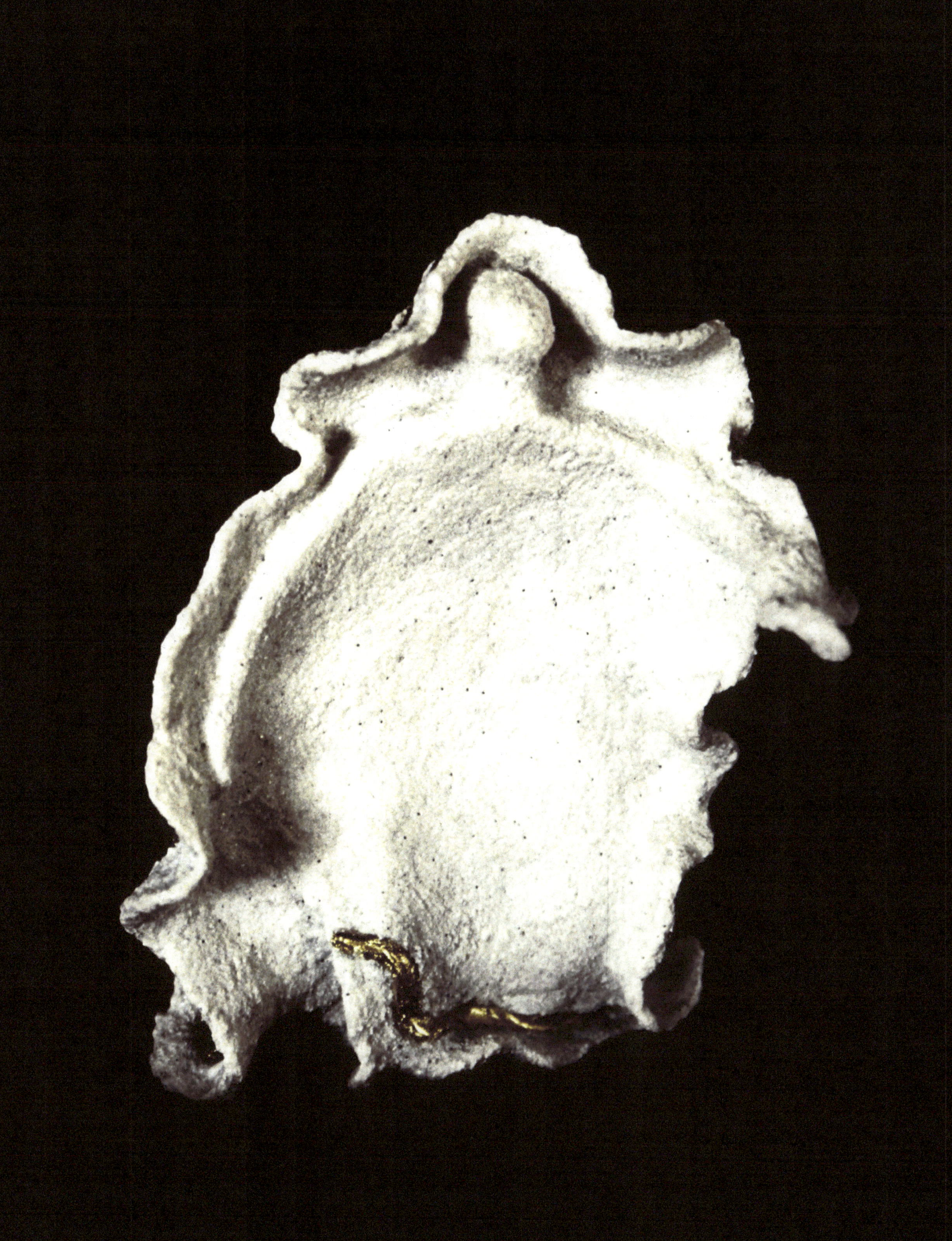

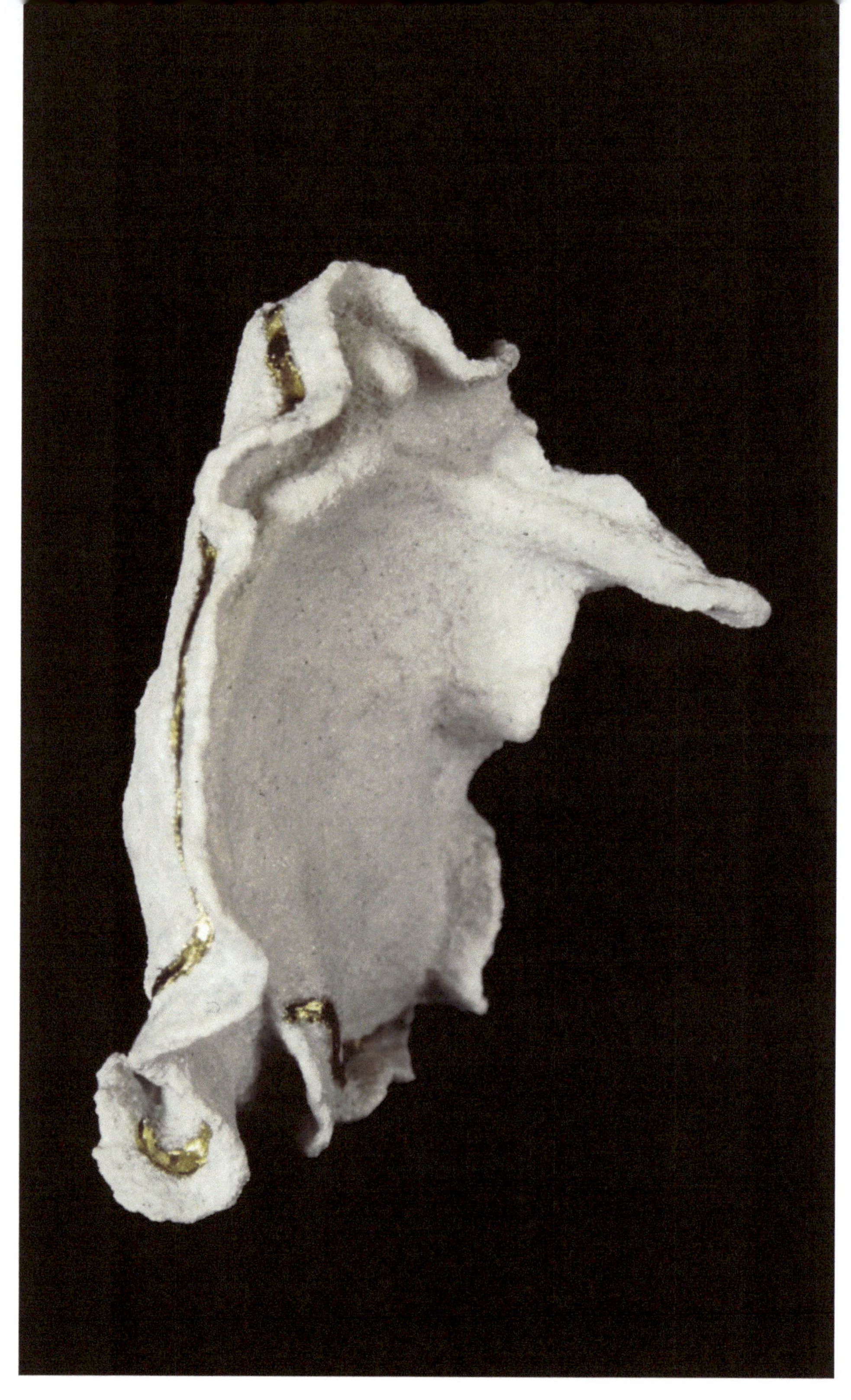

SHE...it is...who Beholds her Kingdom

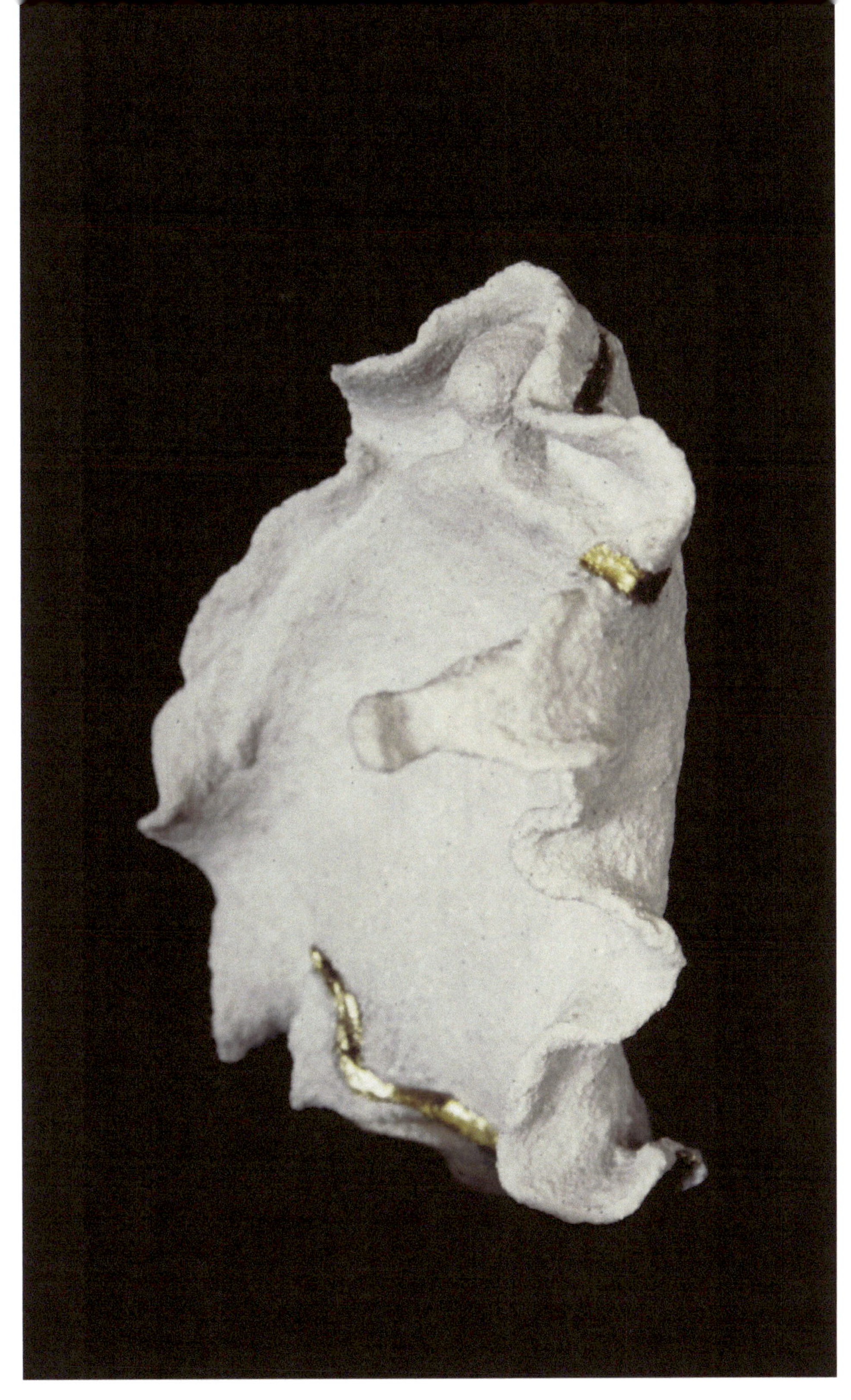

SHE...it is...who Beholds her Kingdom

SHE...who comes in the wind...

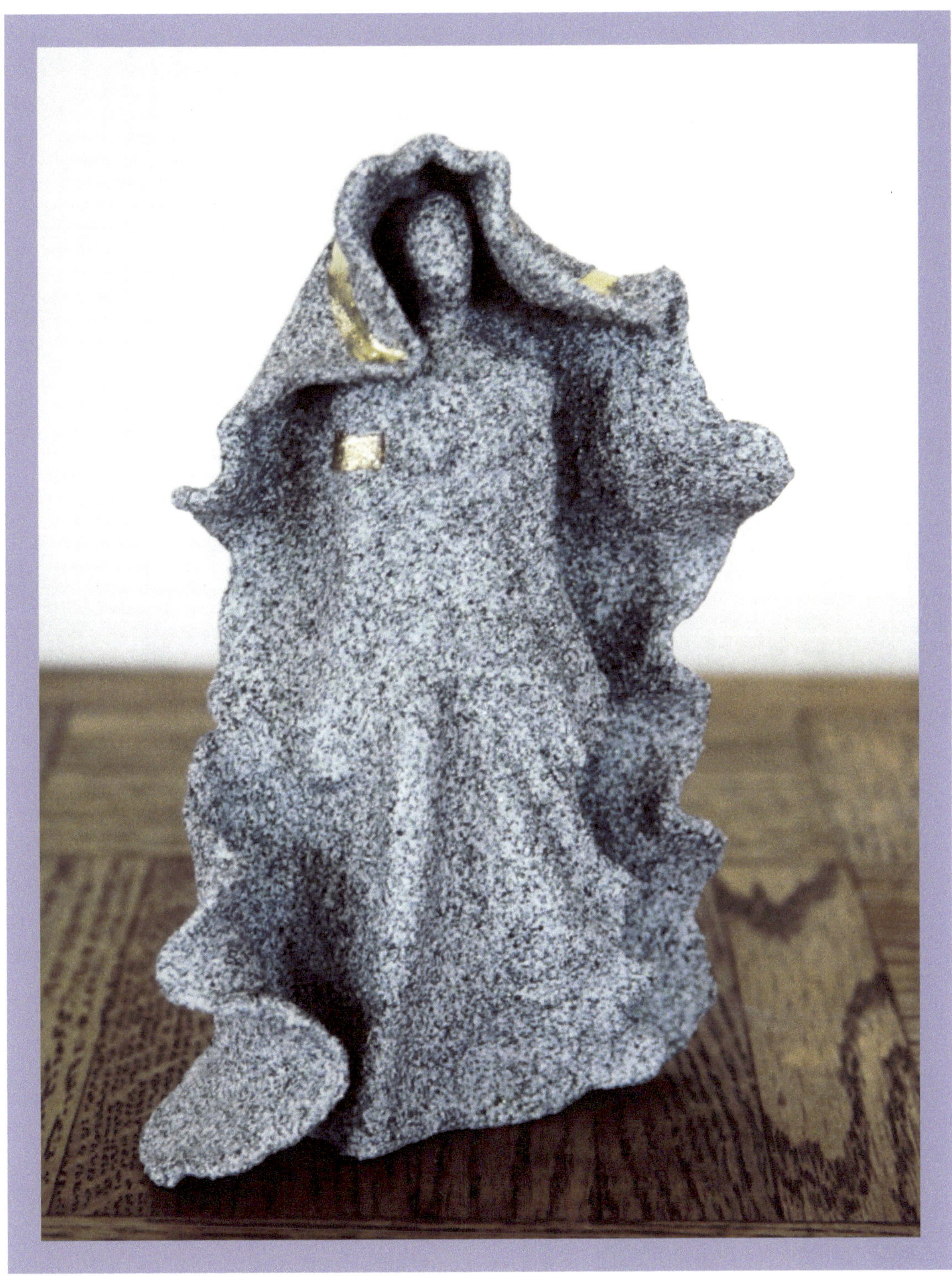

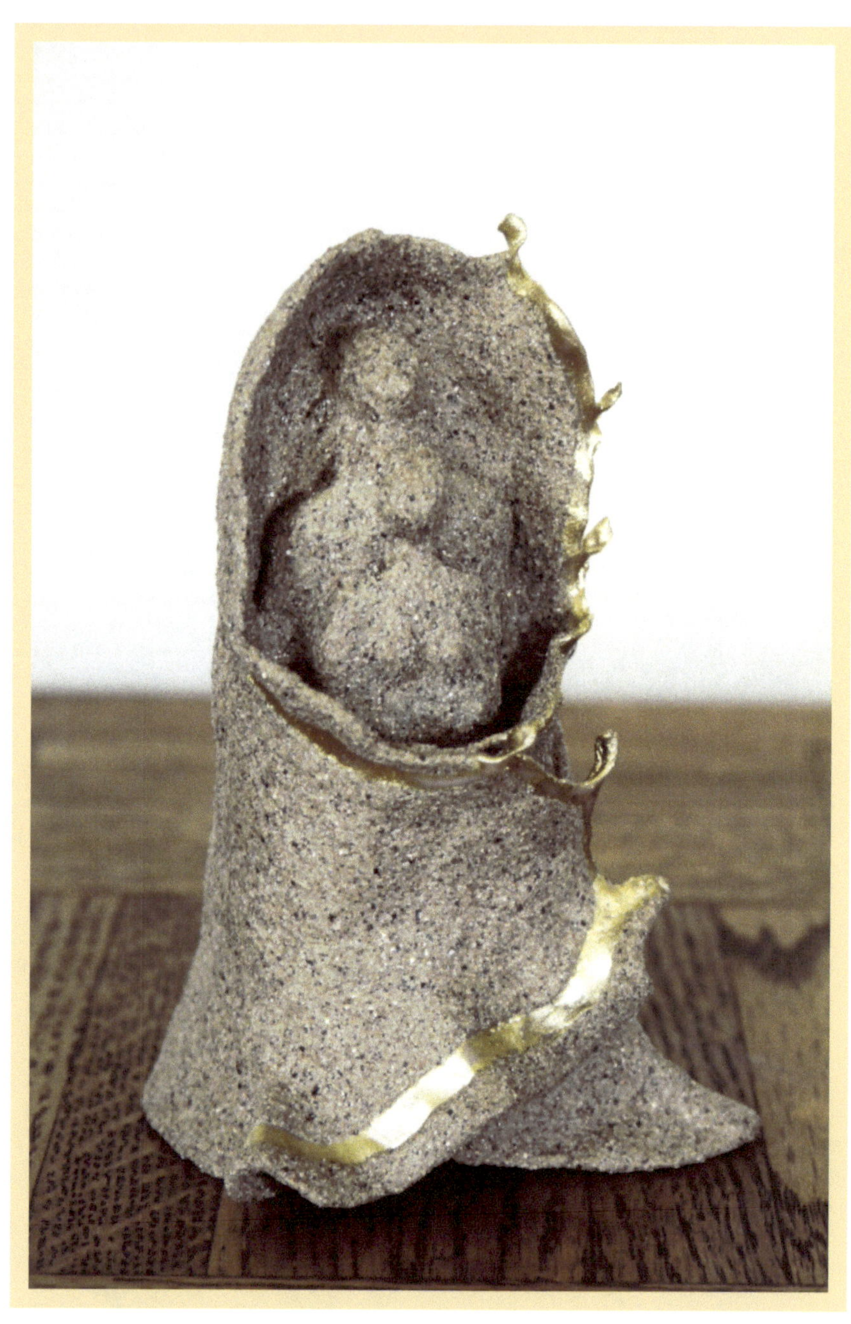

Flaming Mantle of HE and SHE

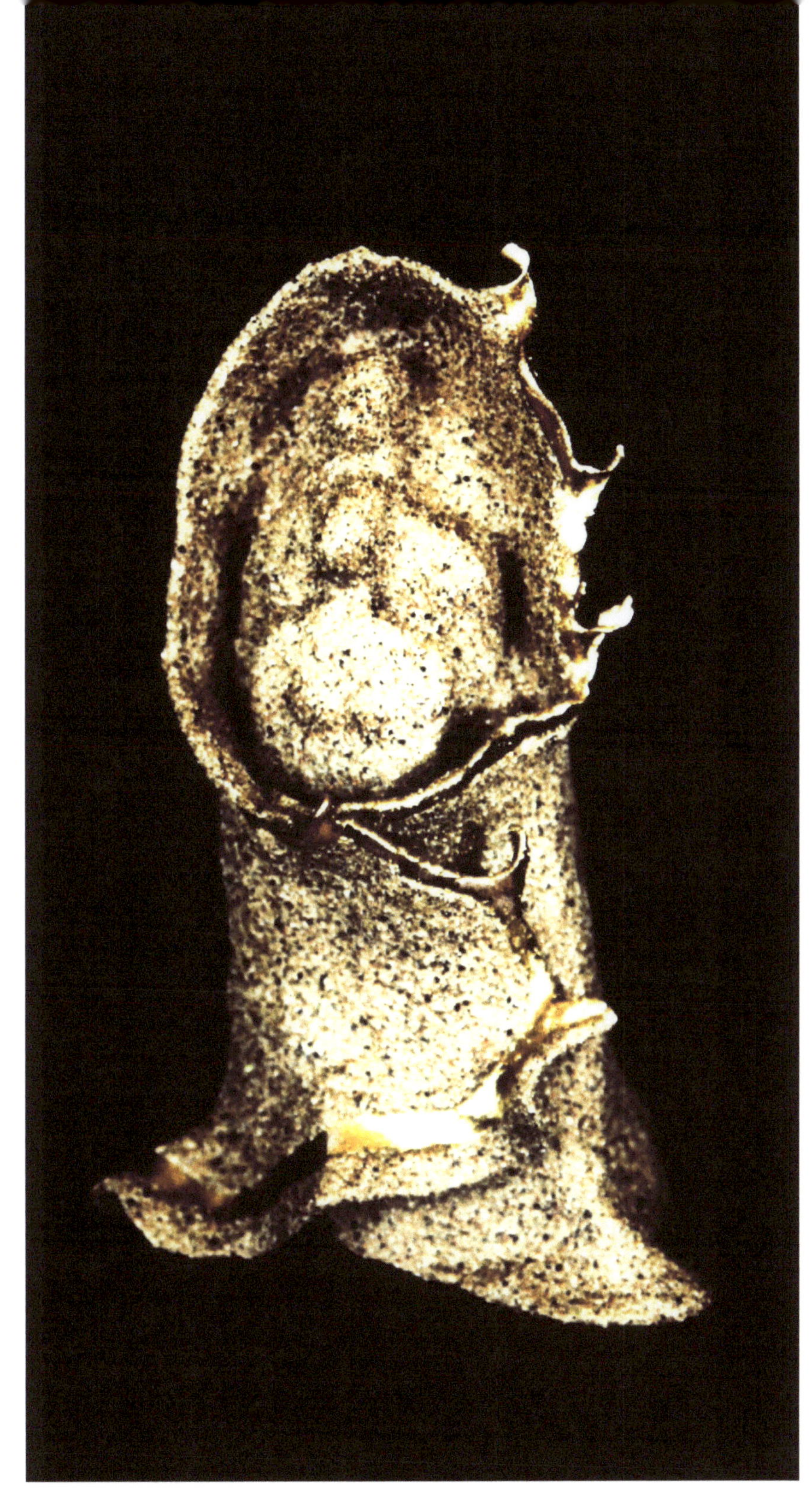

Flaming Mantle of HE and SHE

Mantle of HE and SHE

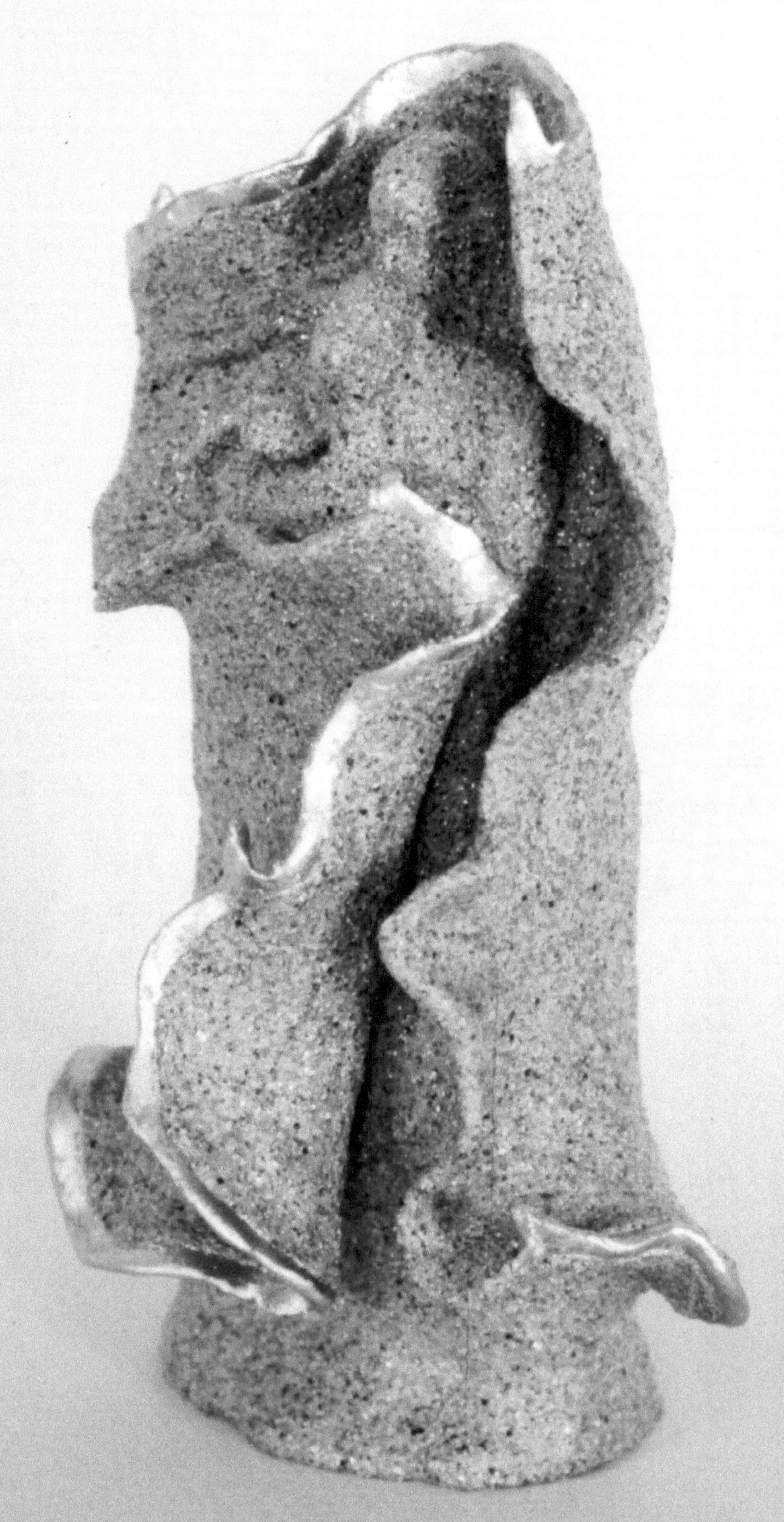

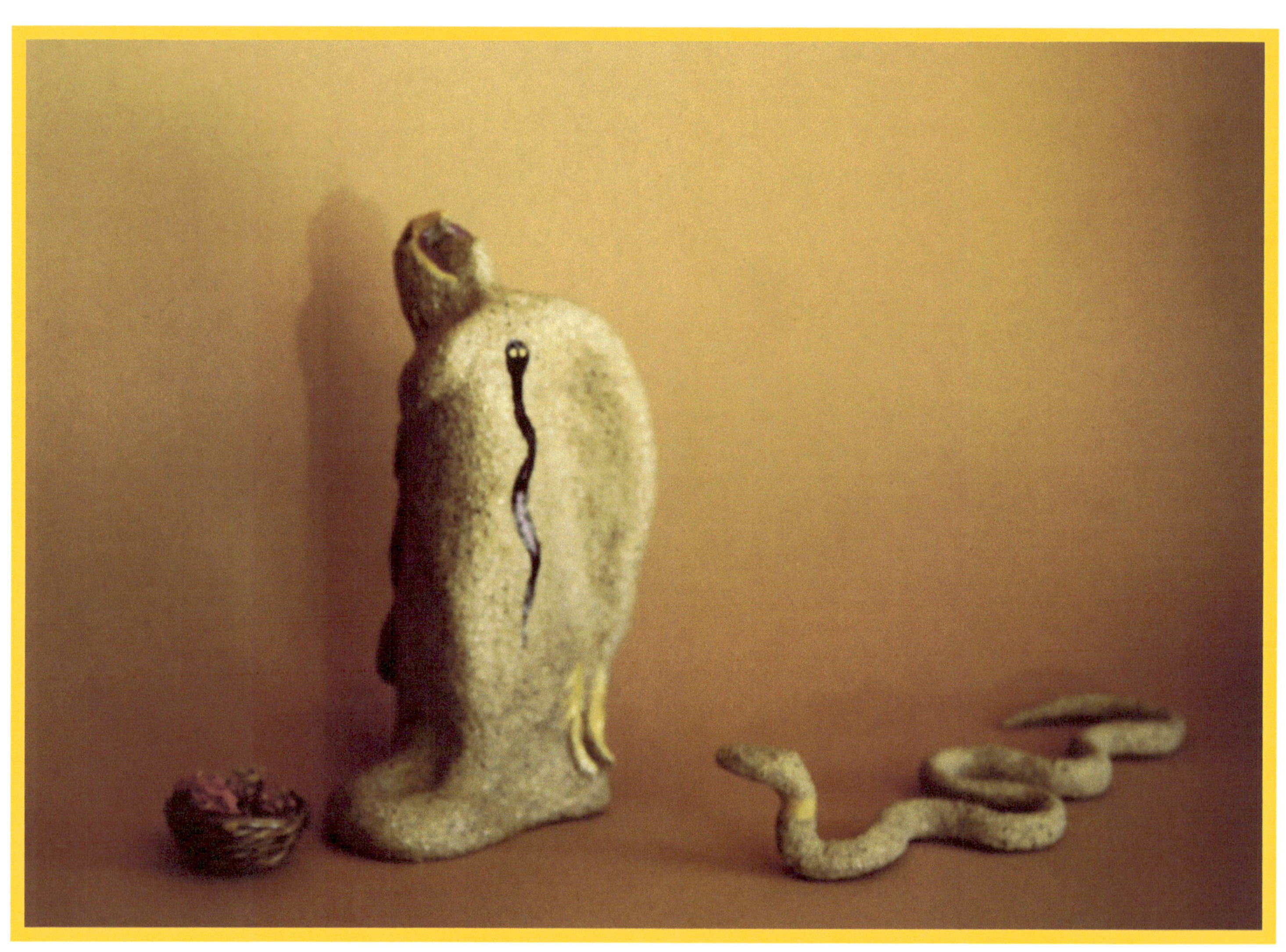

Shaman-SHE...of the stars...

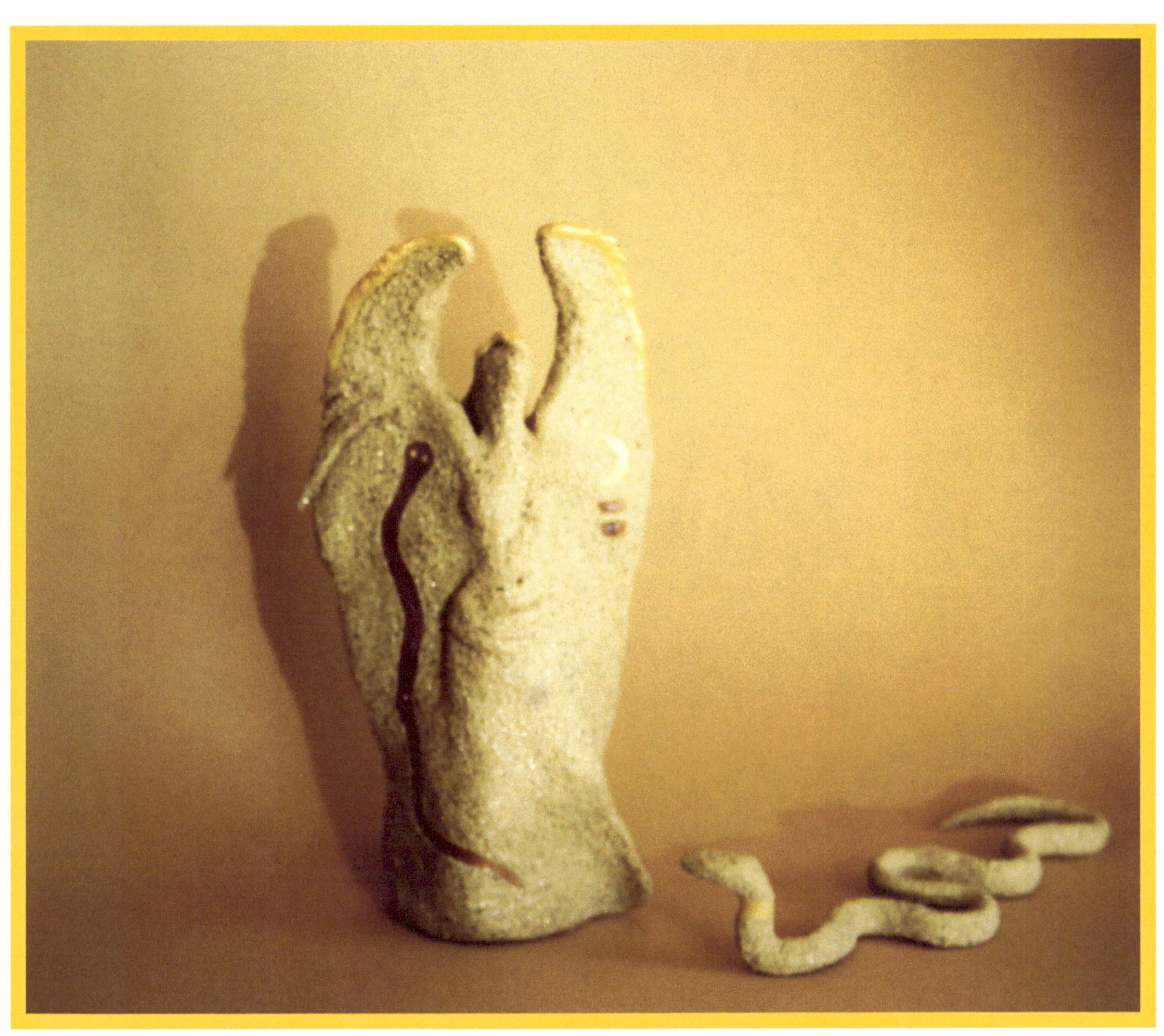

Her Flight

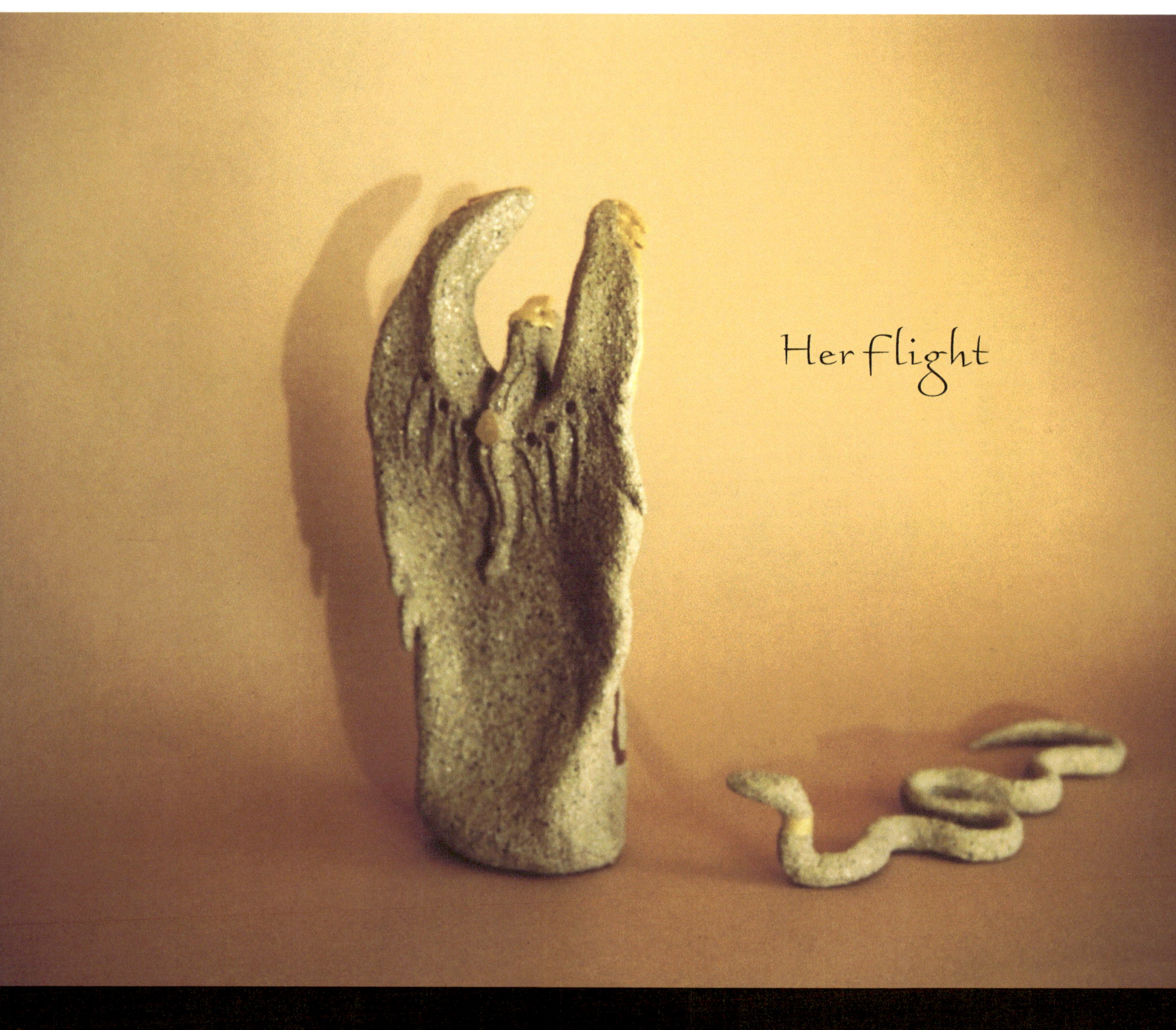
Her Flight

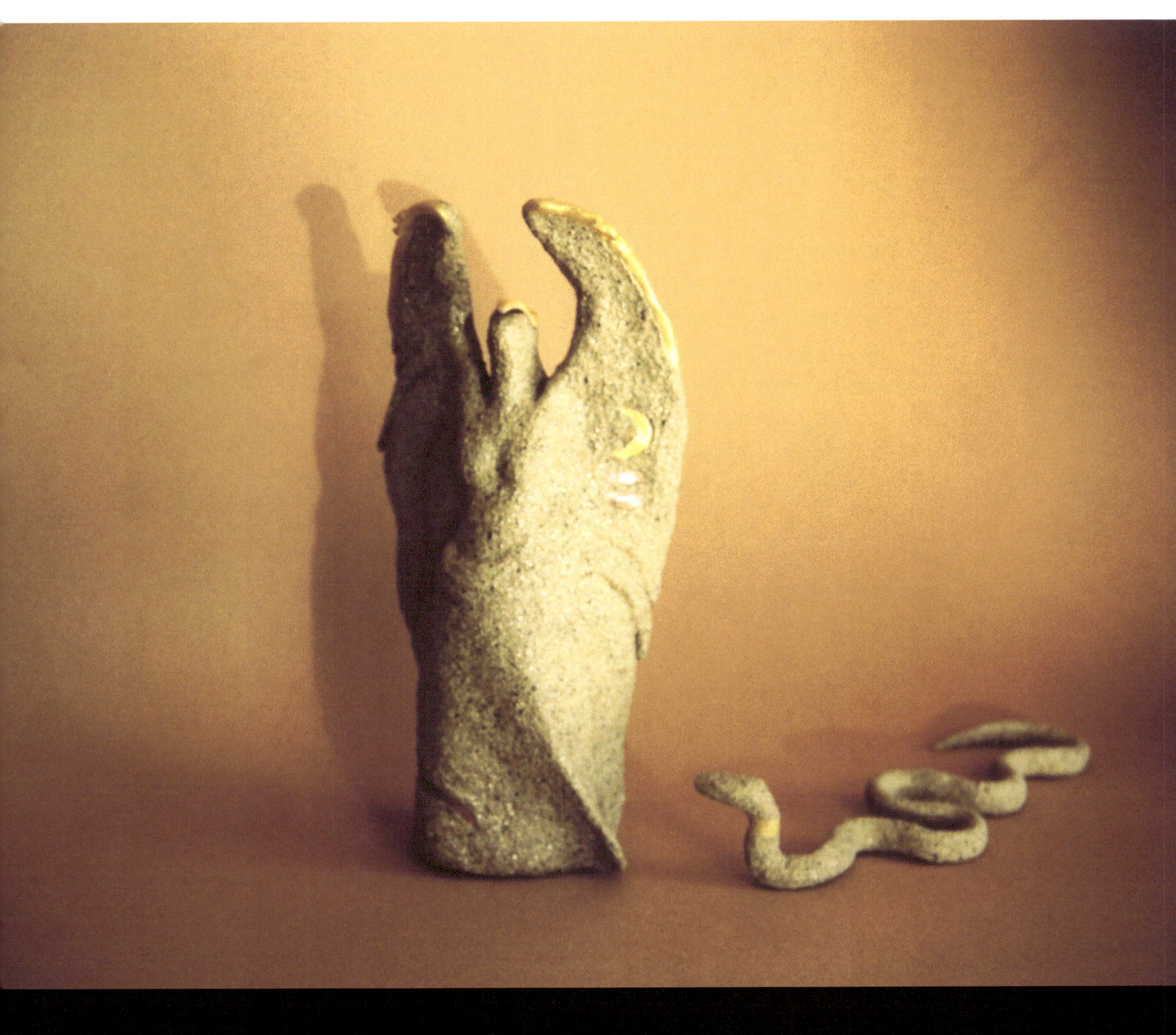

Her Flight

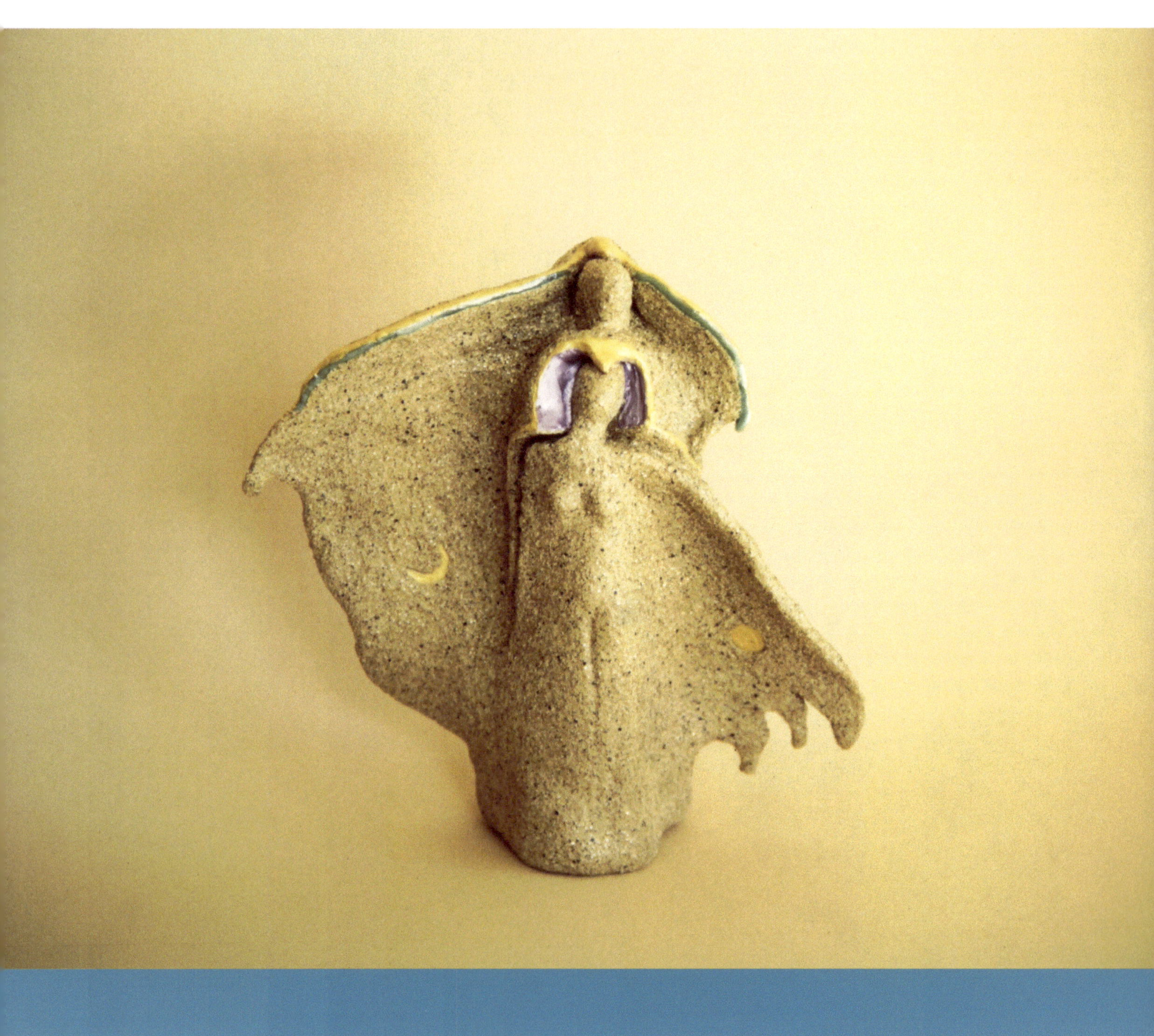

Star-Stone-Two...upon the earth...

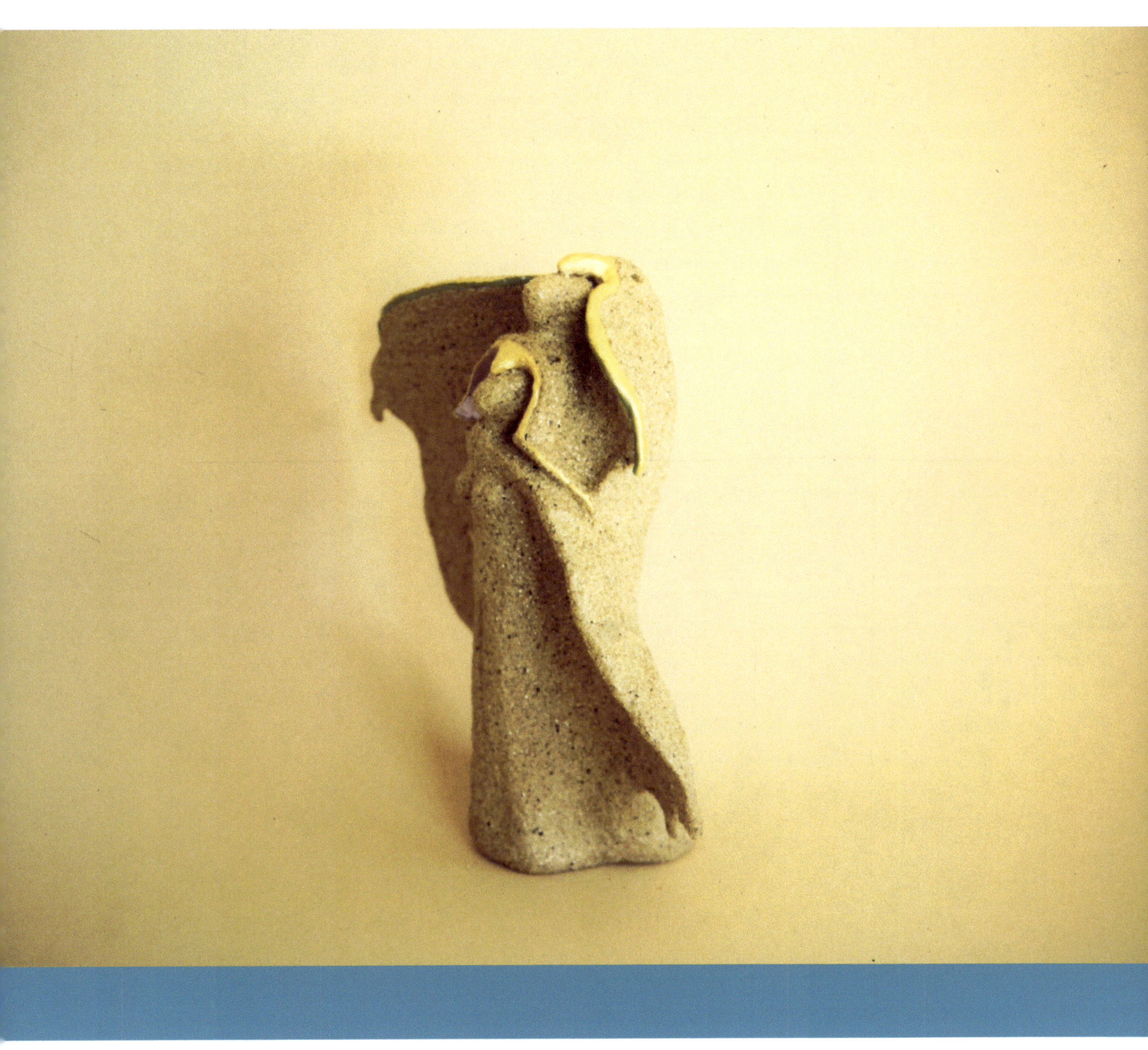

Star-Stone-Two...upon the earth...

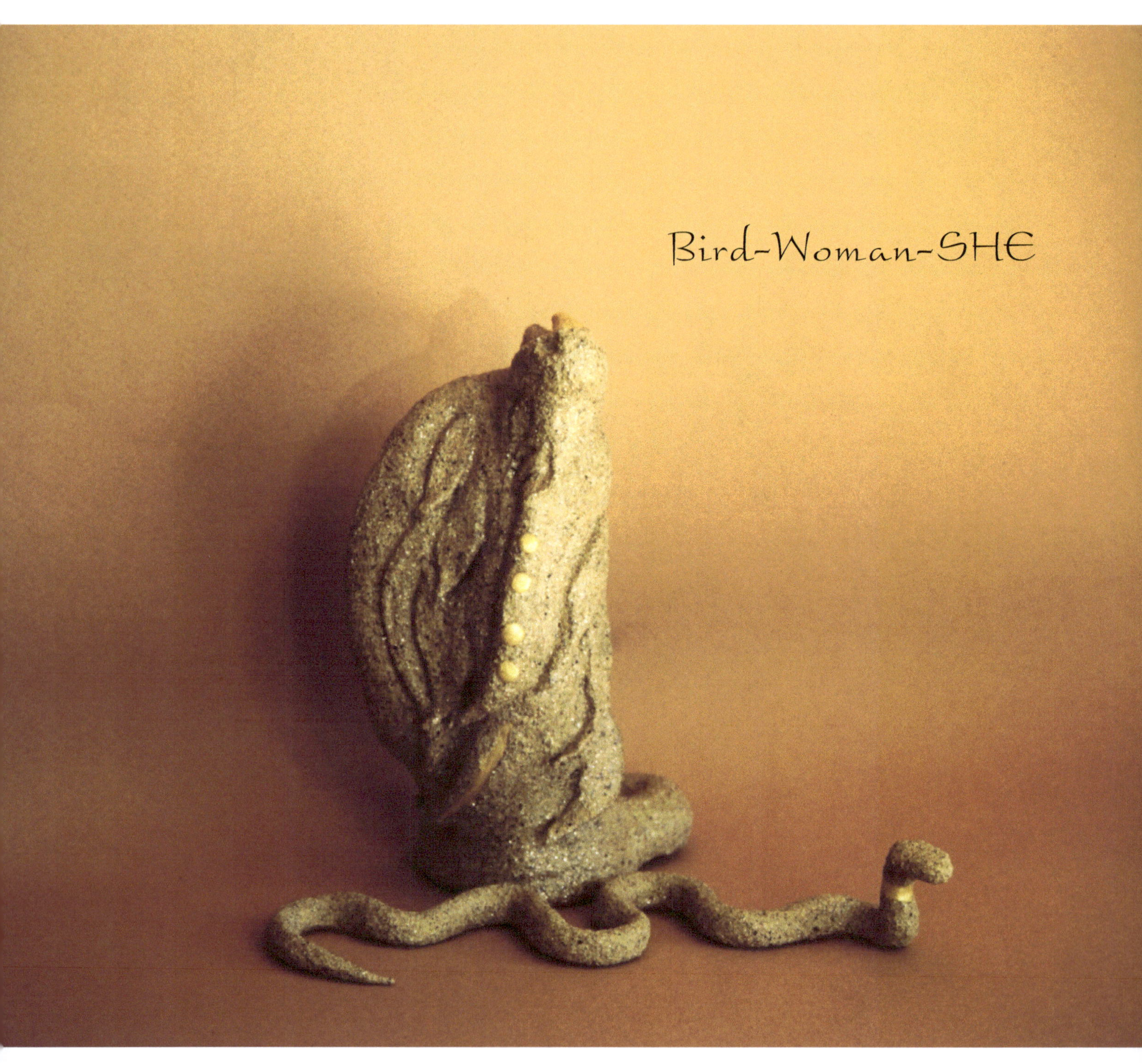
Bird-Woman-SHE

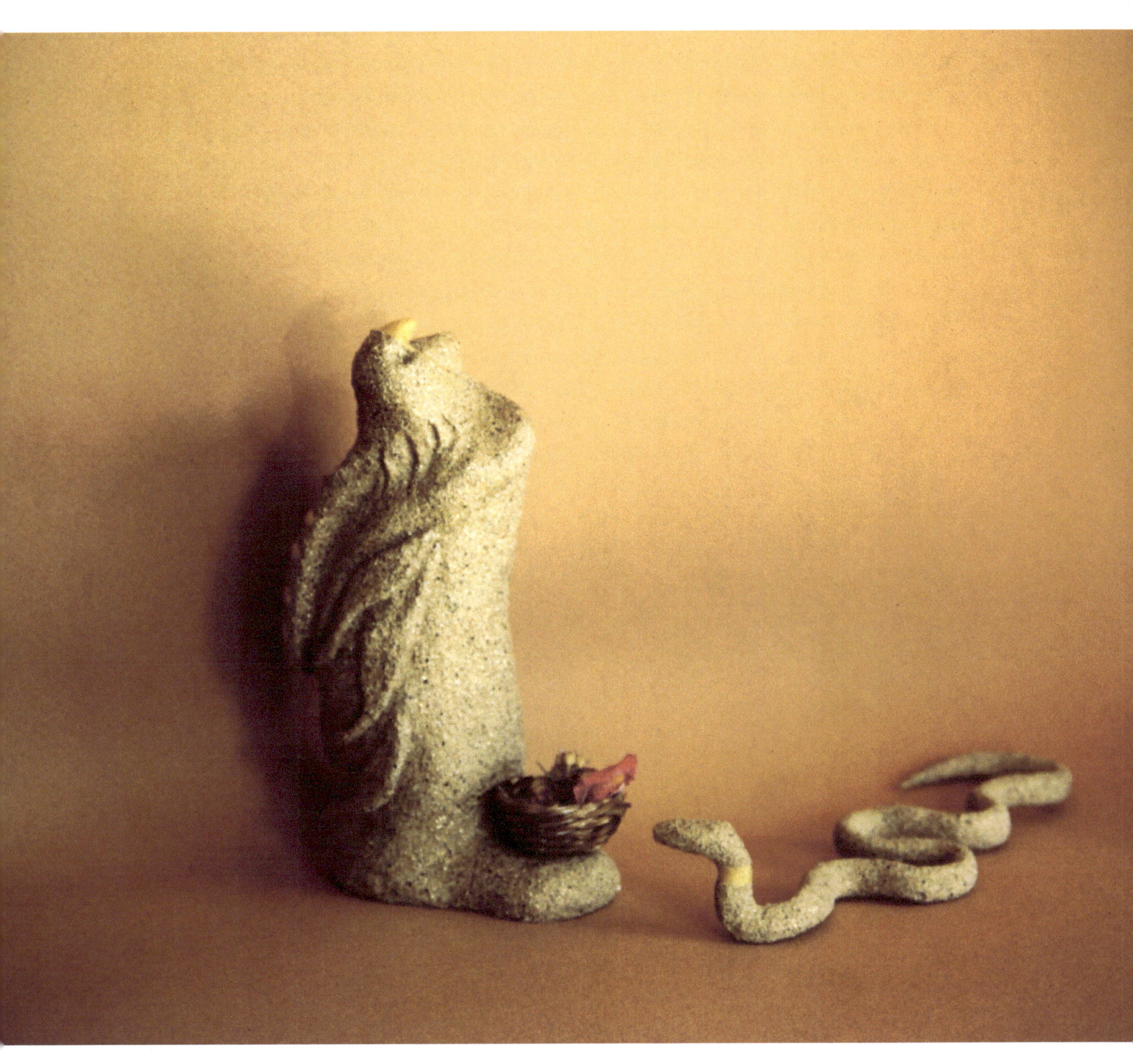

Bird-Woman-SHE

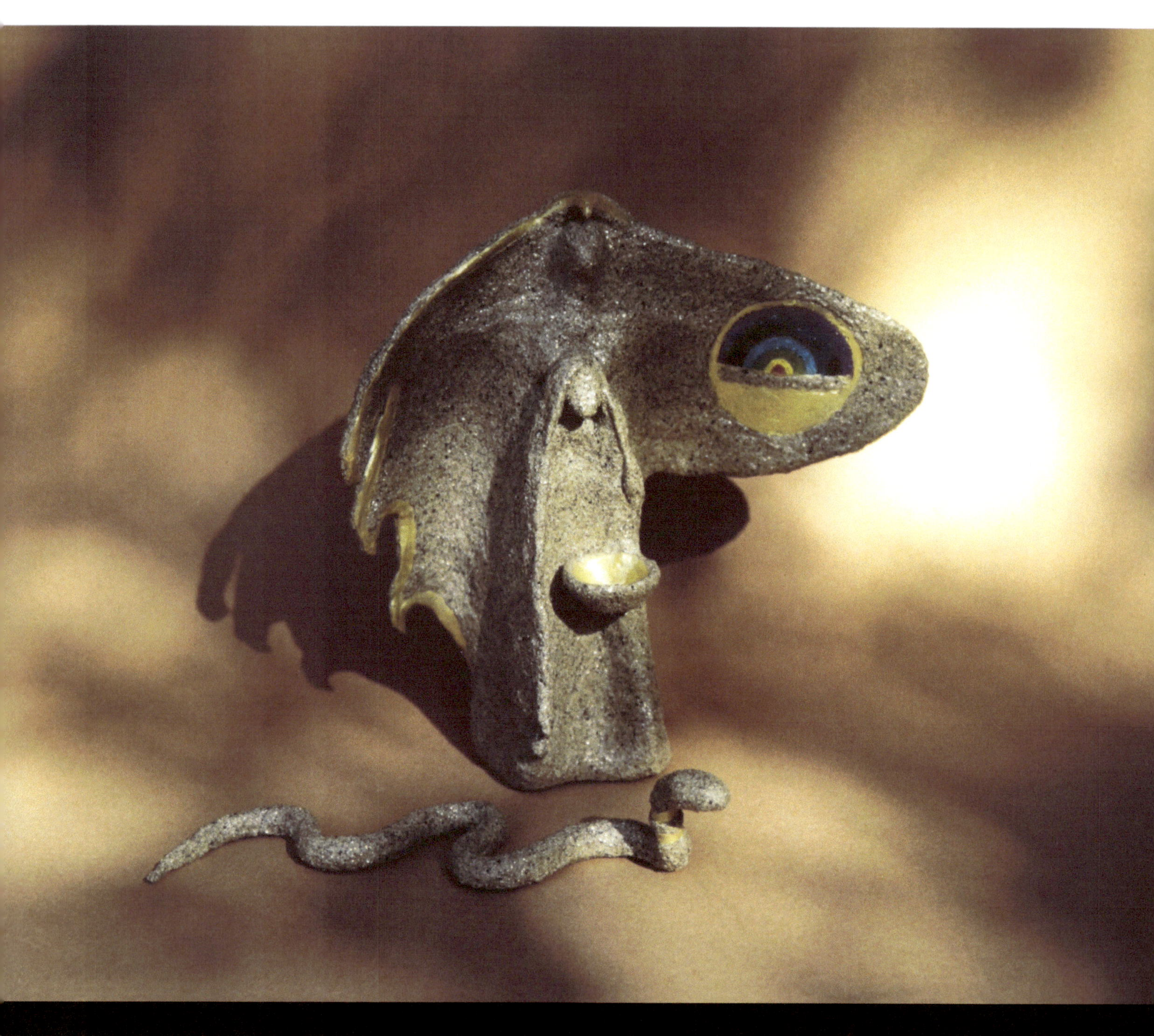

Gift-SHE

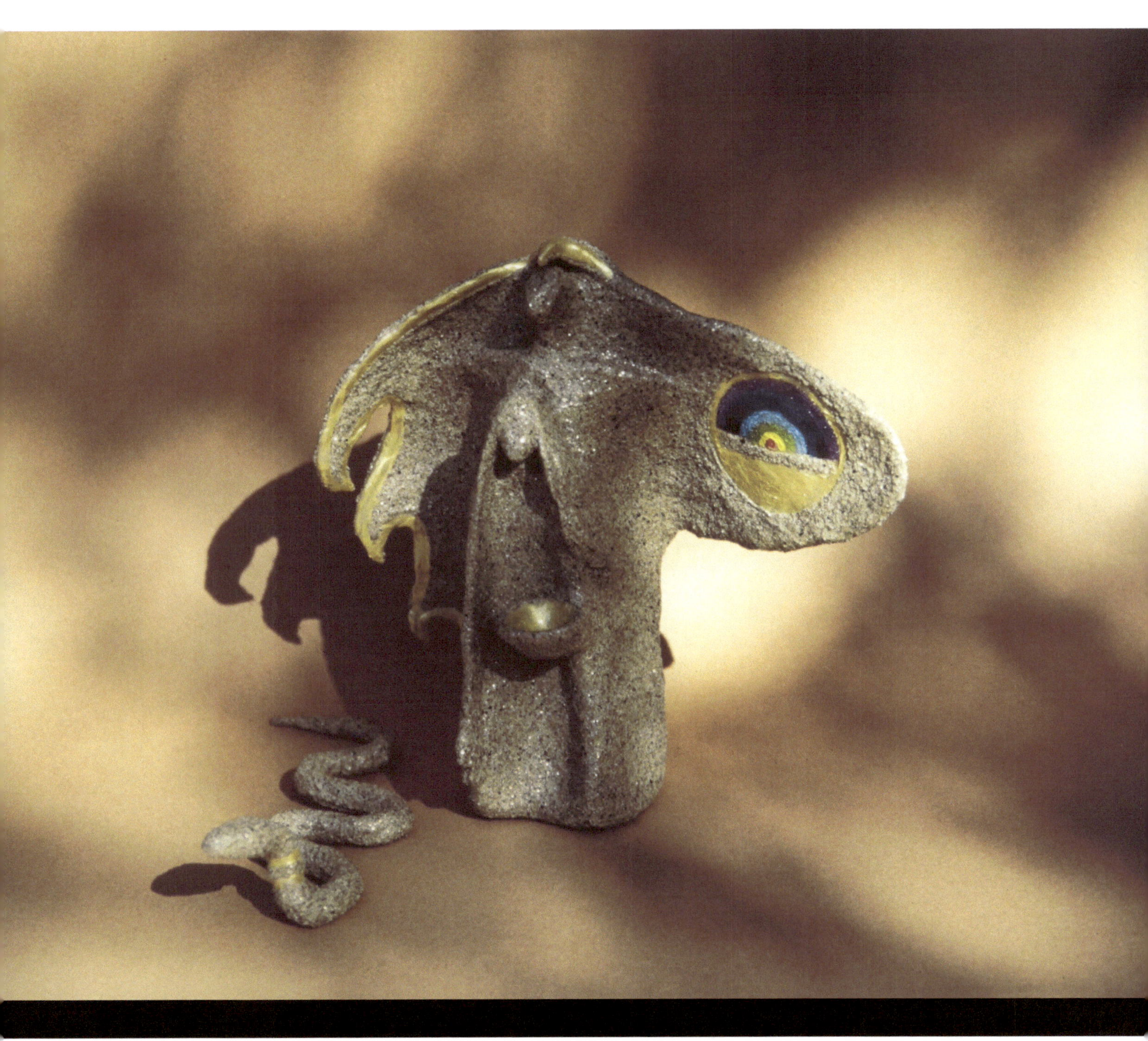

Gift-SHE

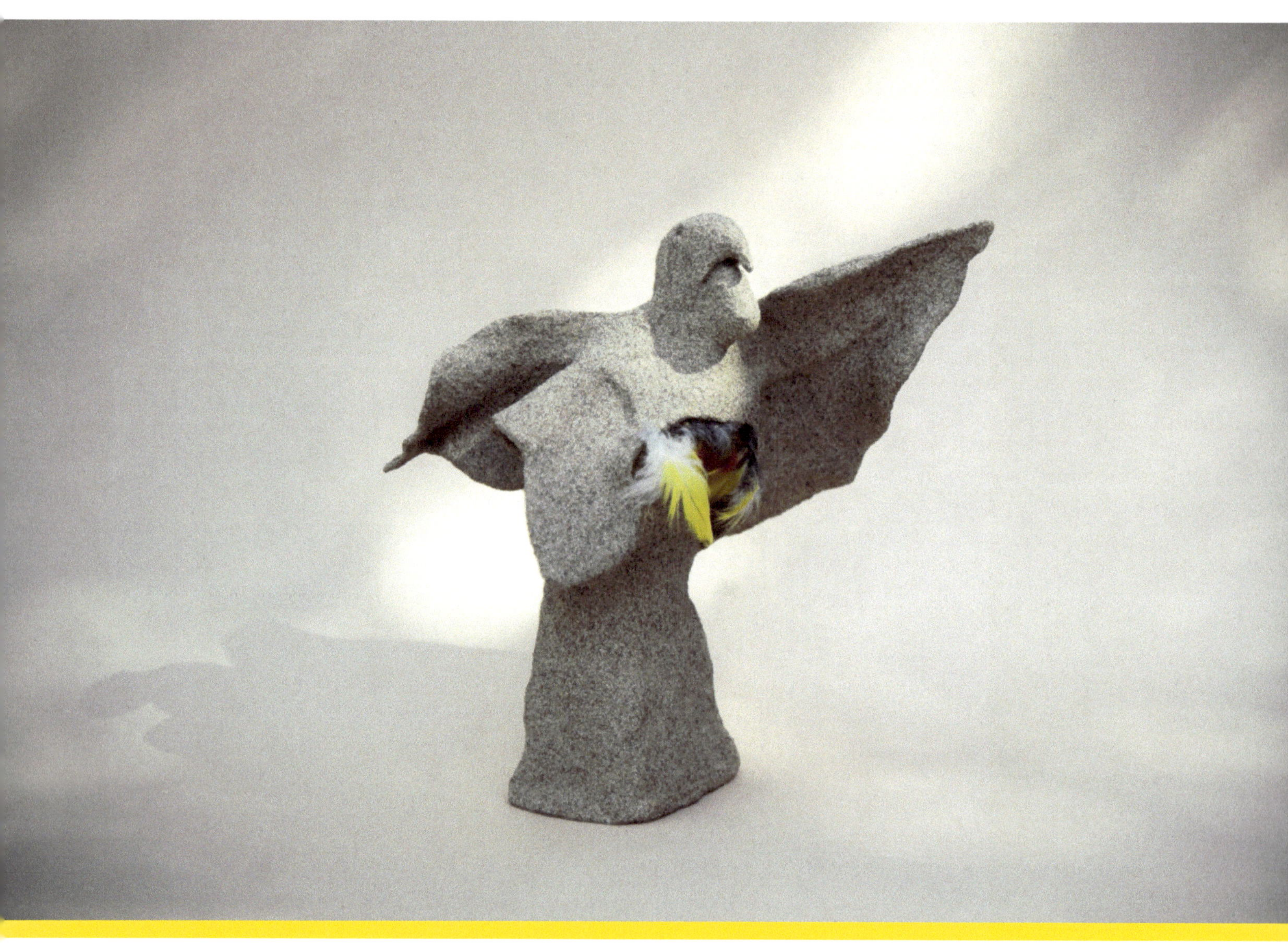

SHE…and the feathered one…

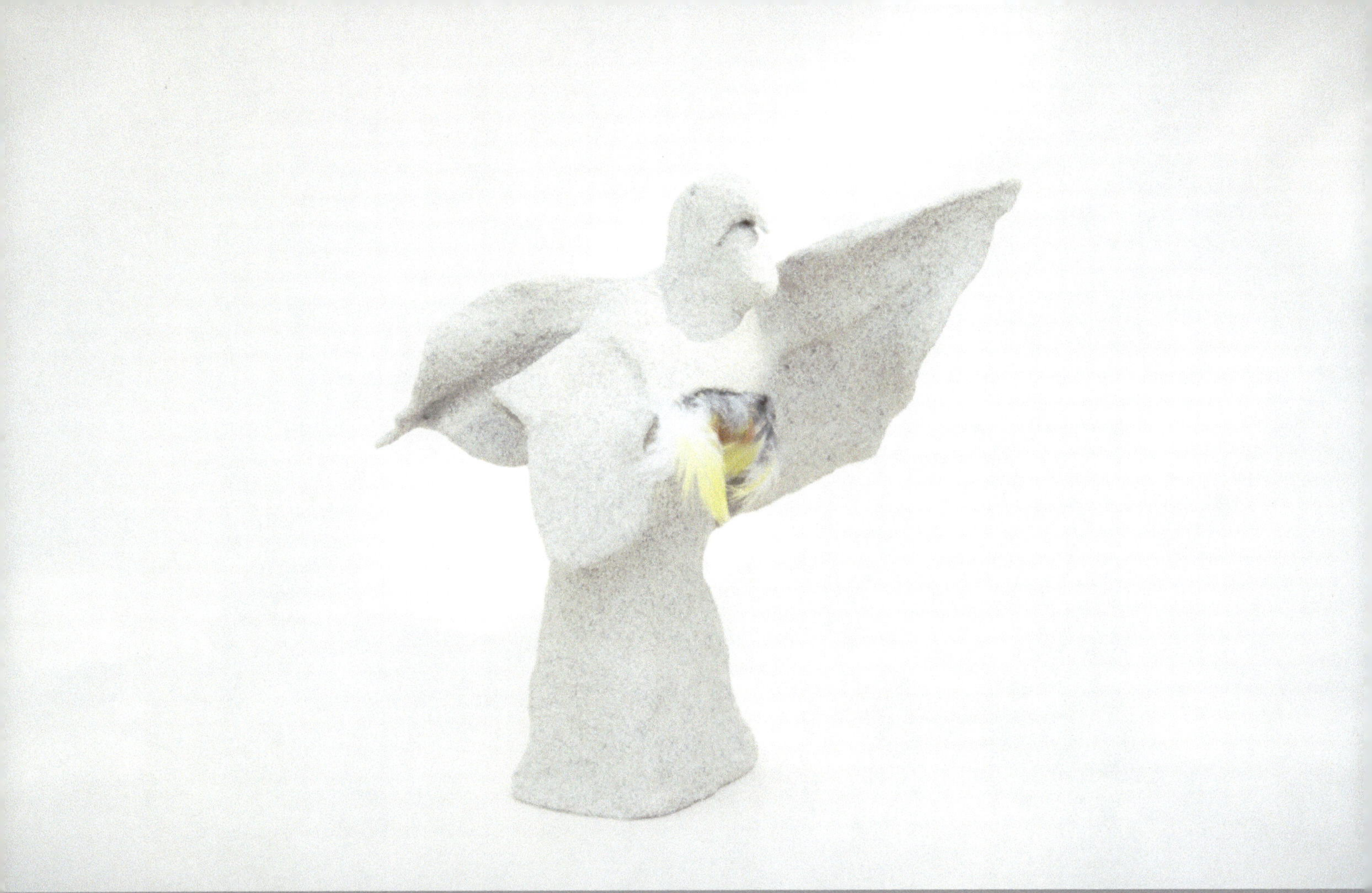

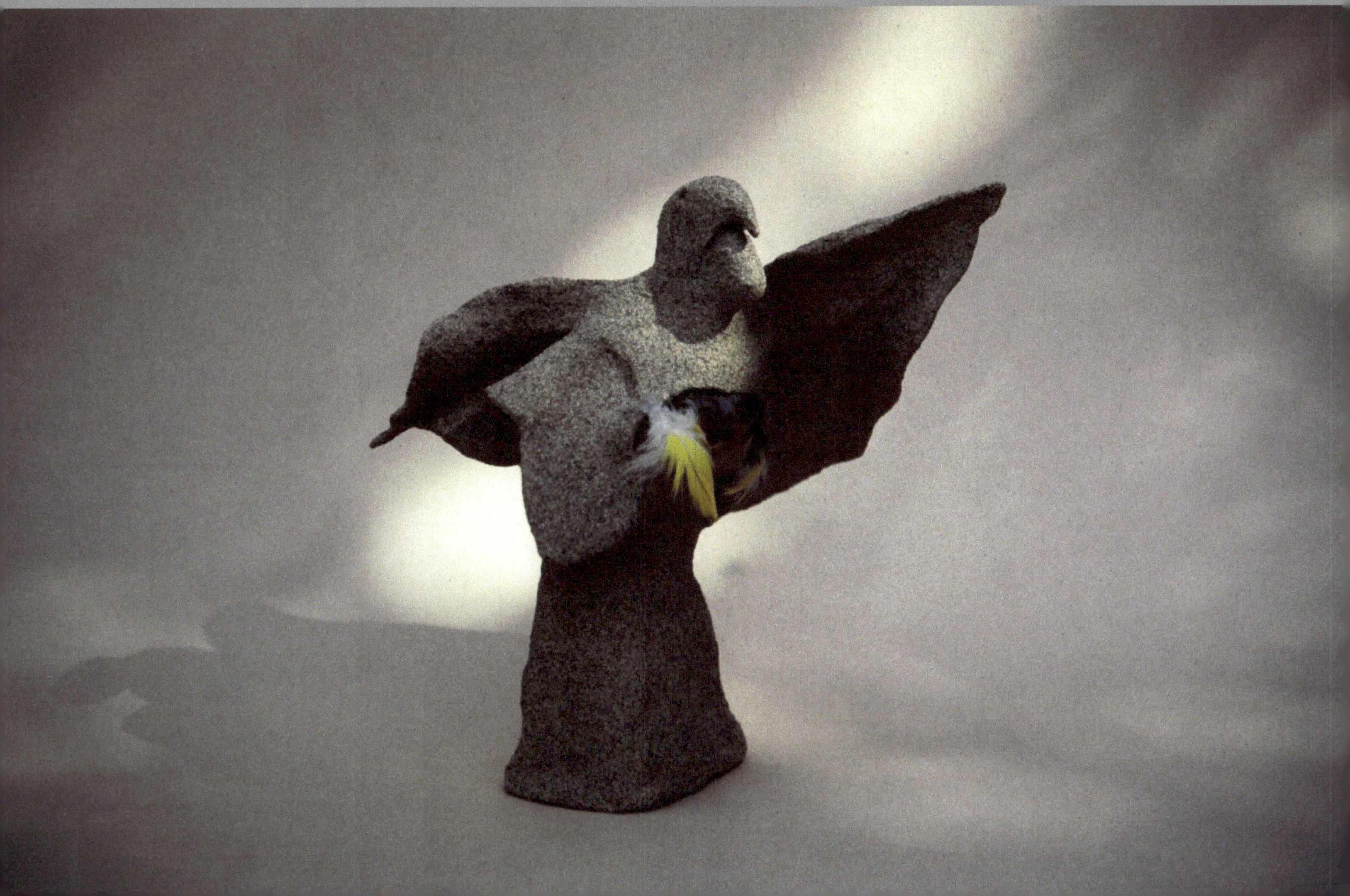

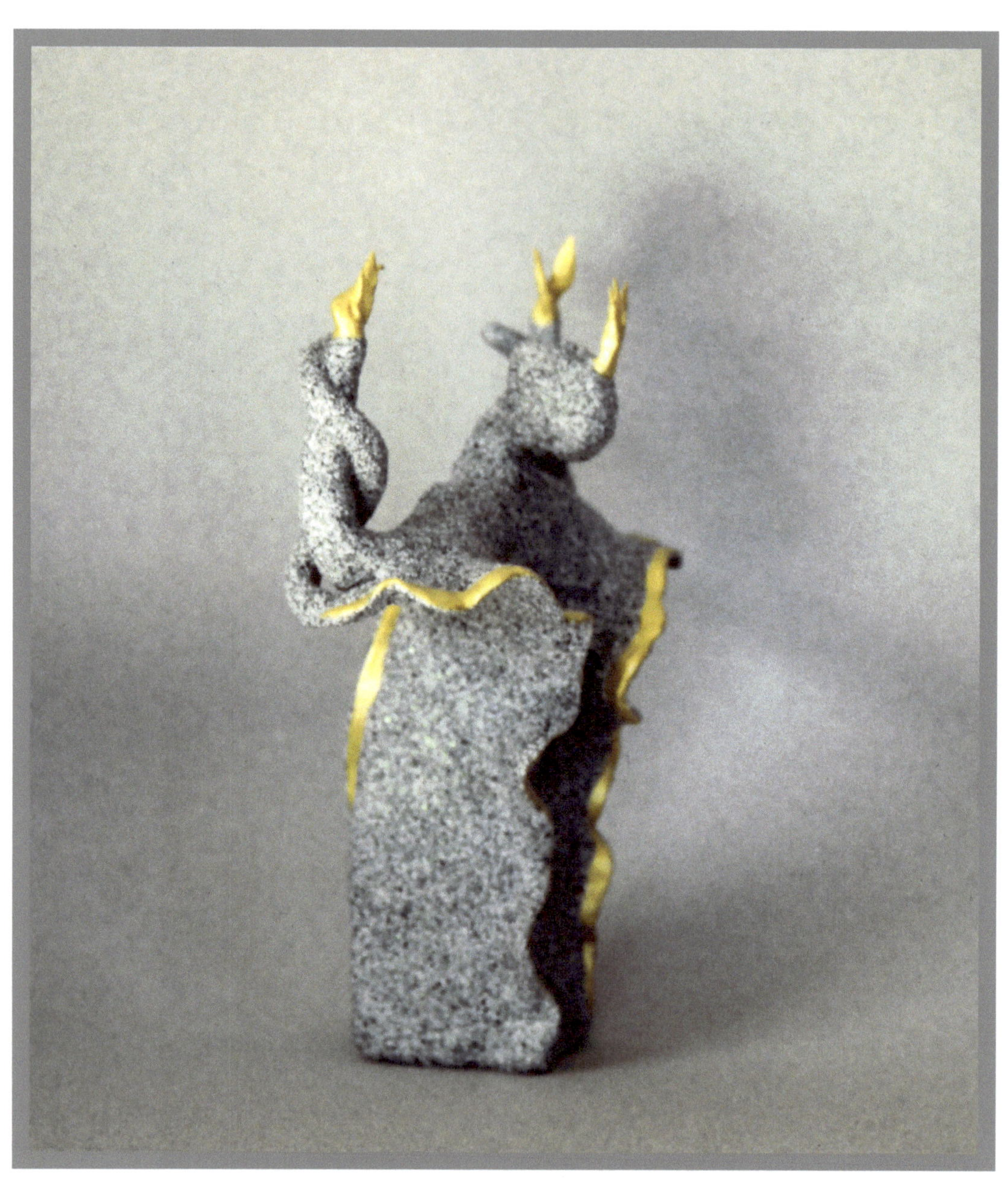

Flame of the Infinite

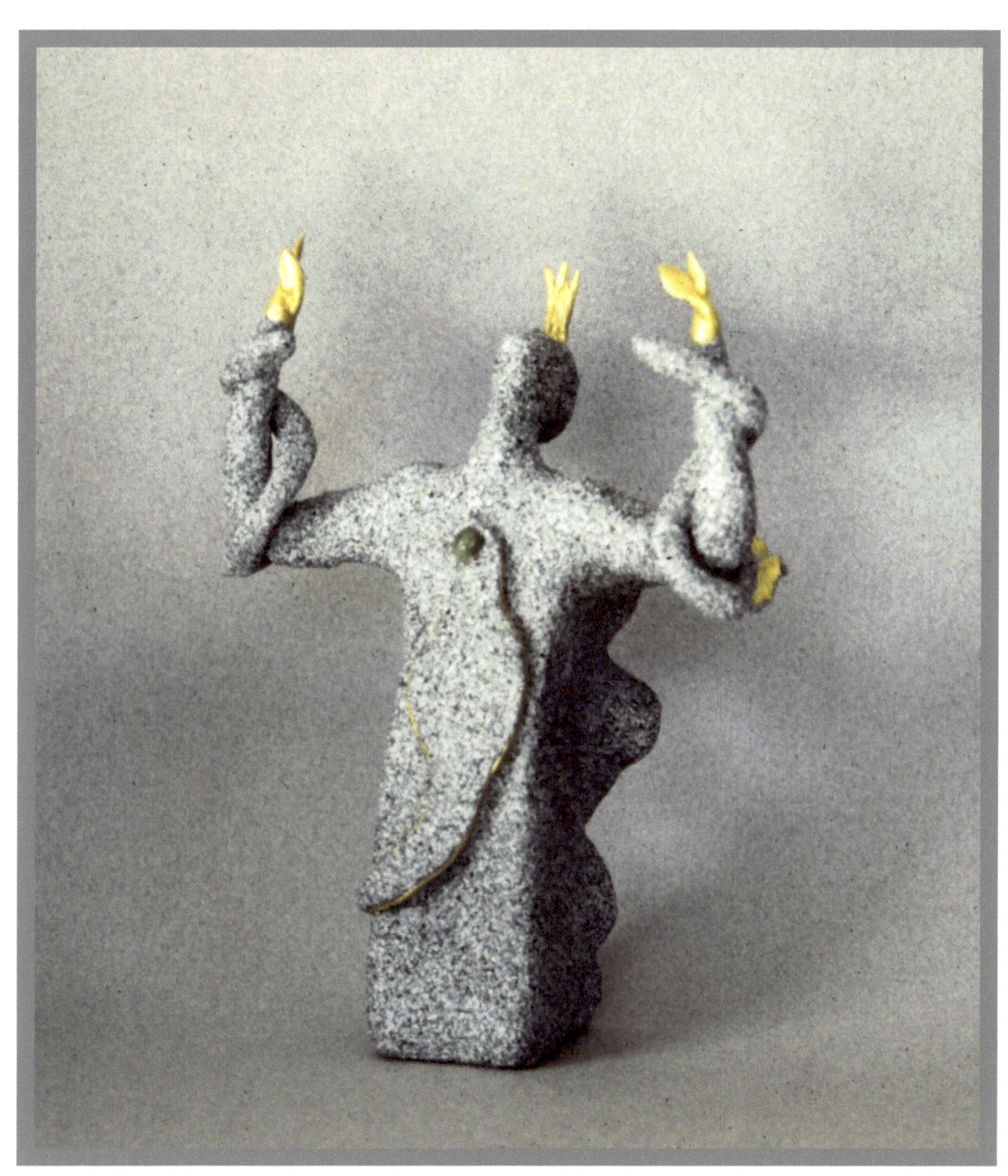

Flame of the Infinite

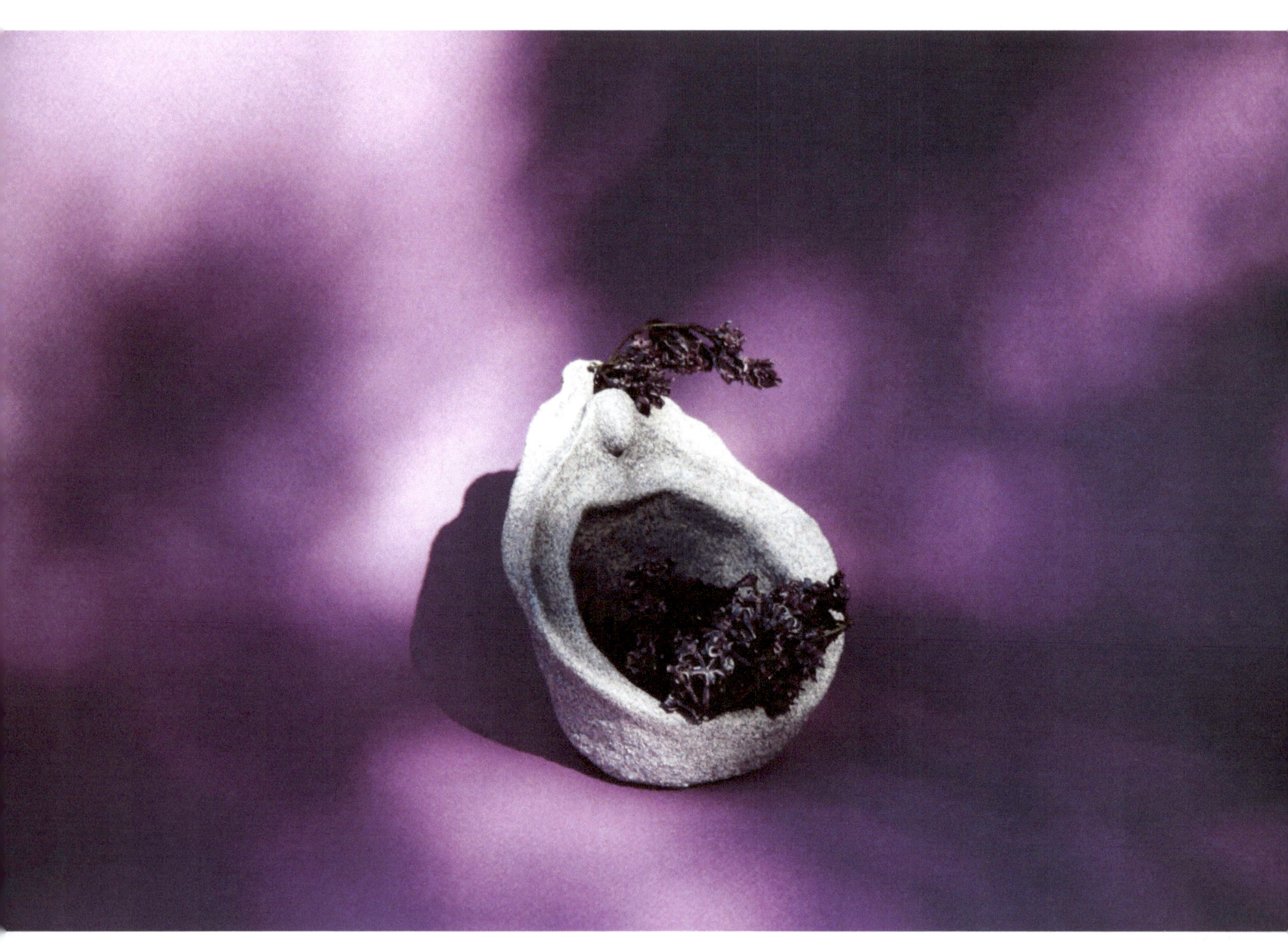

from womb of creation...

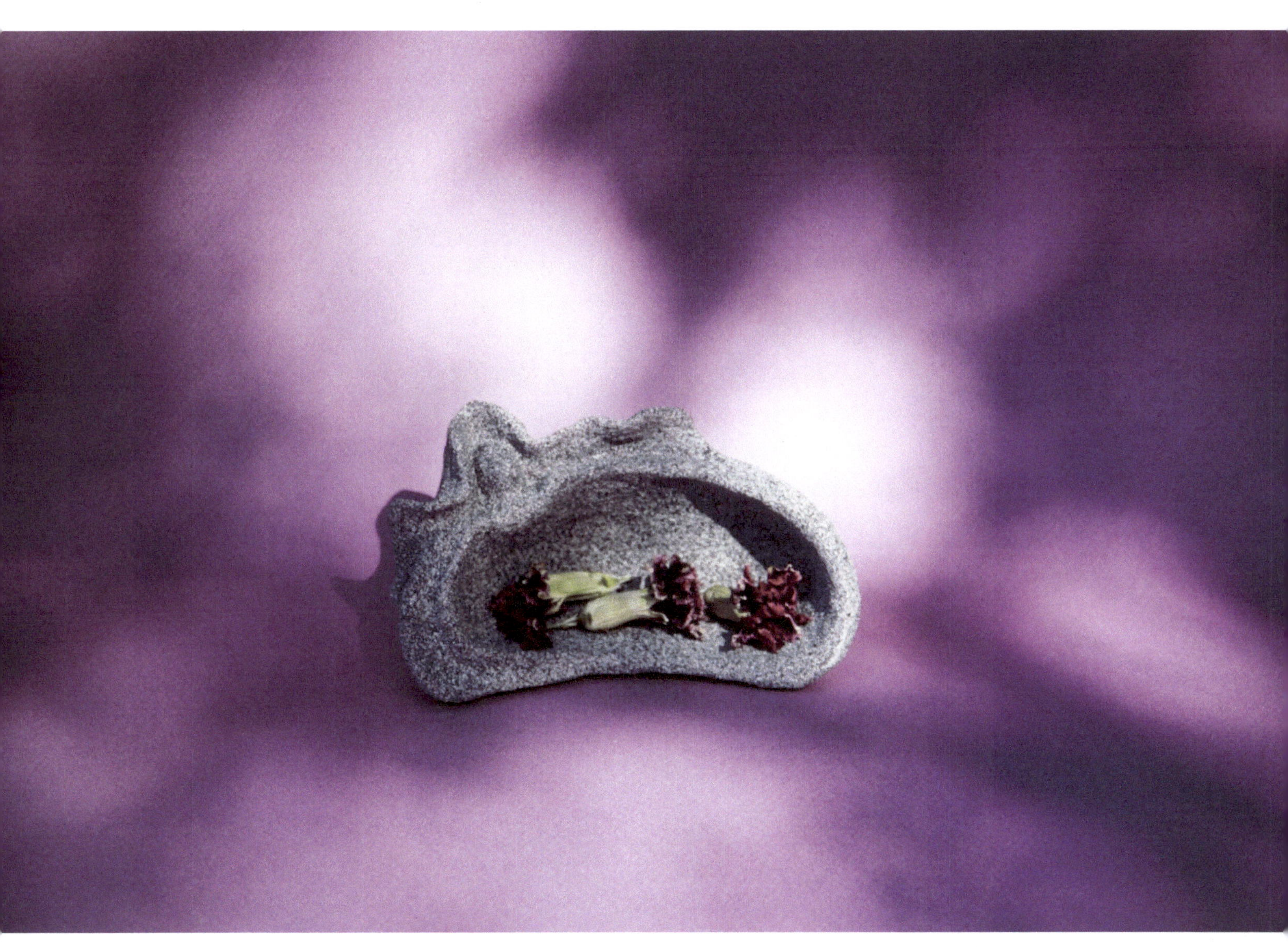

giver of gifts-SHE

Second Phase:
Kachina Cactus Gardens

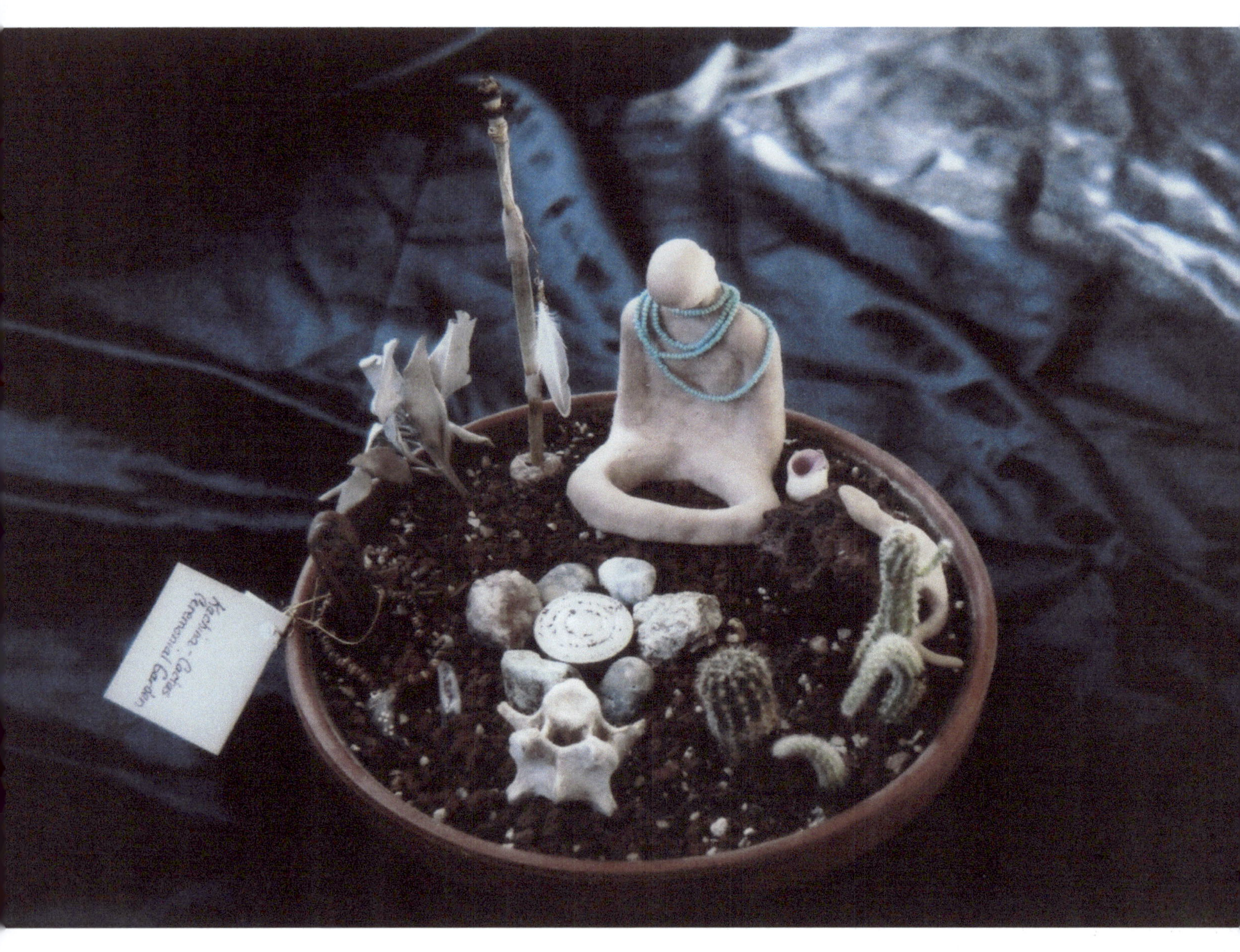

sweat lodge ceremony—He

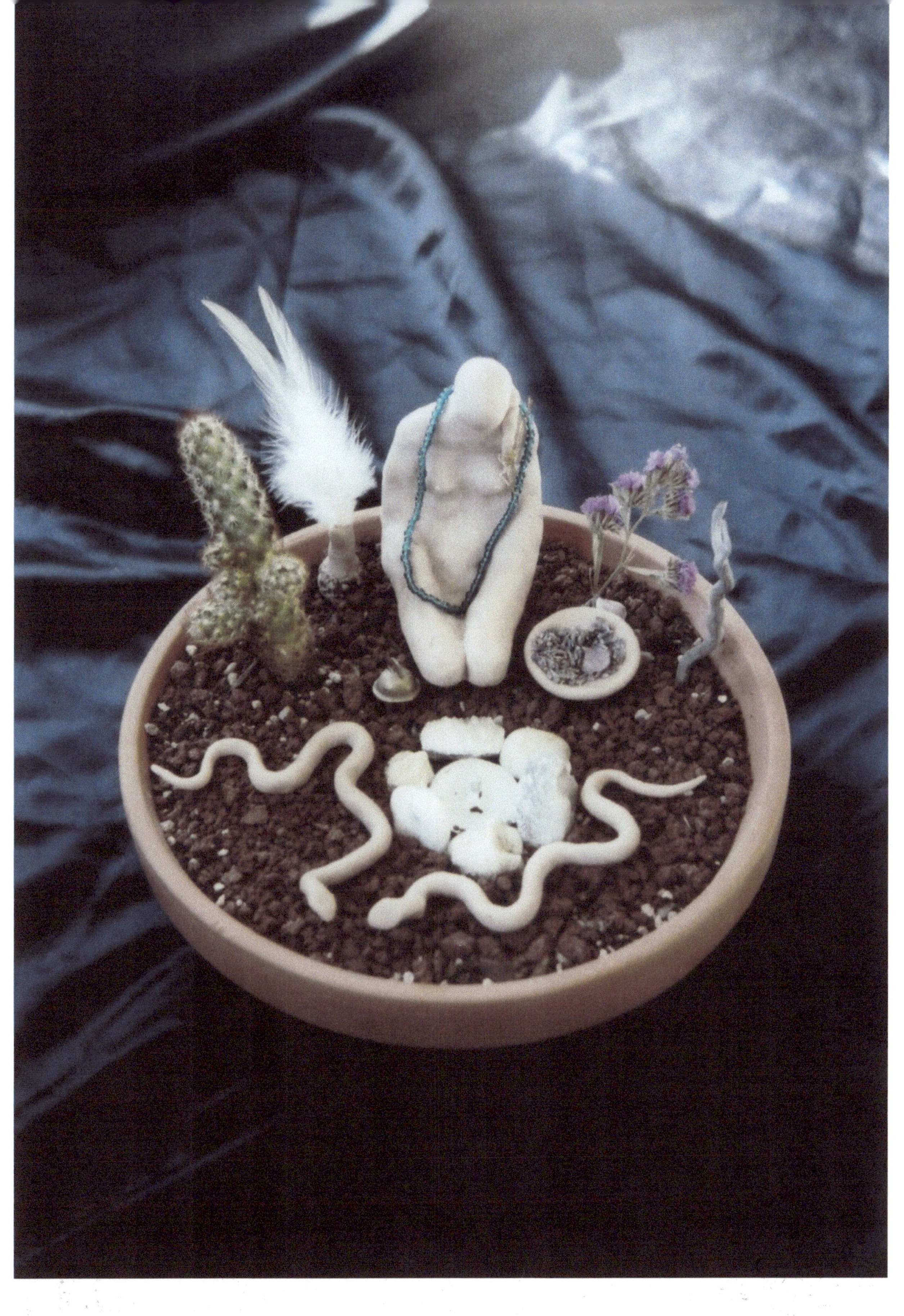

sweat lodge ceremony–She

Ceremony of HE and SHE

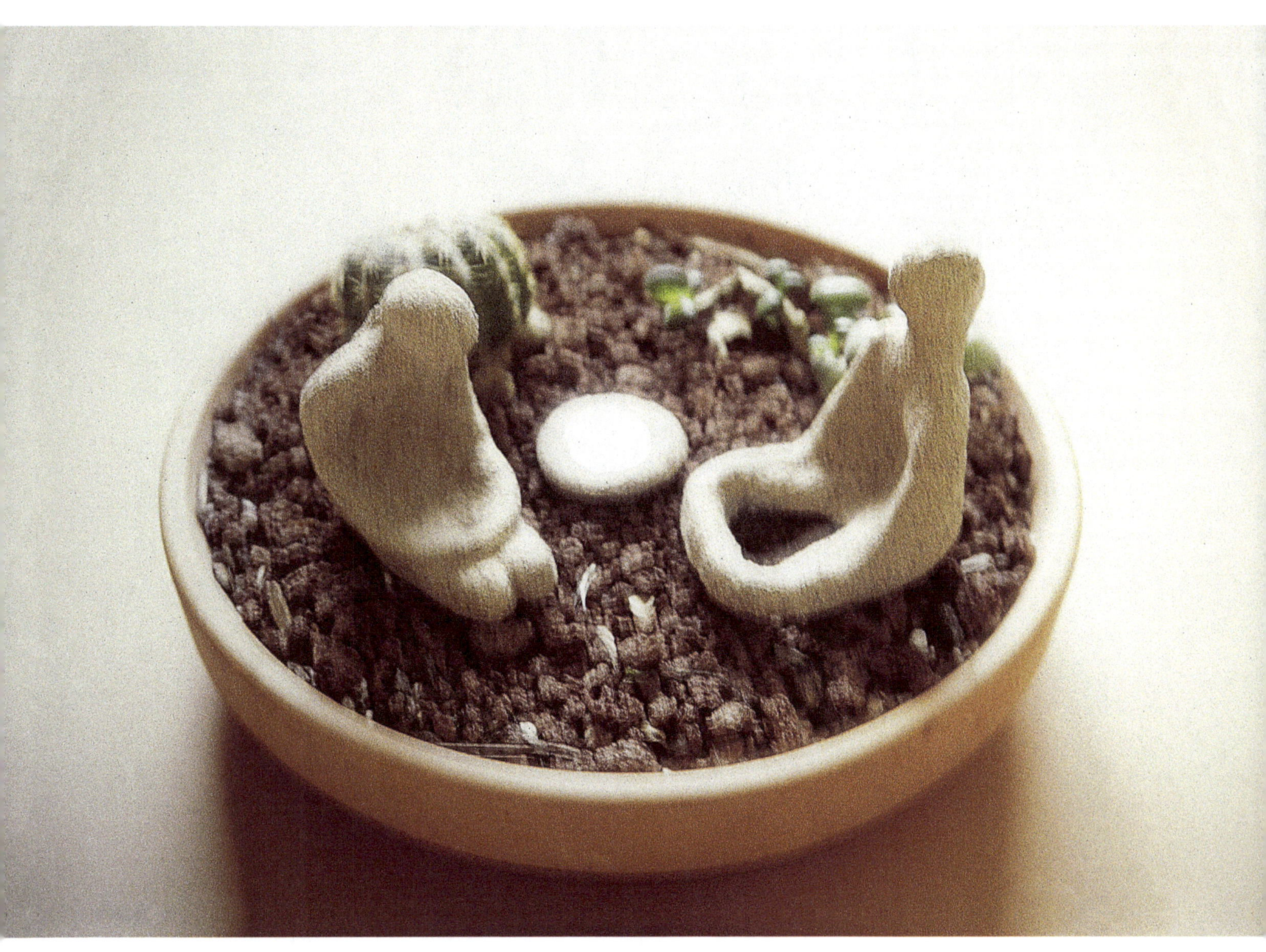

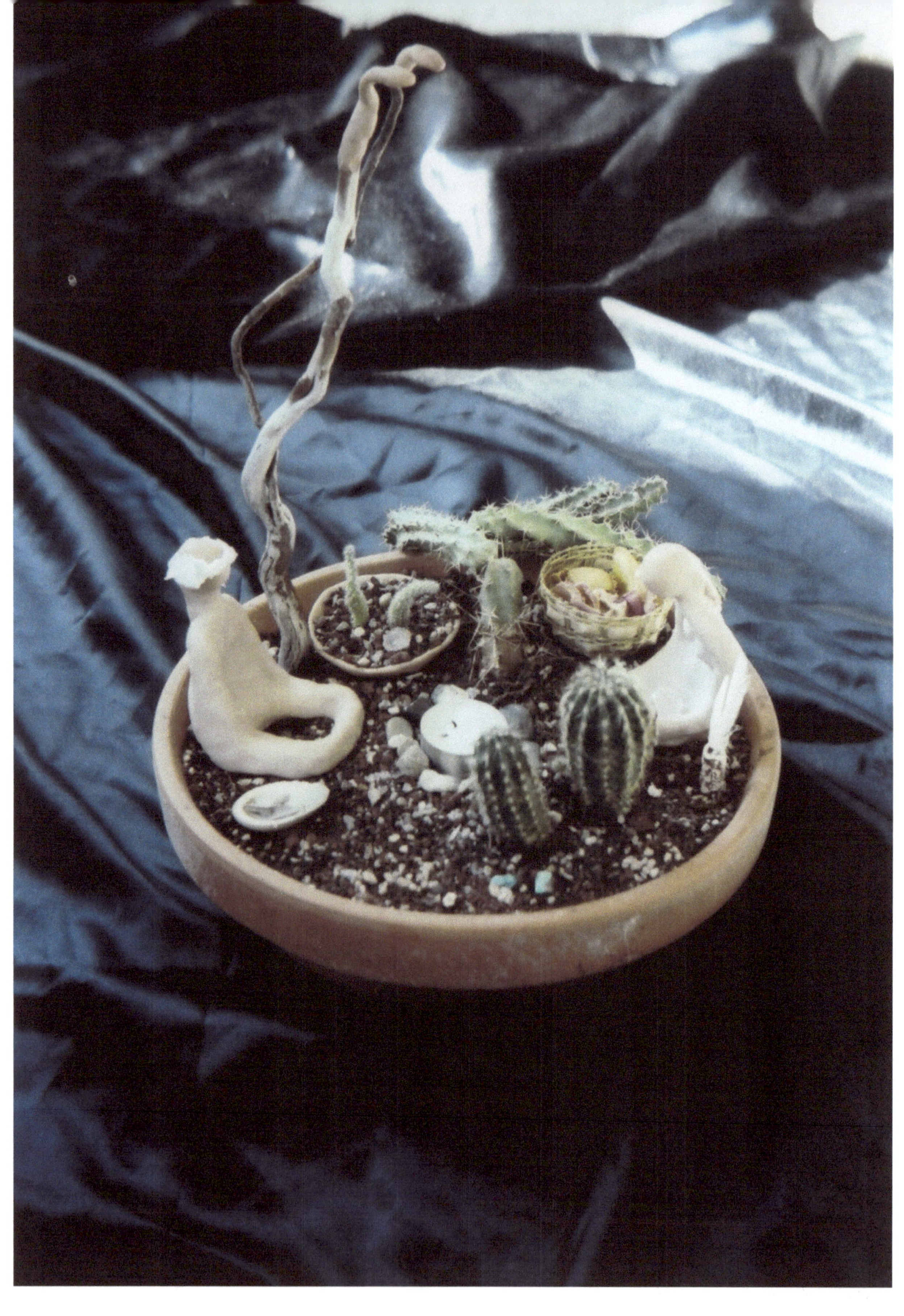

the ceremony

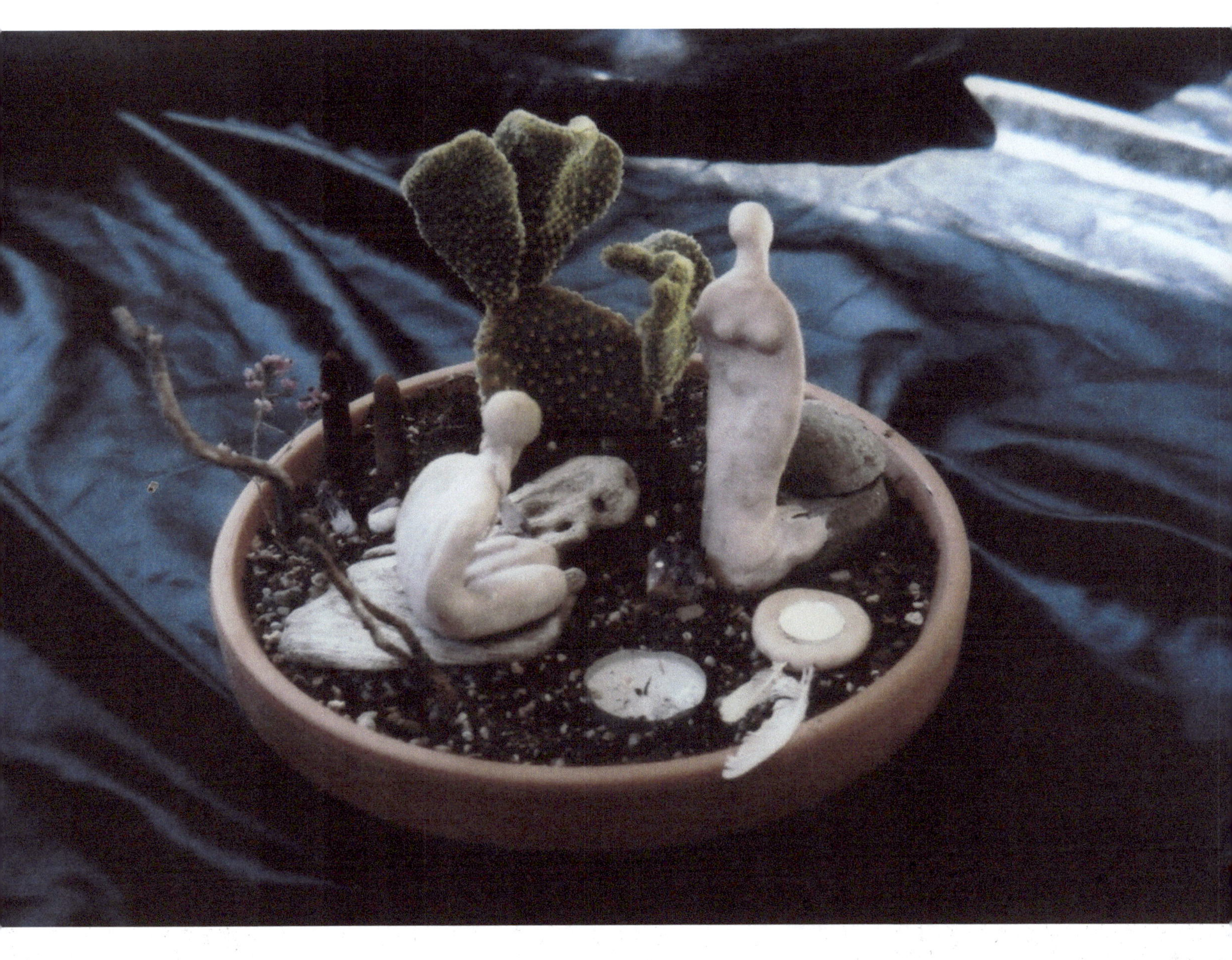

night desert dance of the sacred twos

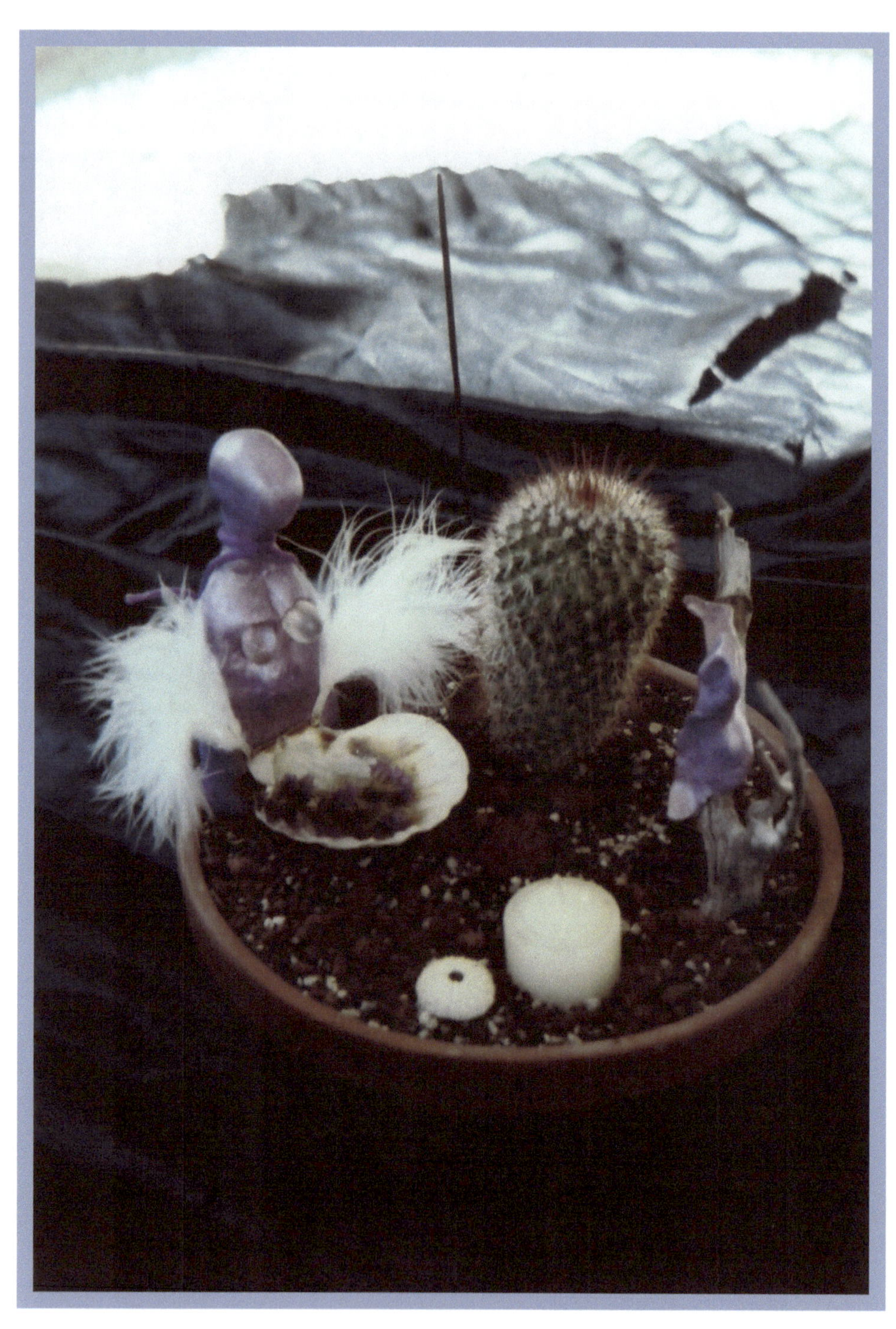

universes borne ceremony

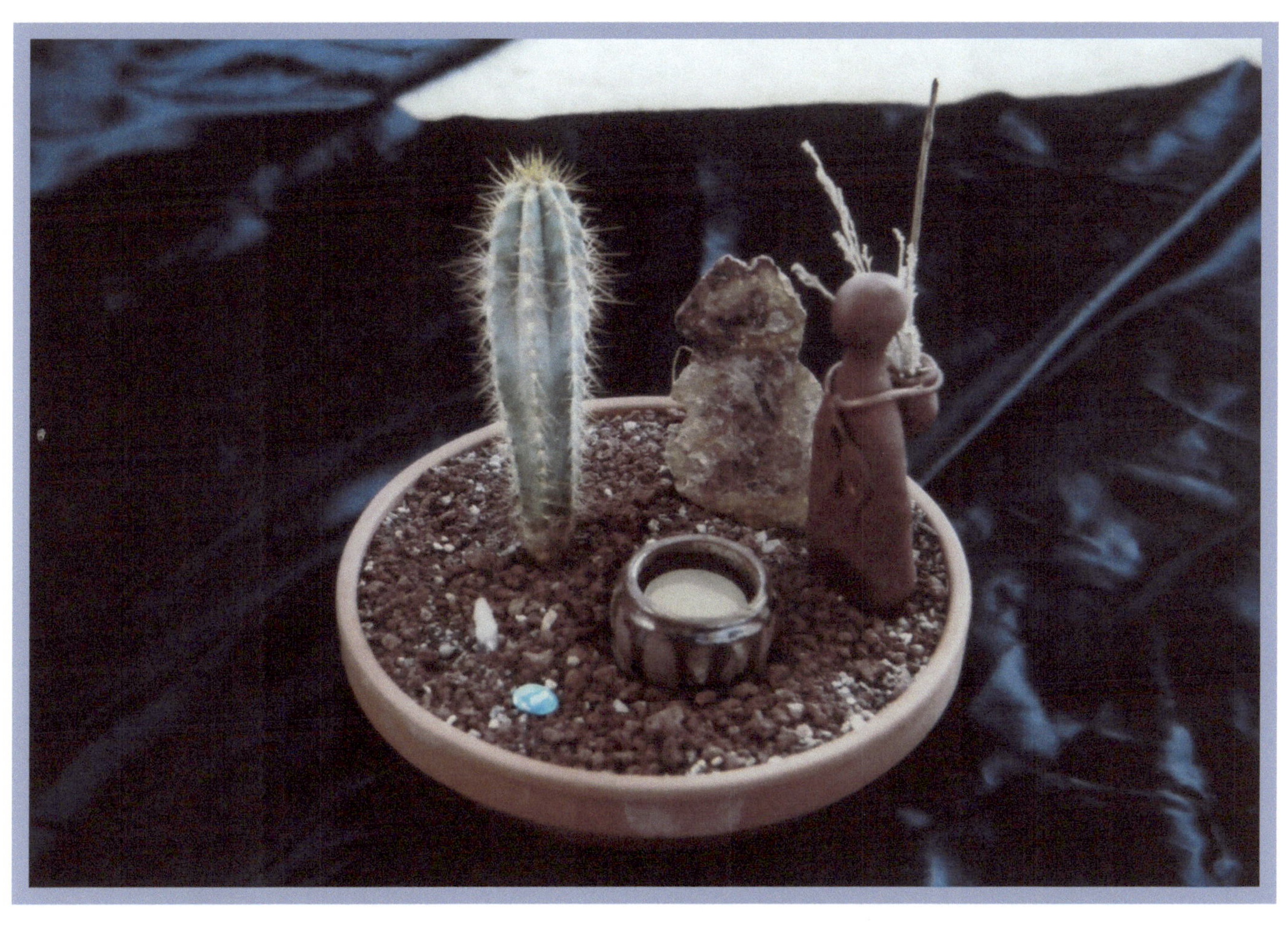

sage goddess ceremony

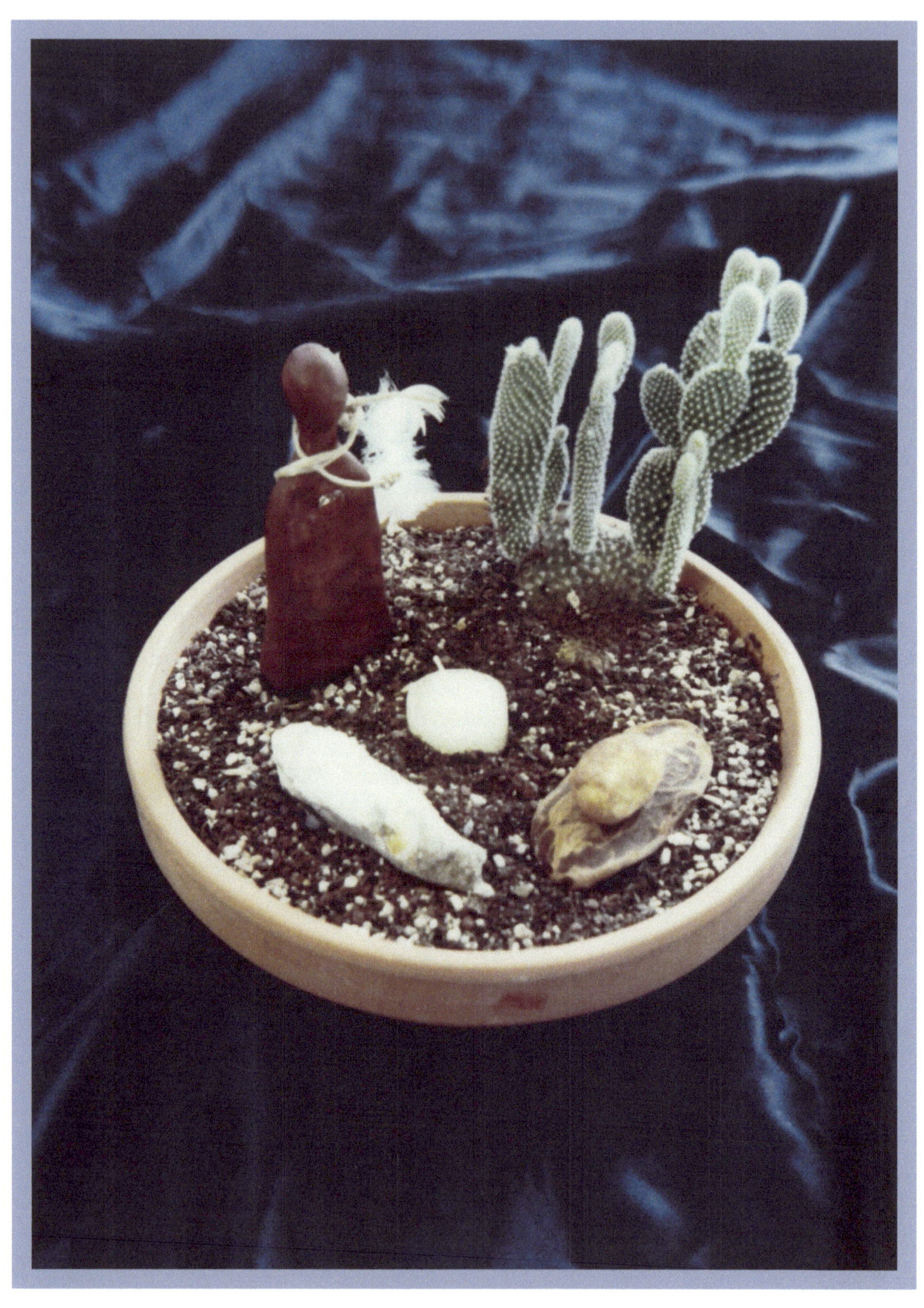

crystal heart ceremony

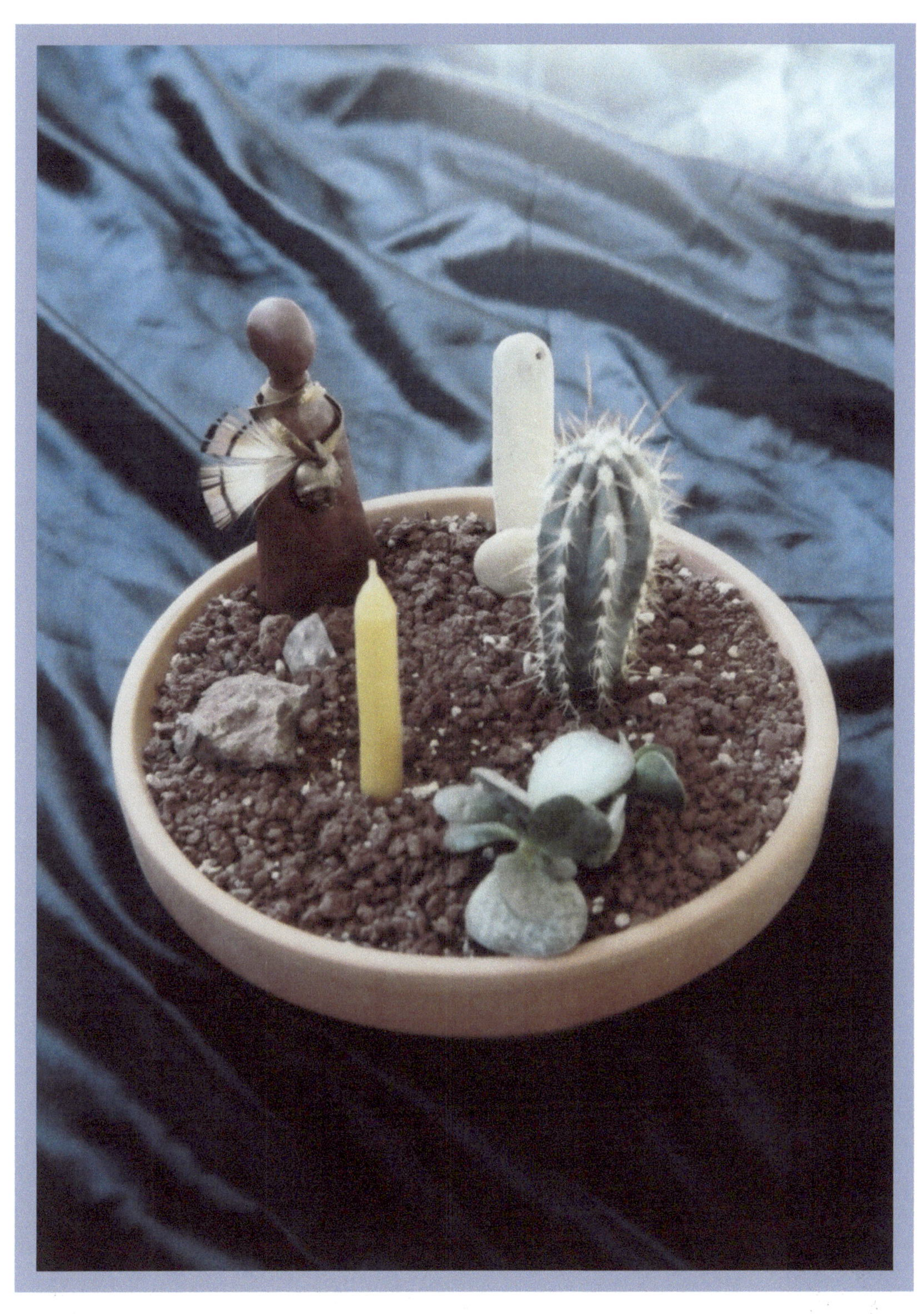

two feathers shield ceremony

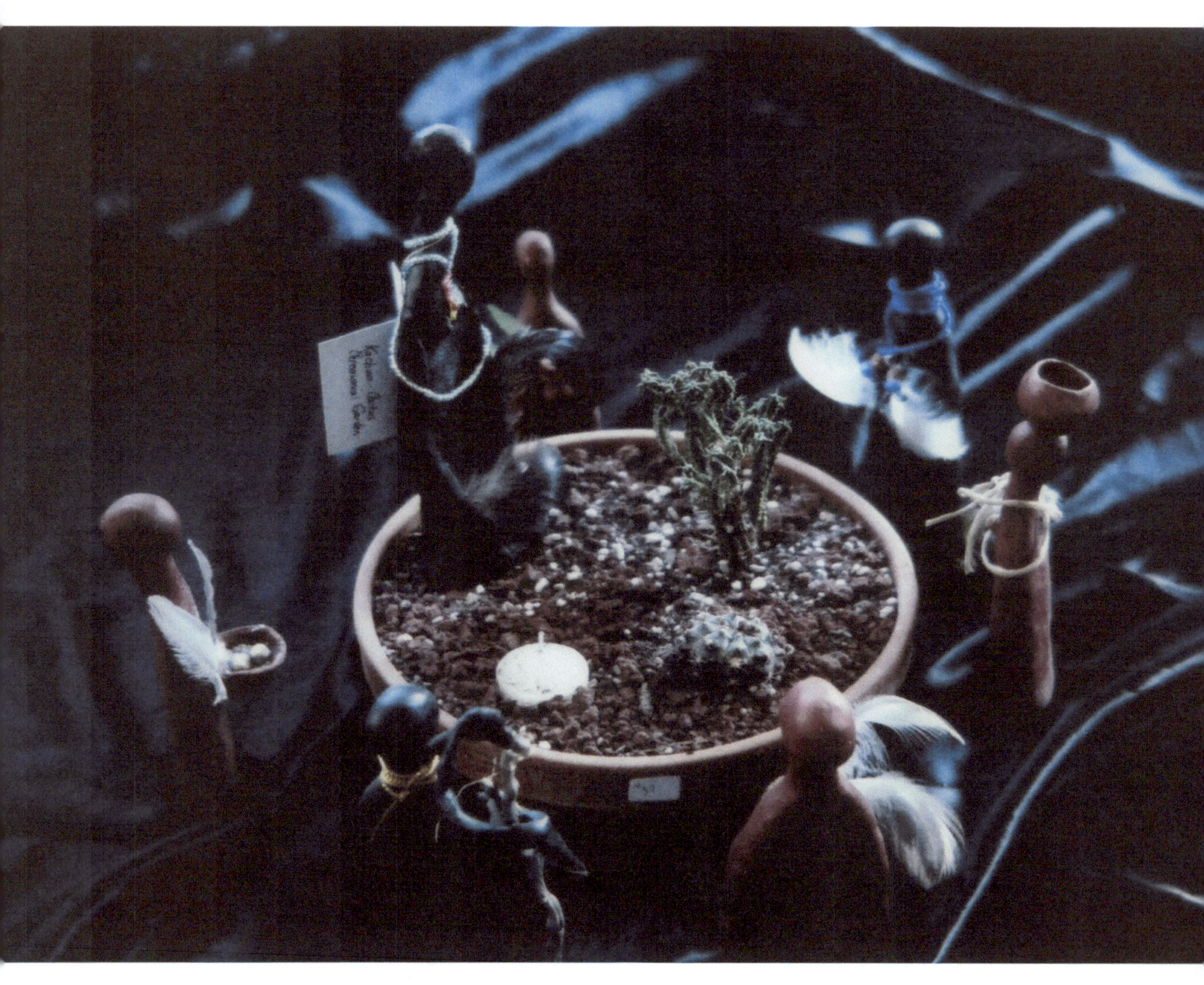

rainbow star kachina in ceremony

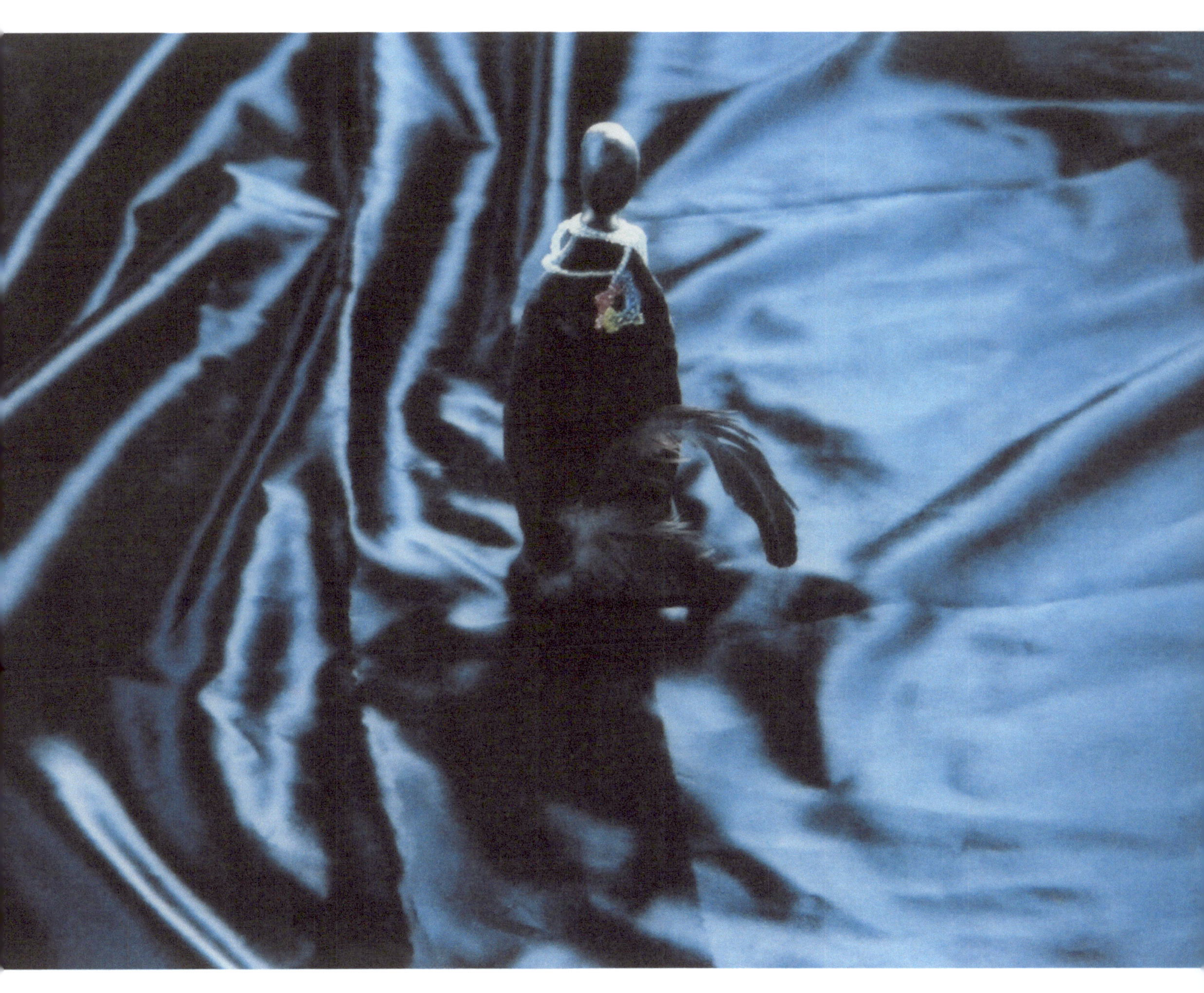

rainbow star kachina

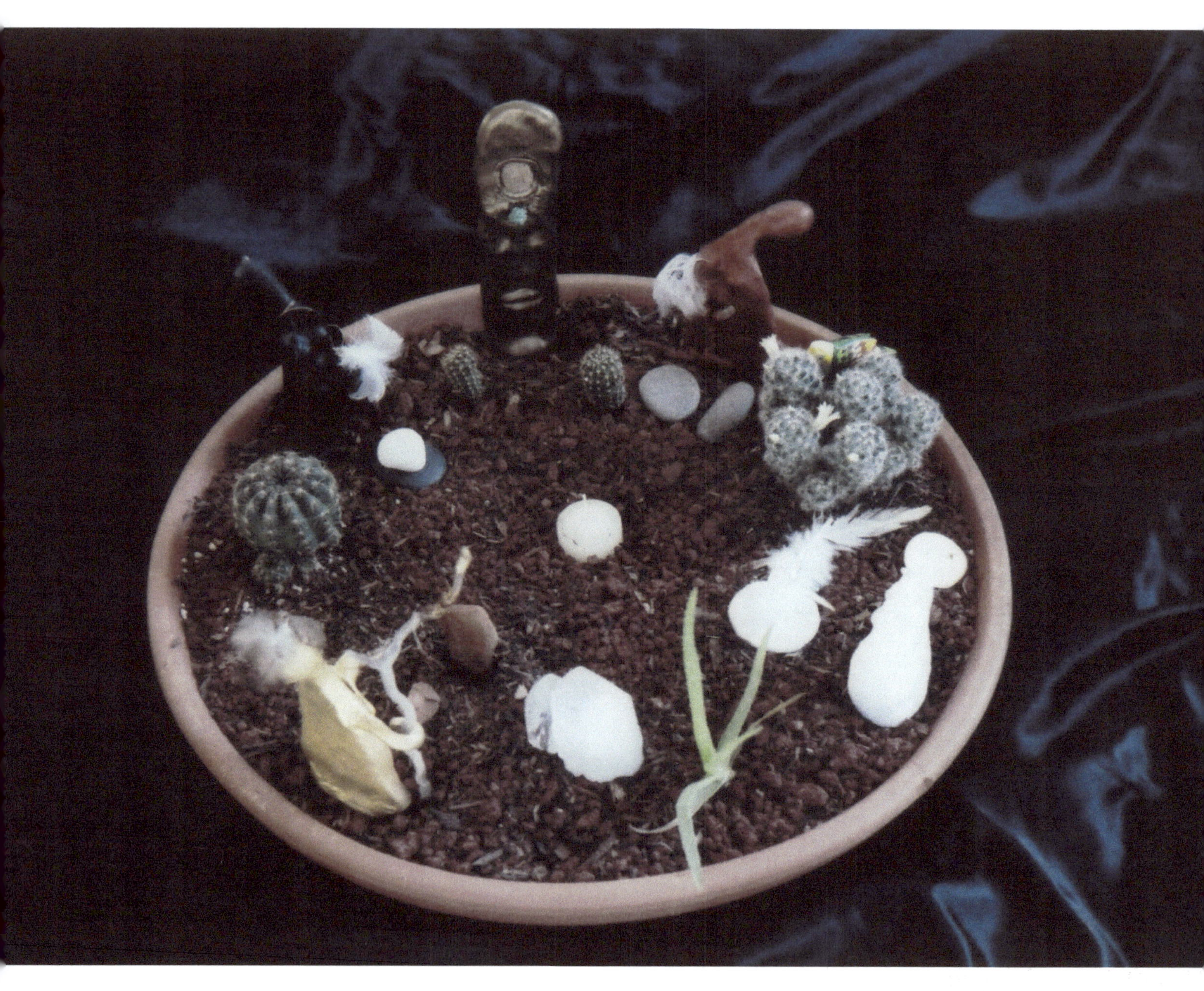

four directions medicine wheel

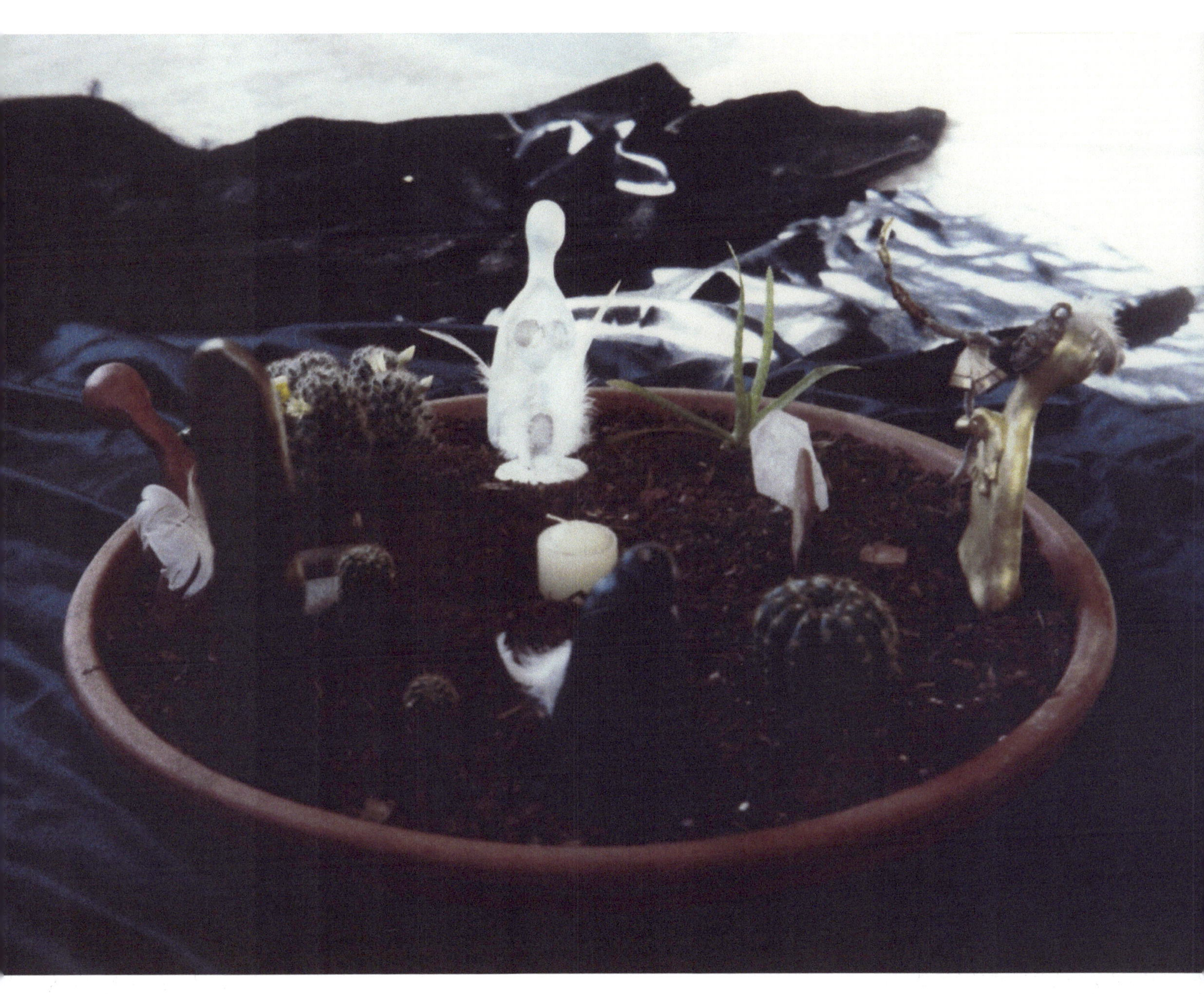

breasted one

Third Phase:
figures in Living Ceremony

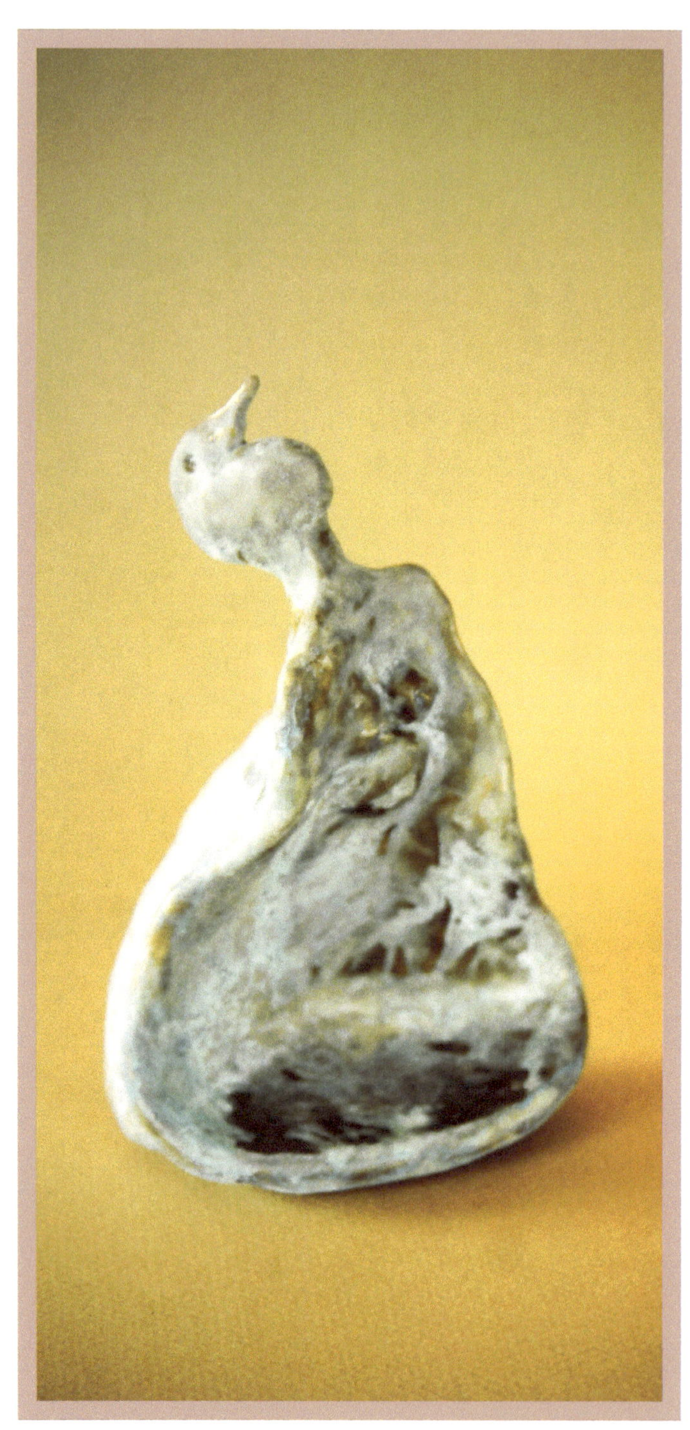

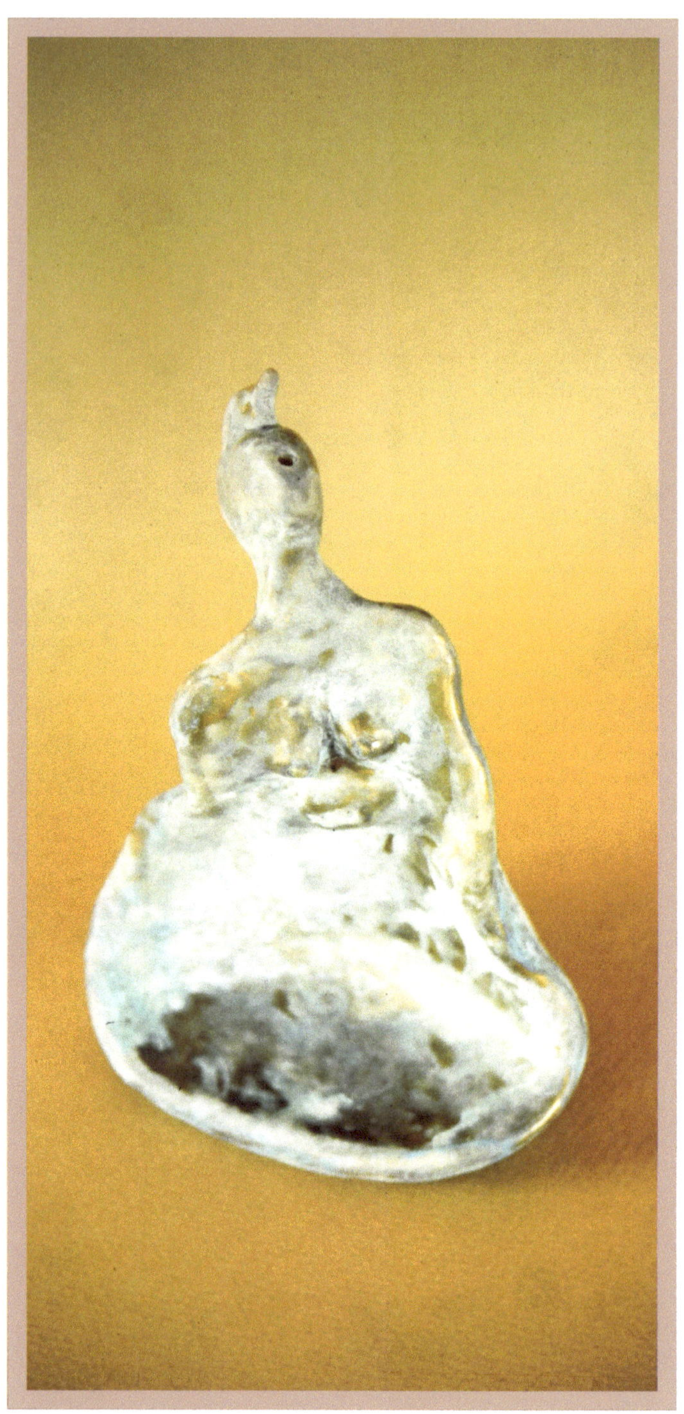

SHE...who sounds in creation...

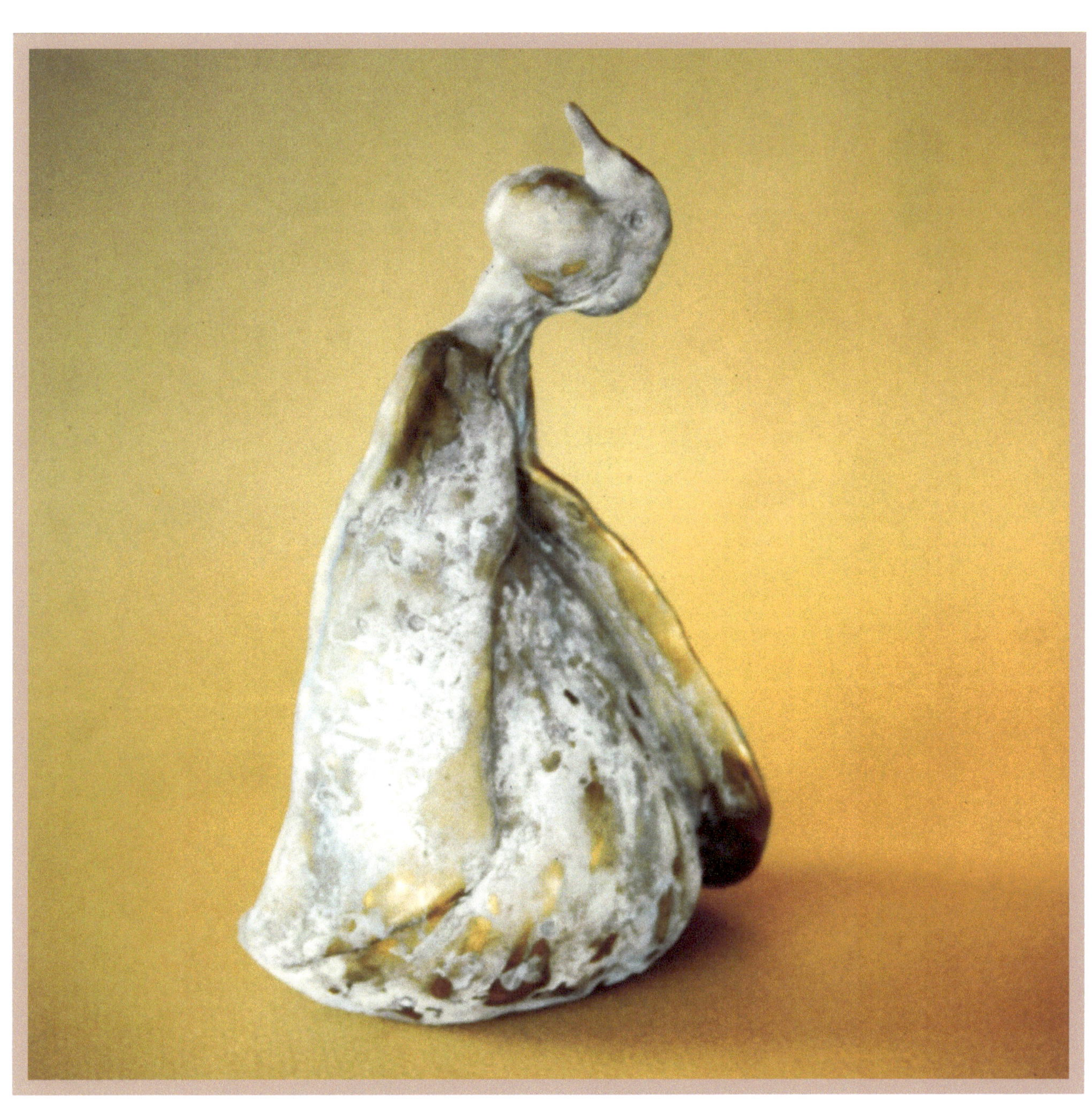

SHE...who sounds in creation...

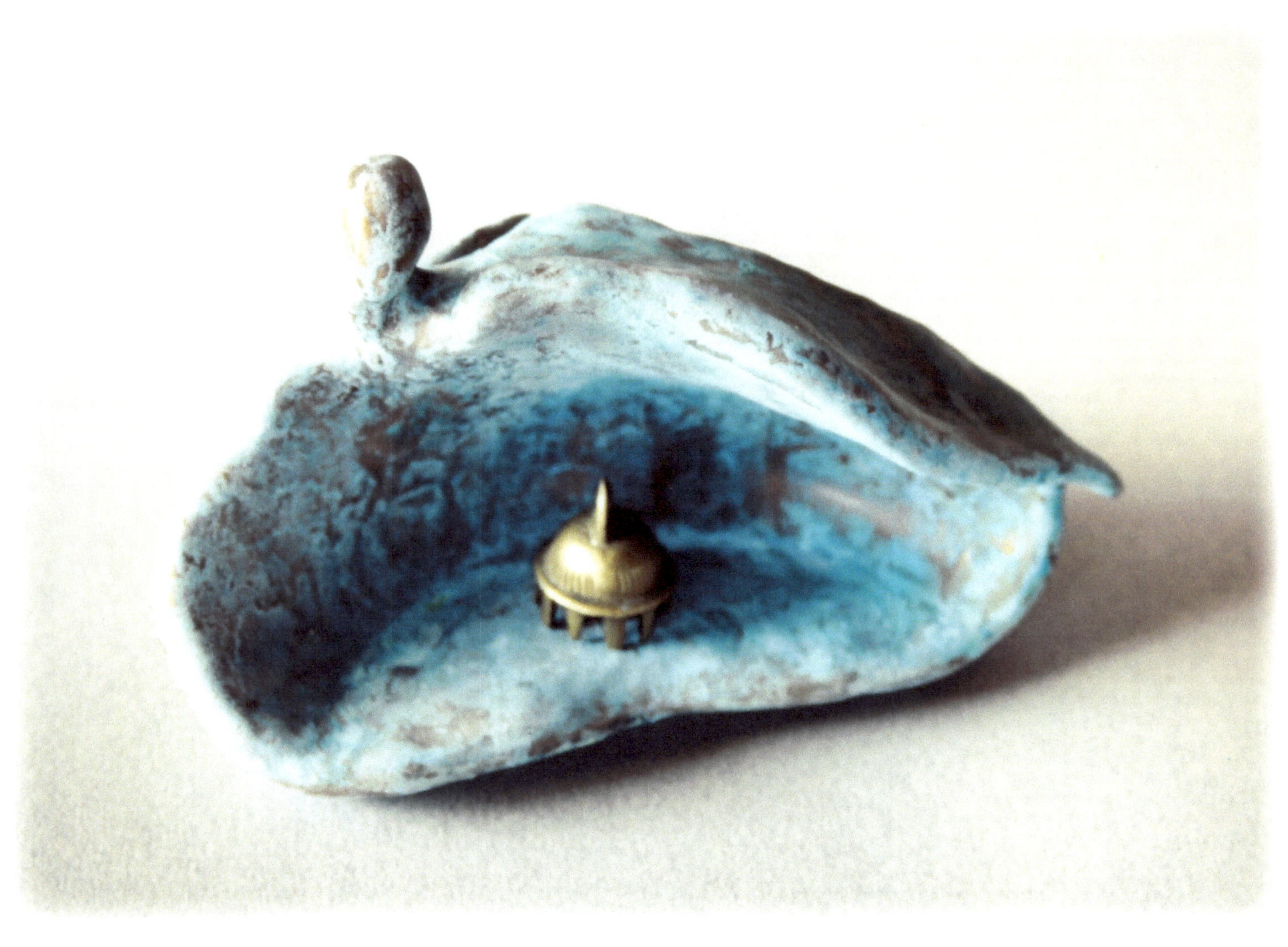

winged ceremony

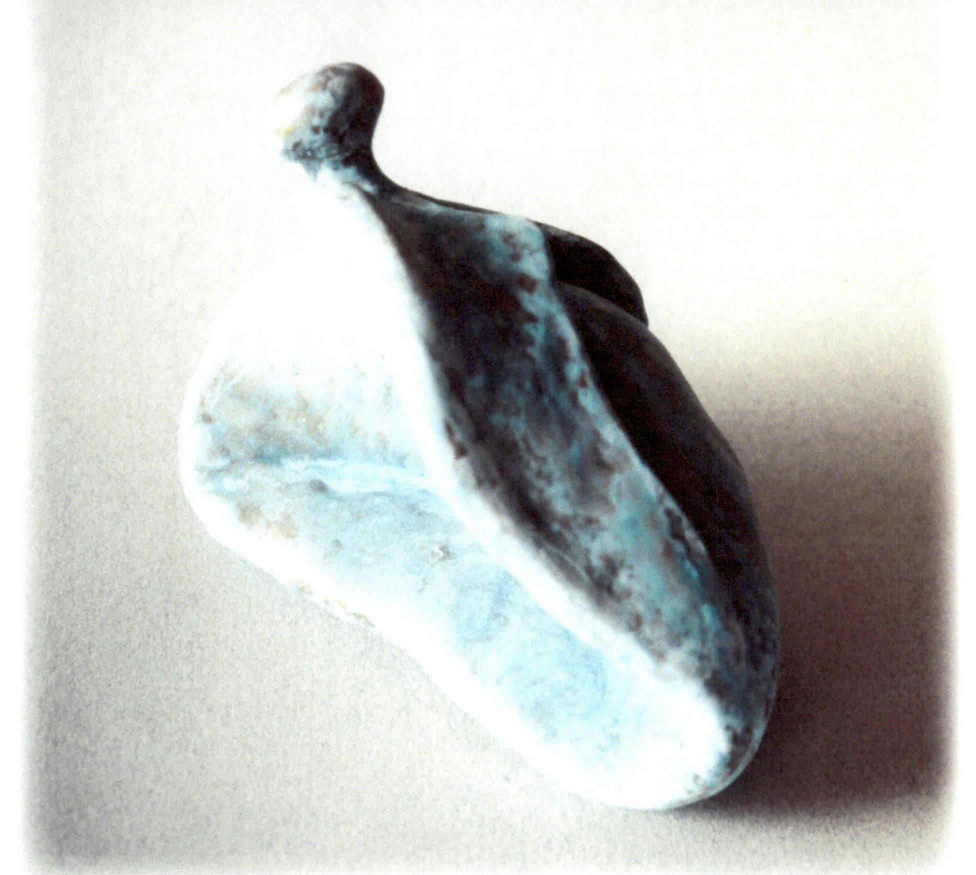

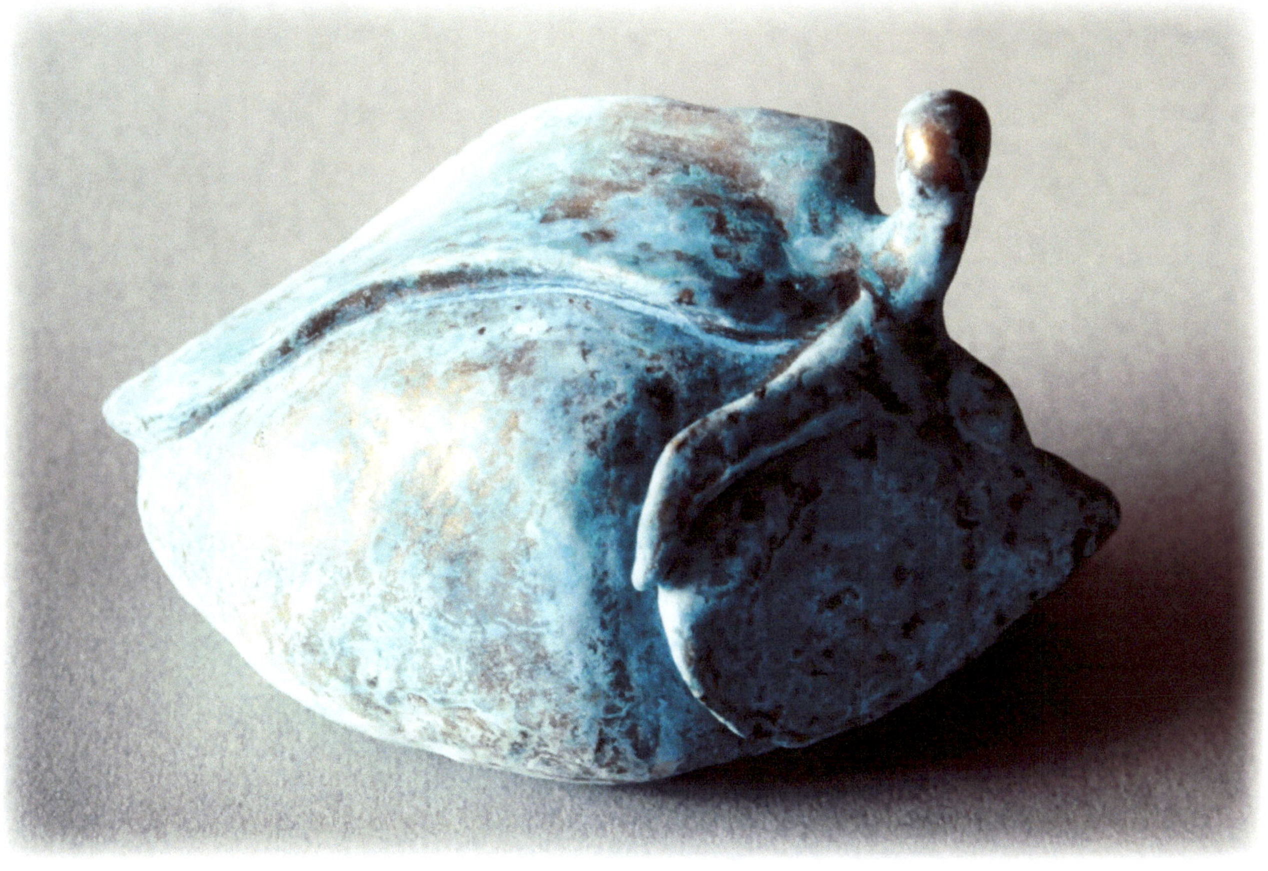

winged ceremony

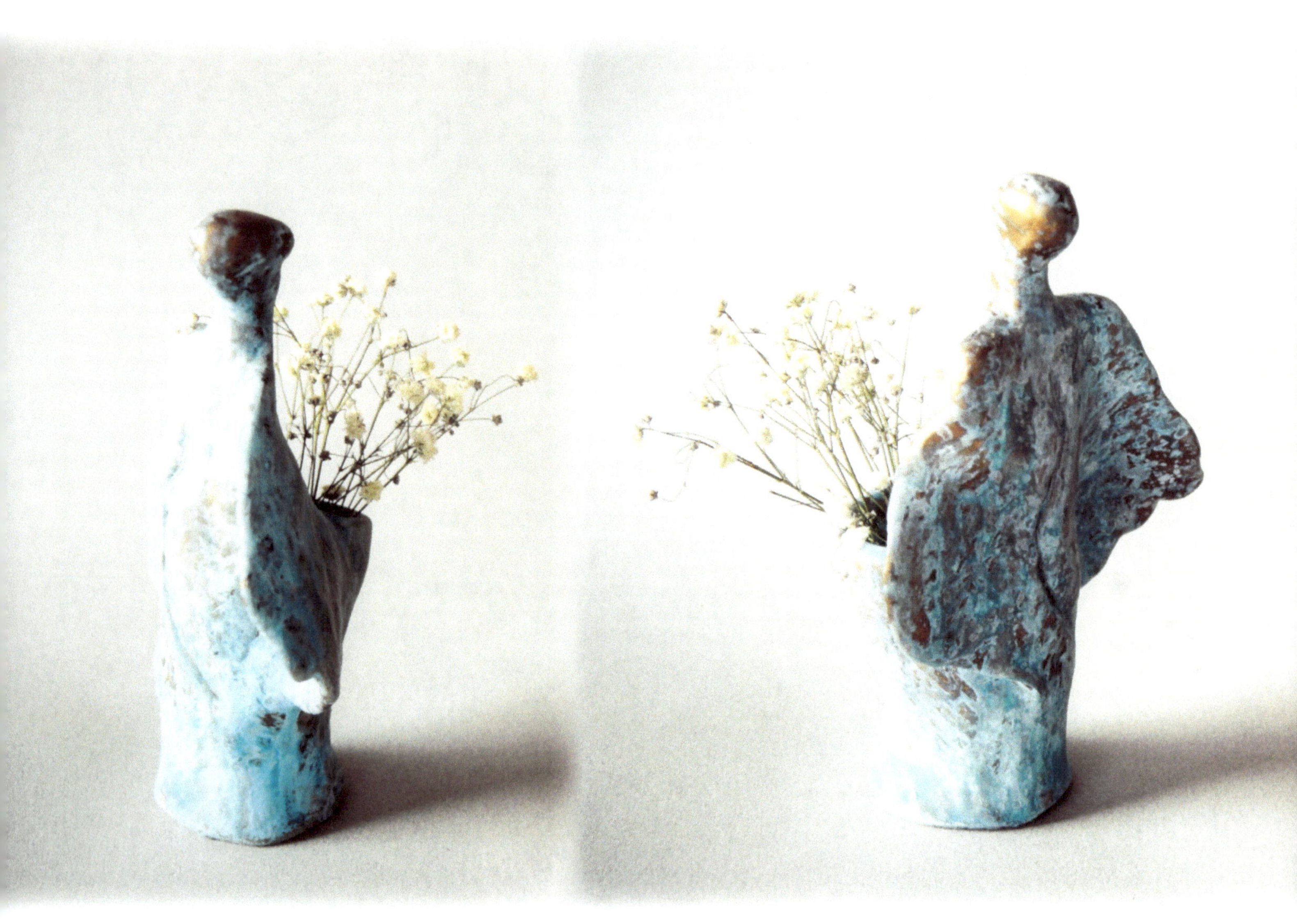

SHE...who gathers...

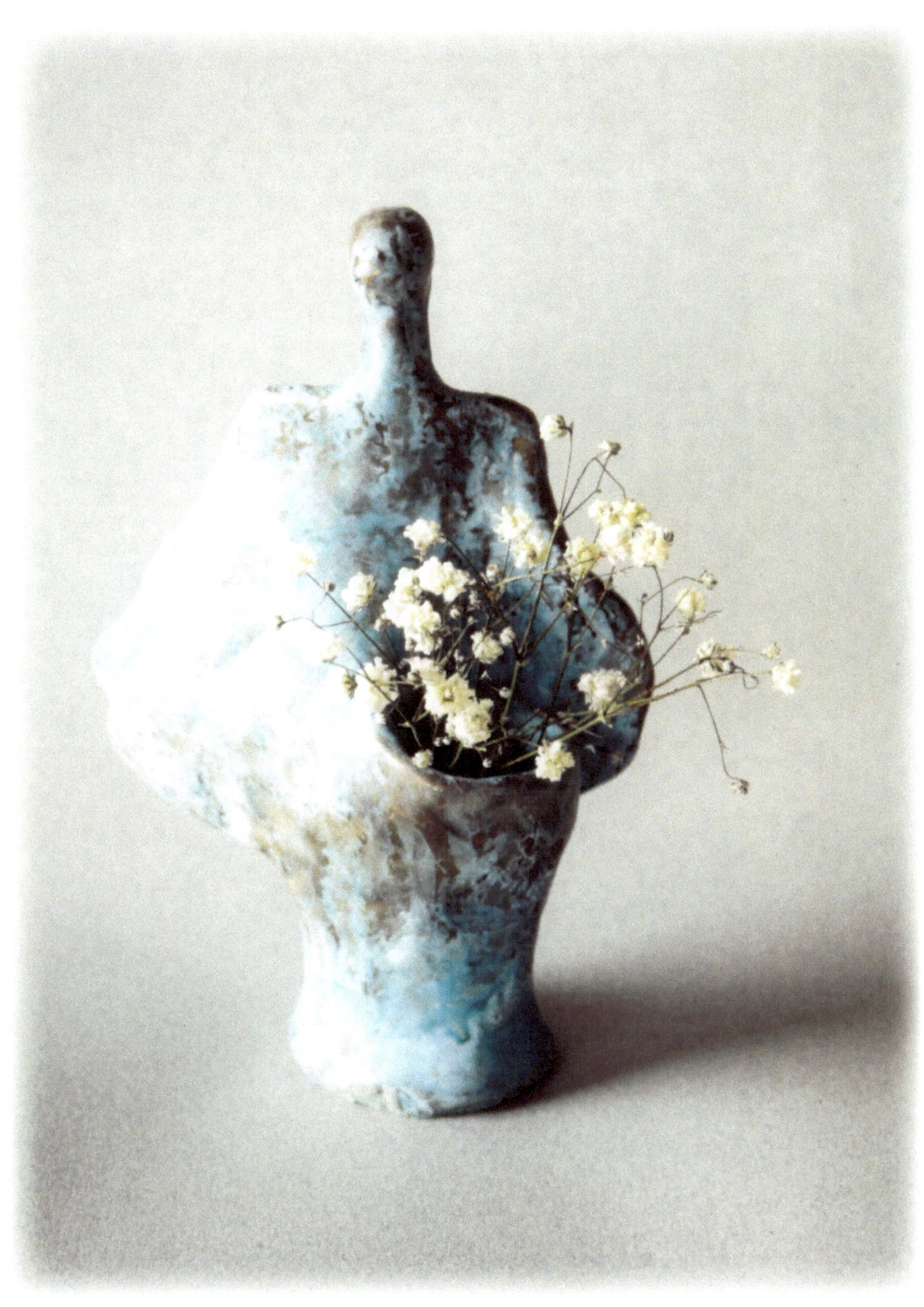

SHE…who gathers…

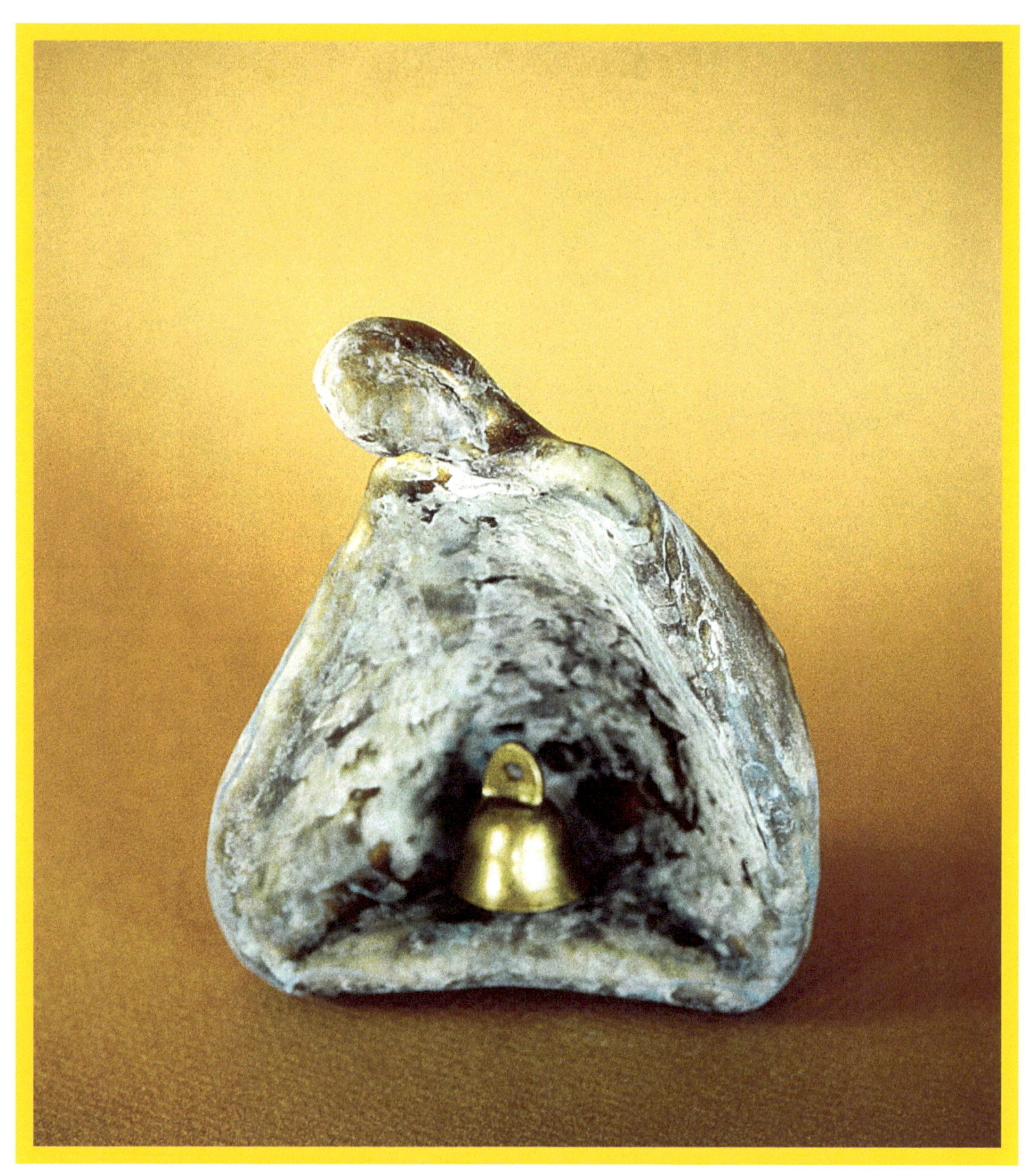

winged-essence-SHE

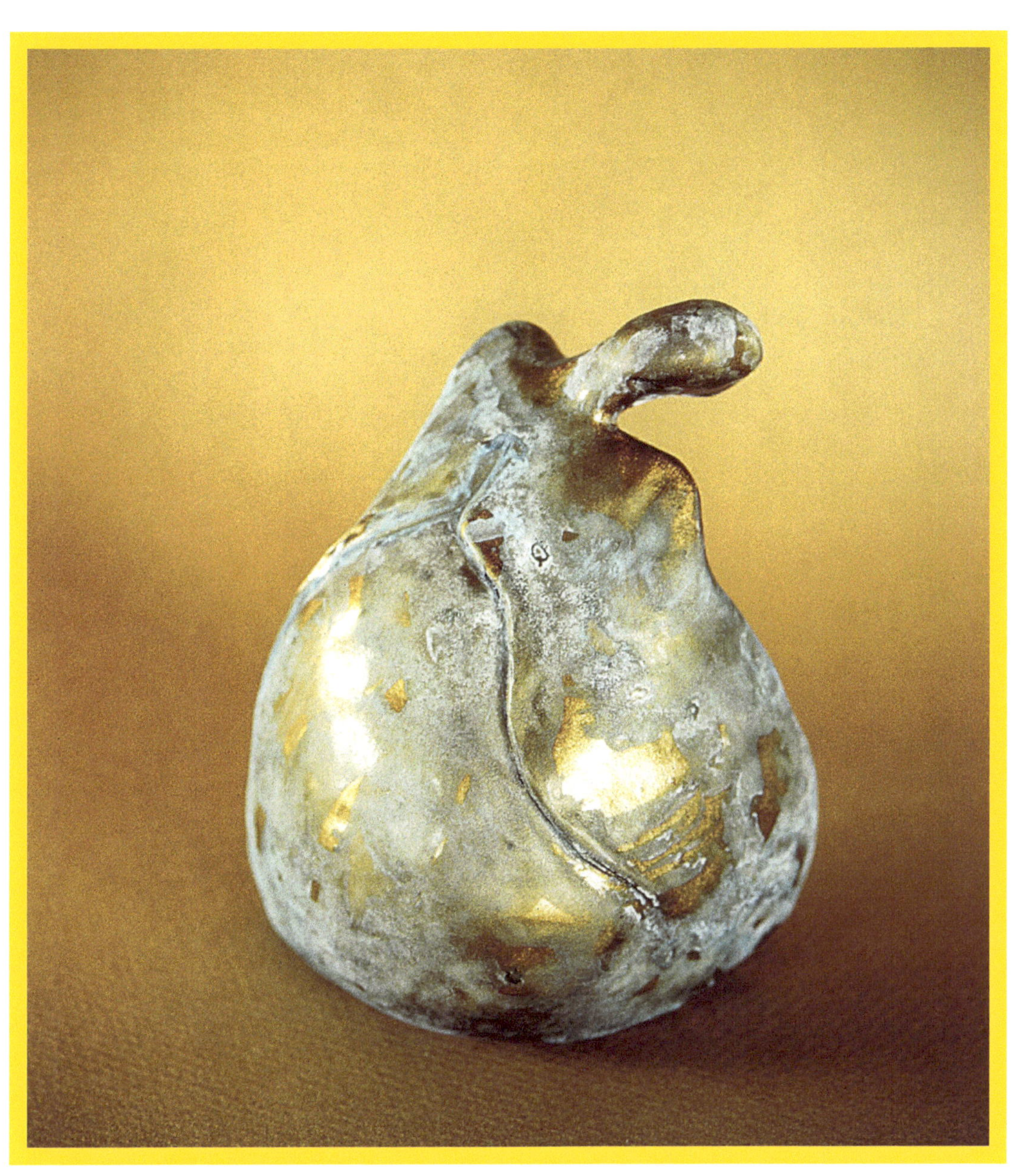

winged-essence-SHE

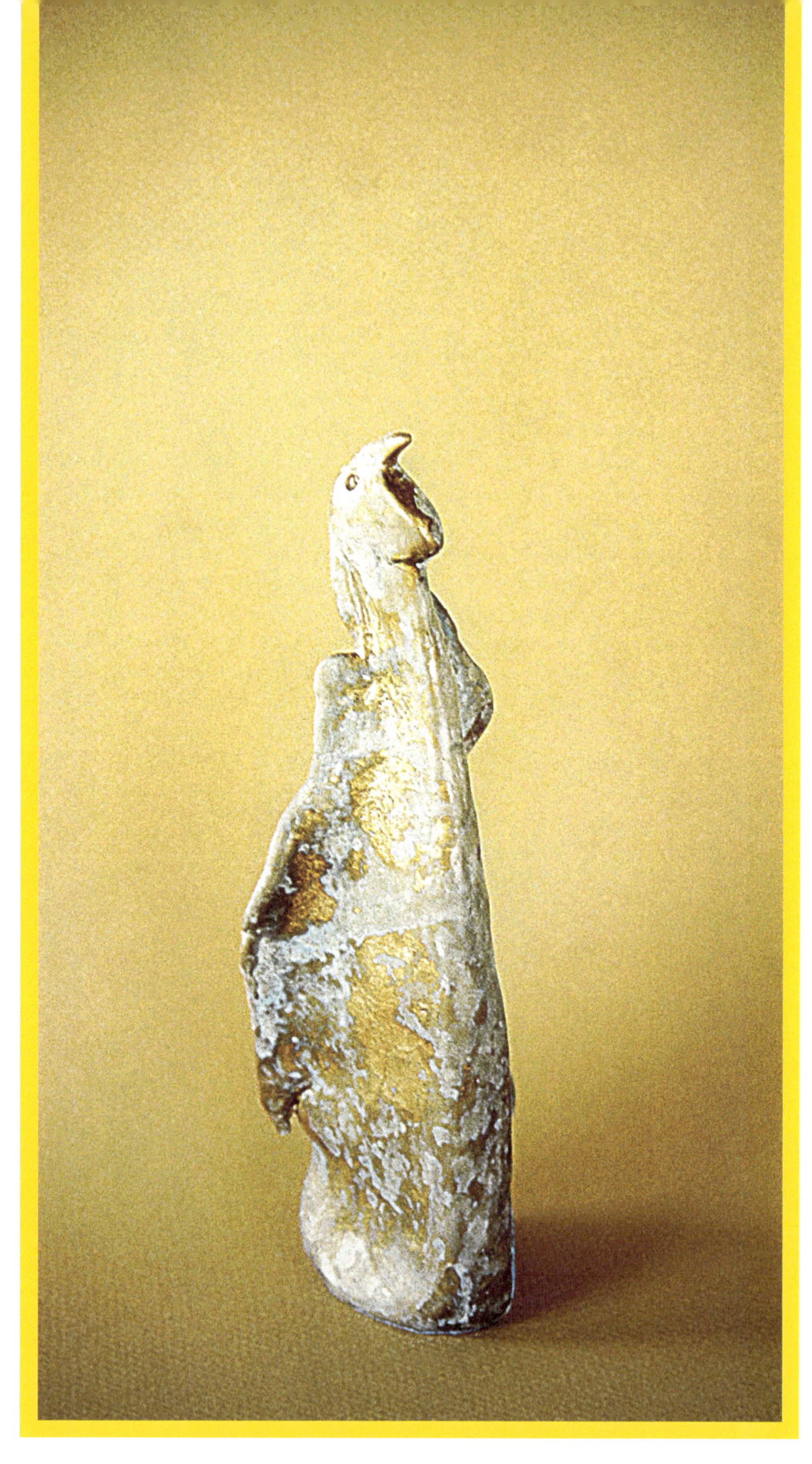

Bird-Tribe-SHE

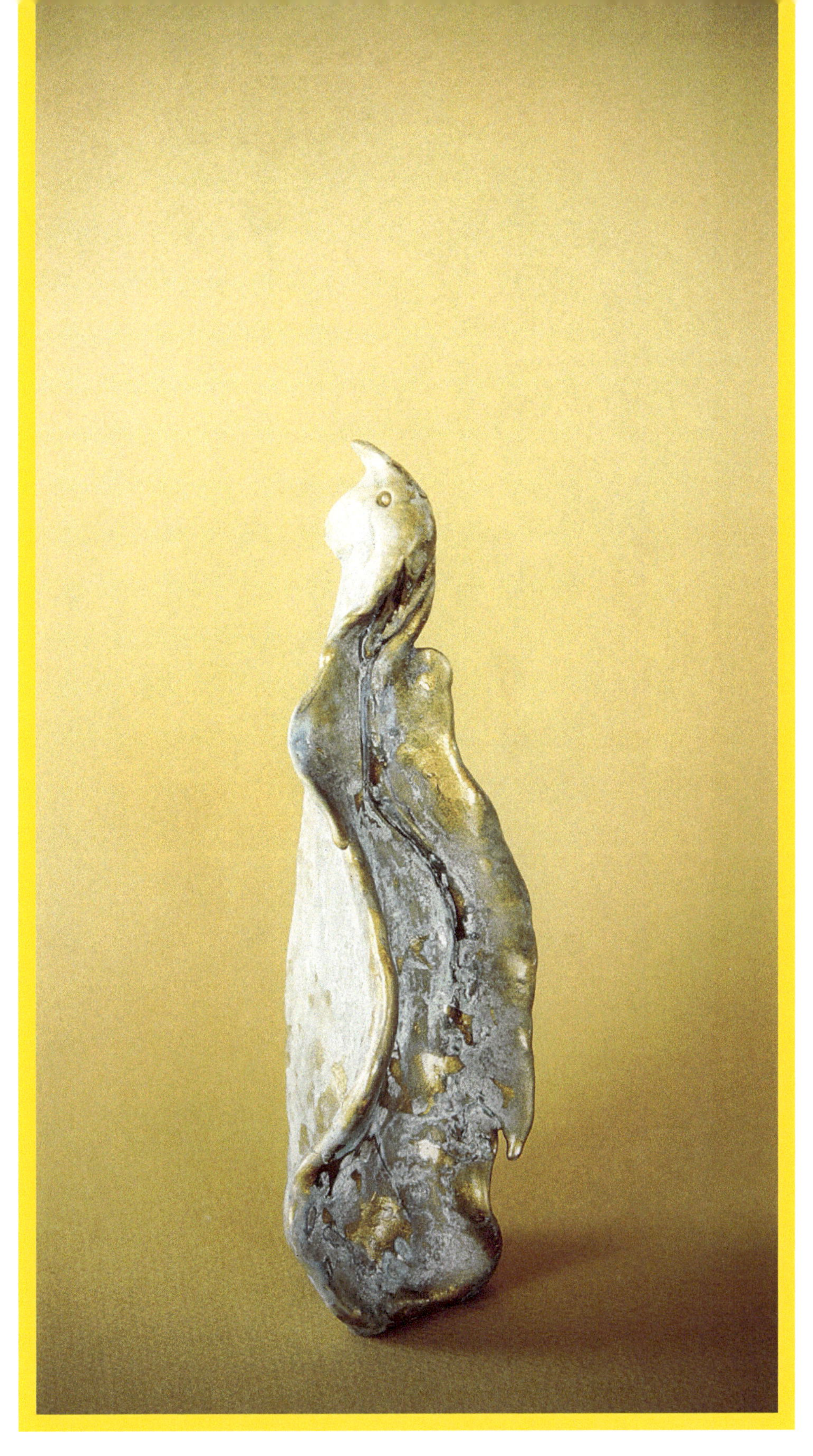

Bird-Tribe-SHE

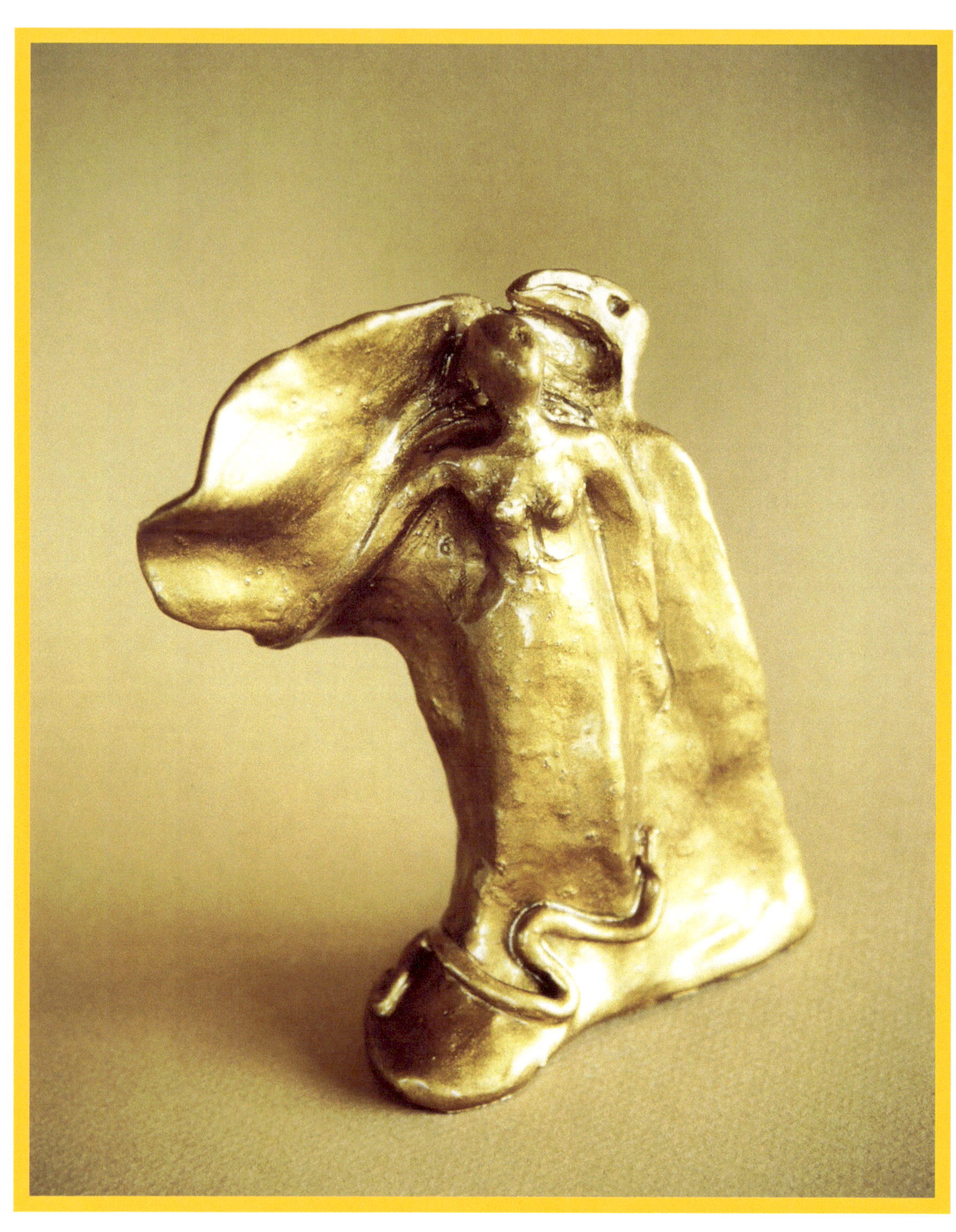

Bird-Tribe-SHE...in ceremony...

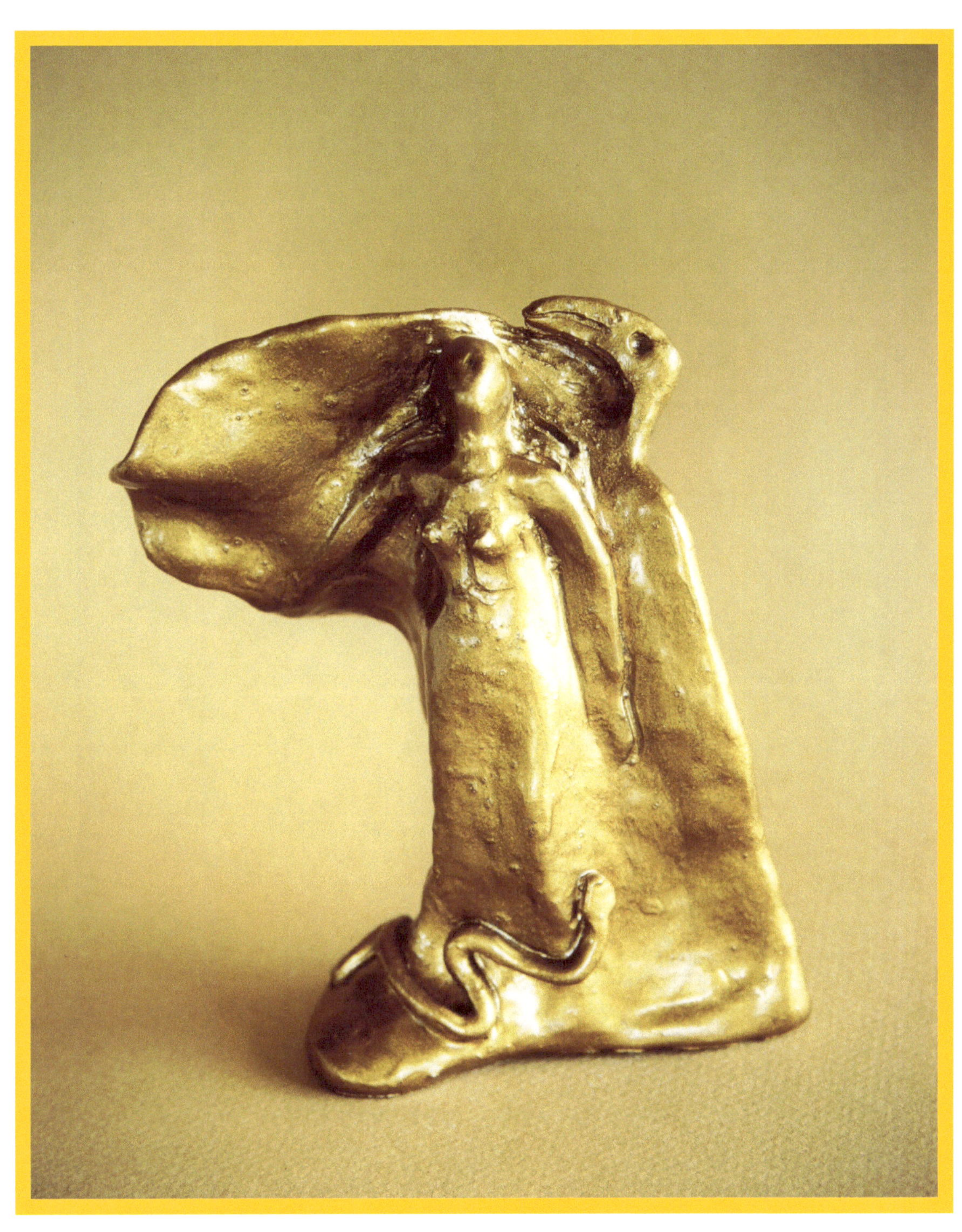

Bird-Tribe-SHE…in ceremony…

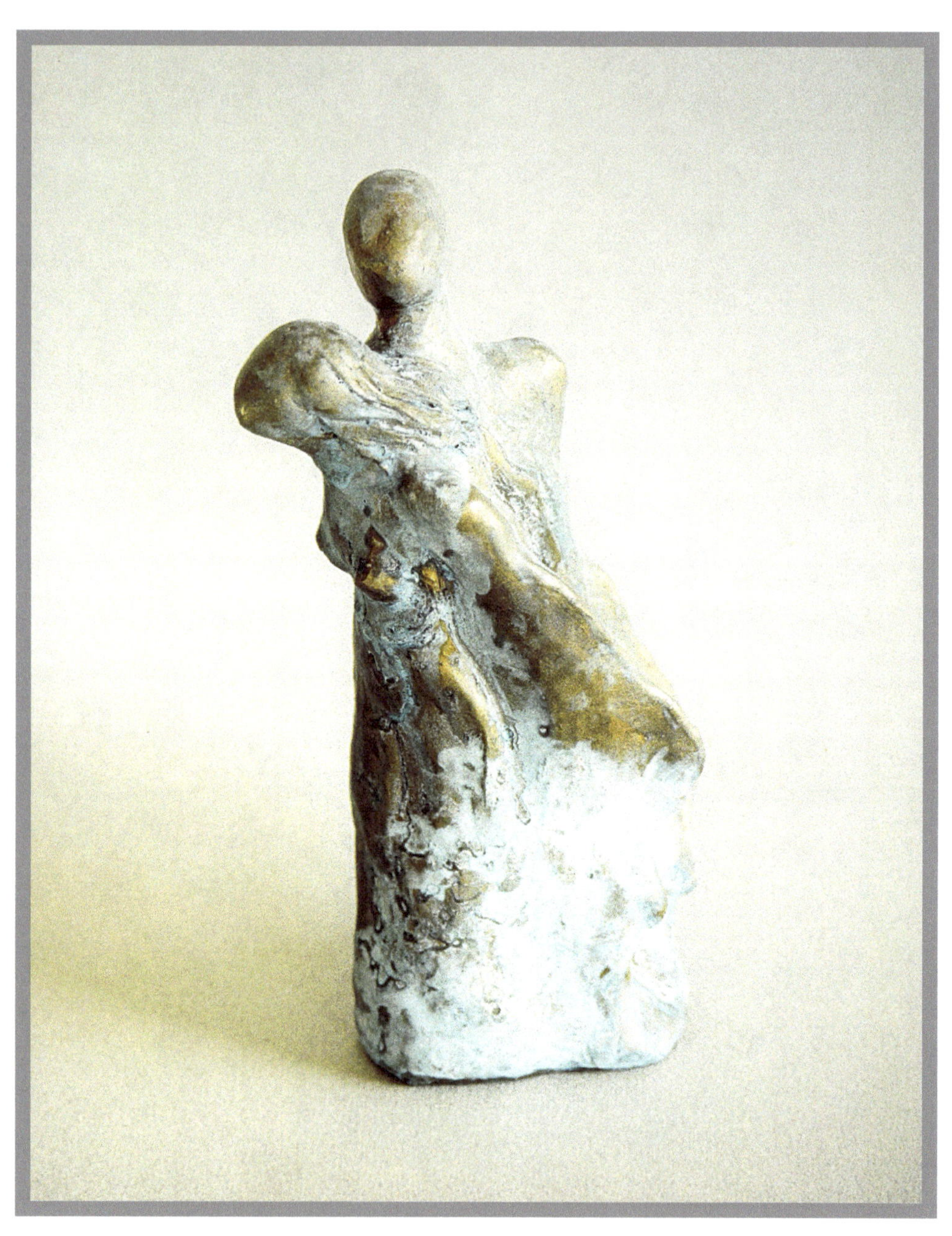

HE and SHE...
in ceremony with the caduceus...

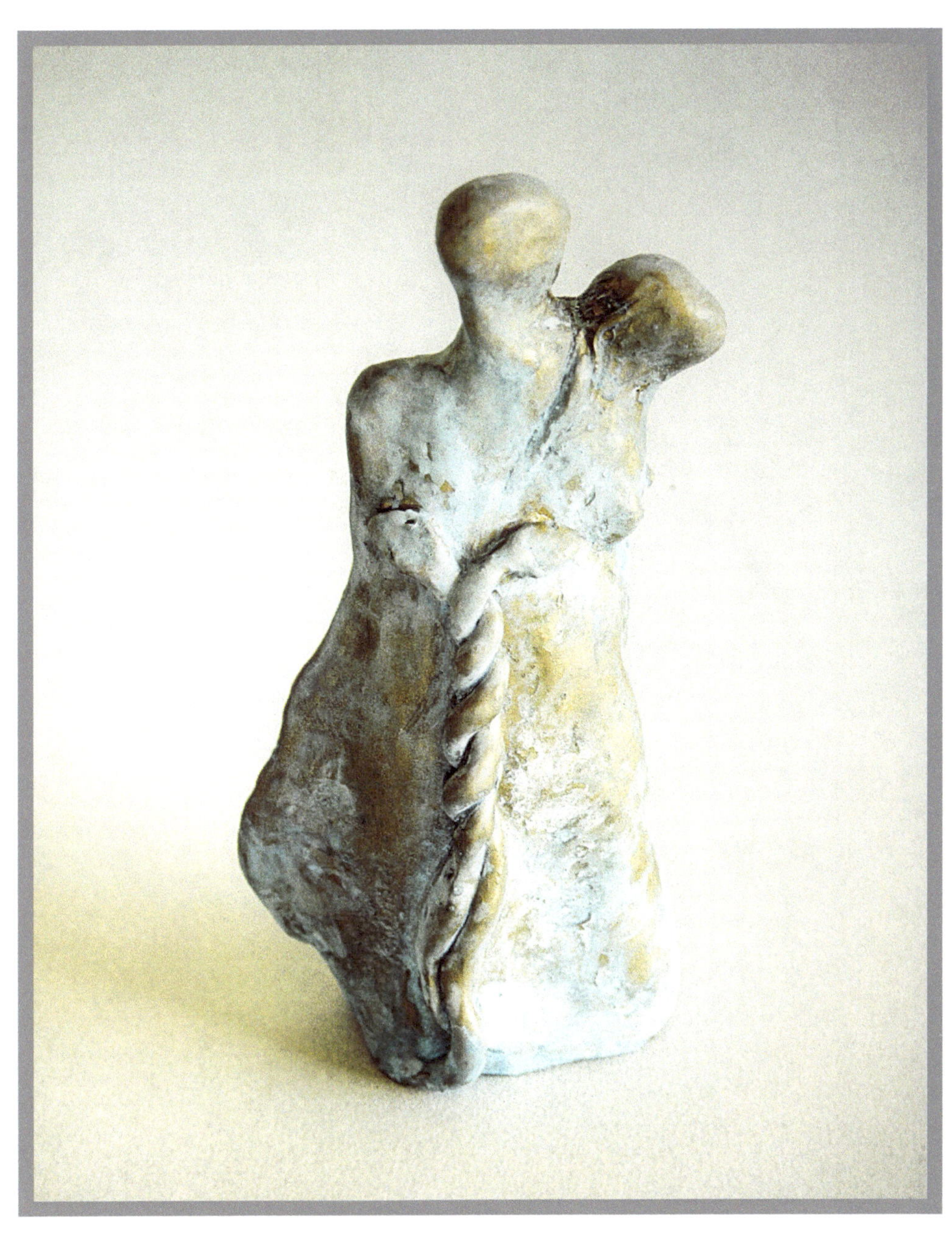

HE and SHE...
in ceremony with the caduceus...

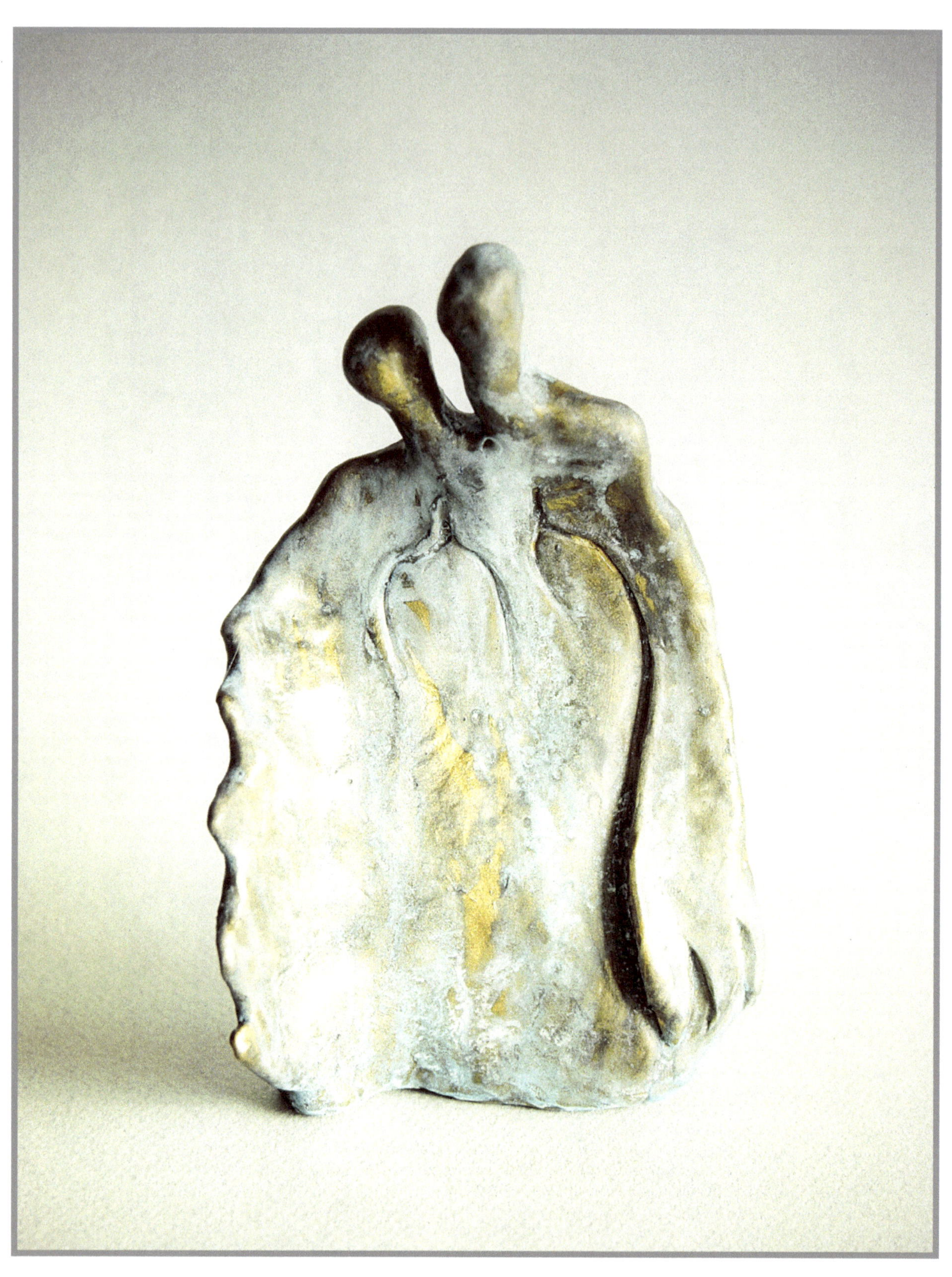

HE and SHE...of the winged nation...

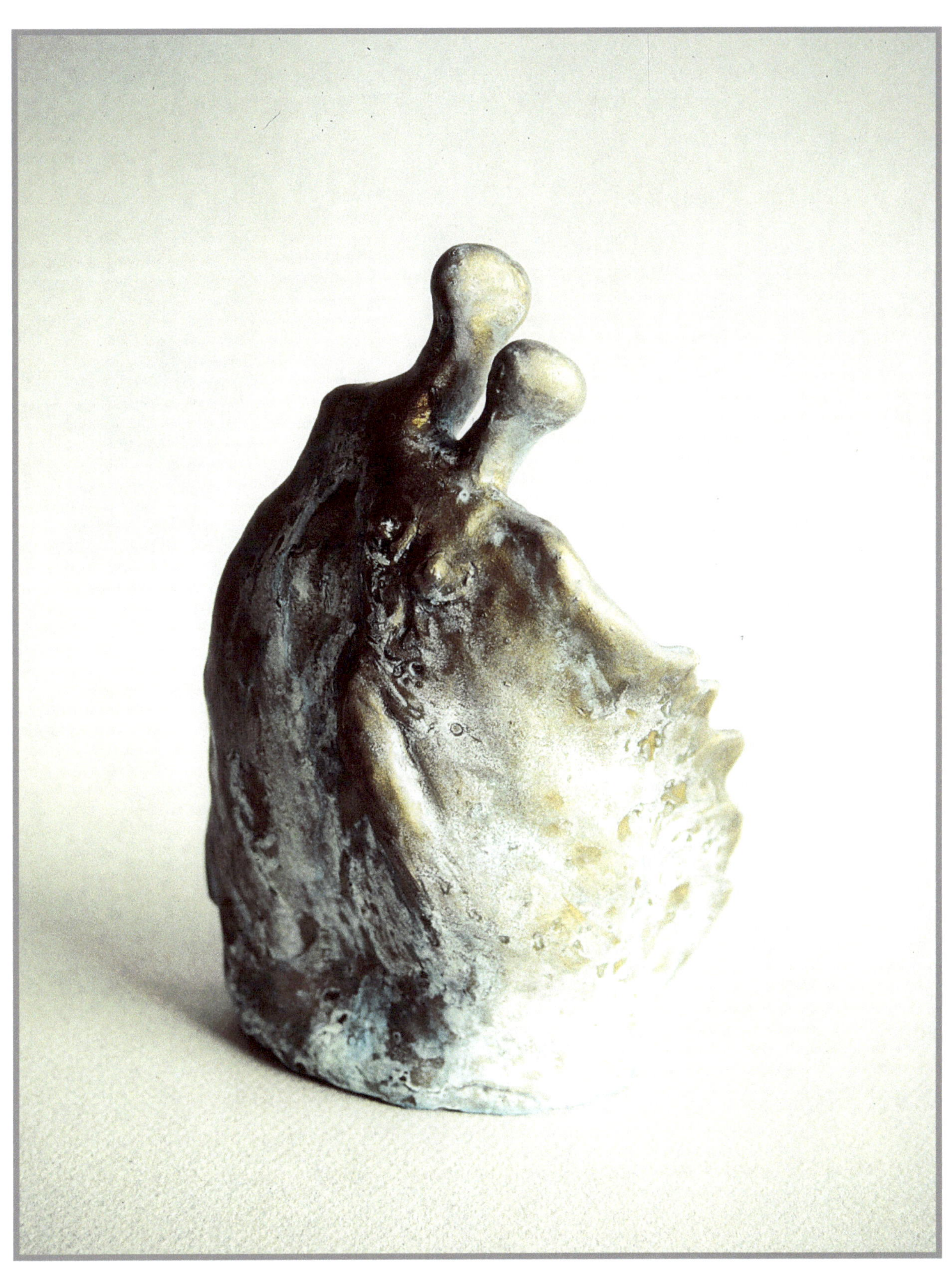

HE and SHE...of the winged nation...

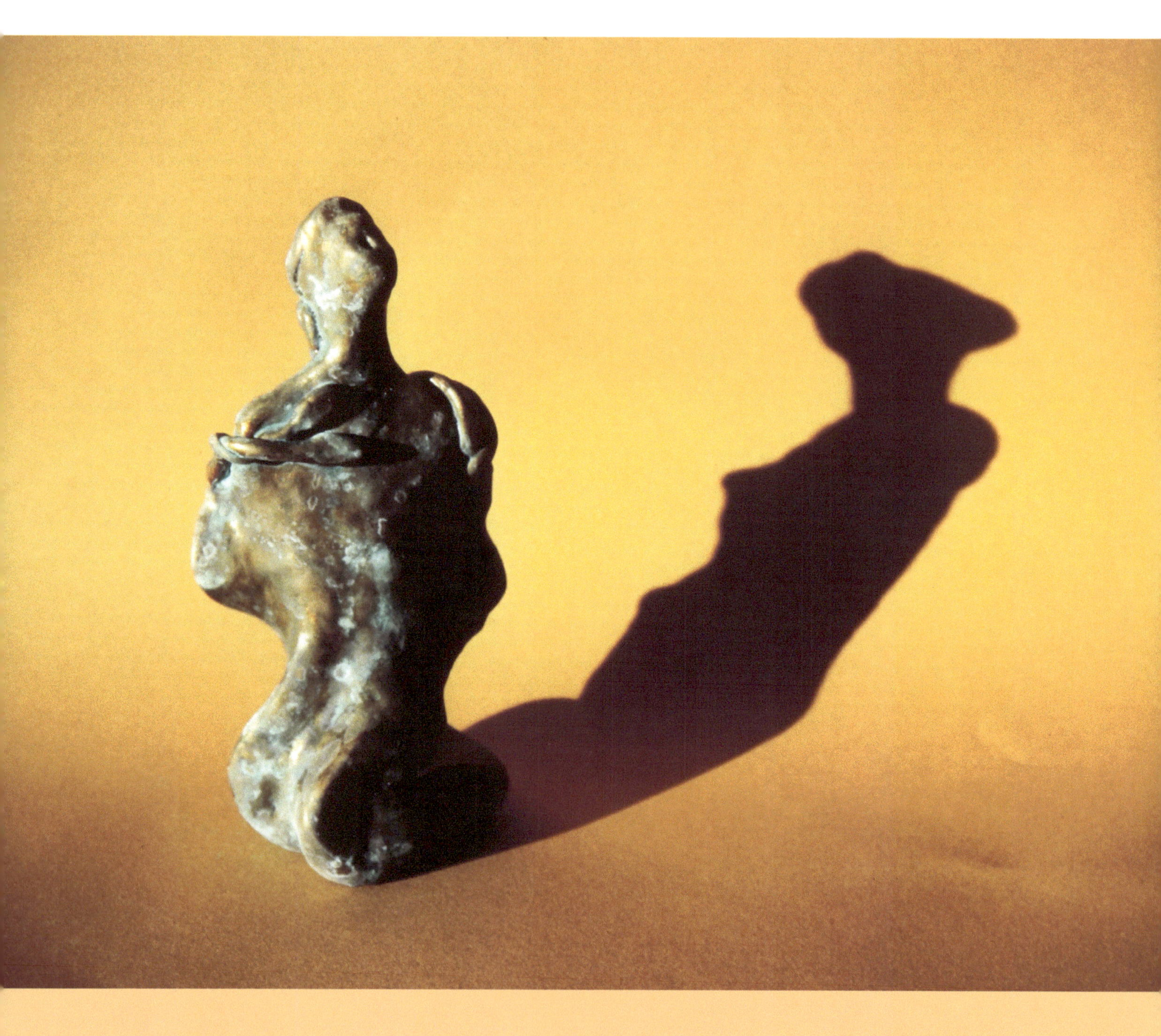

Song of the Winged Serpent

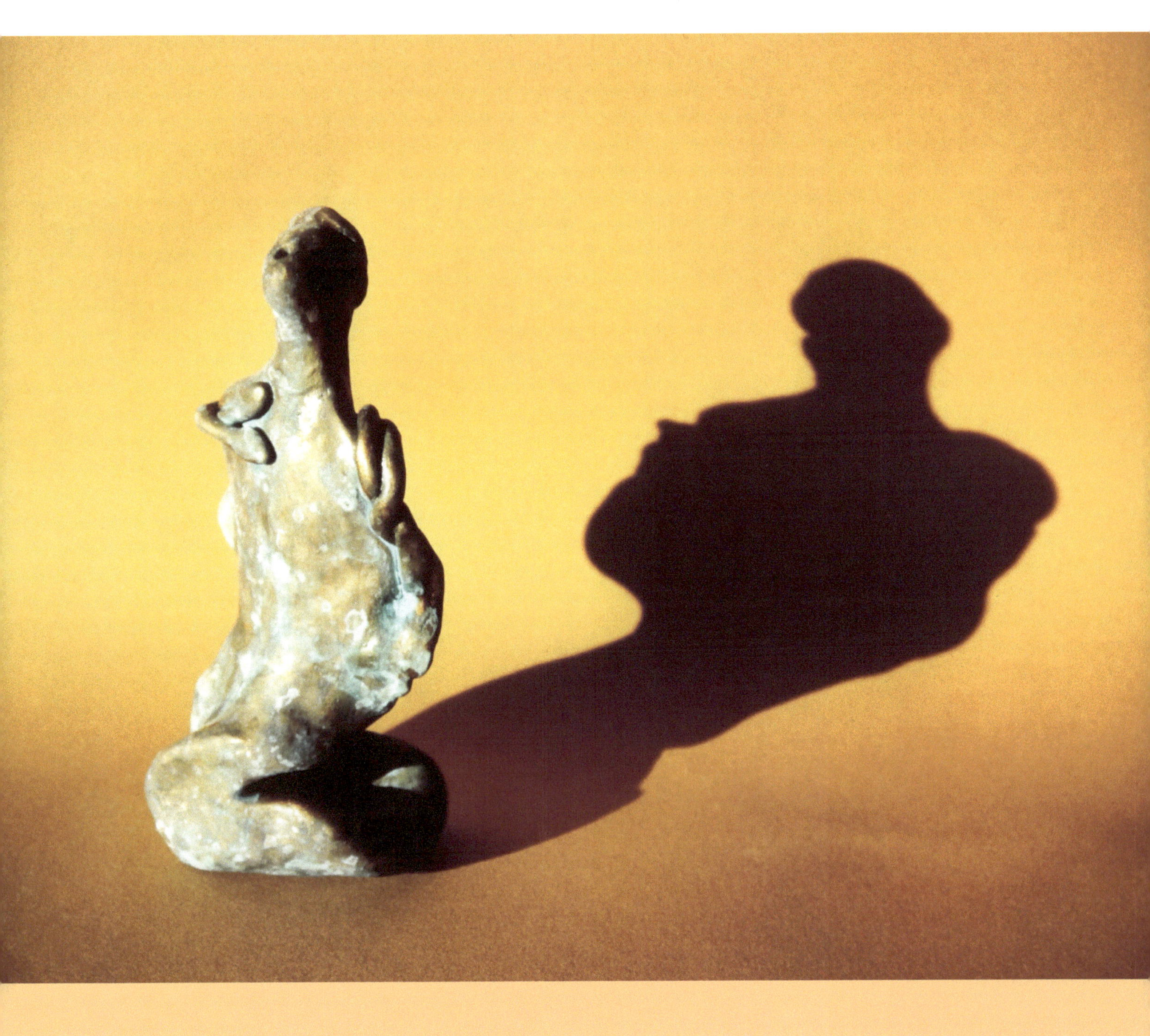

Song of the Winged Serpent

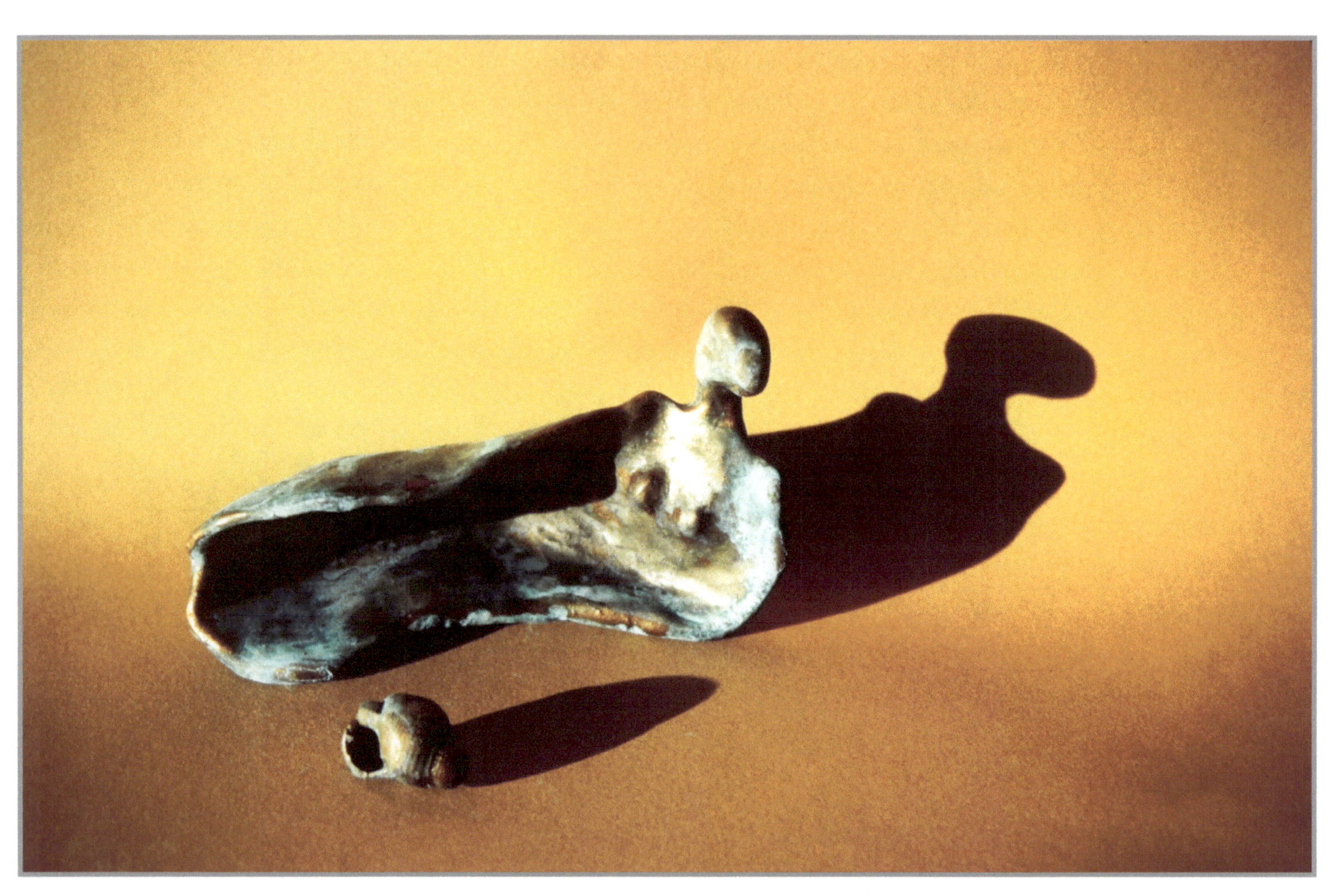

Ceremony with the shell...

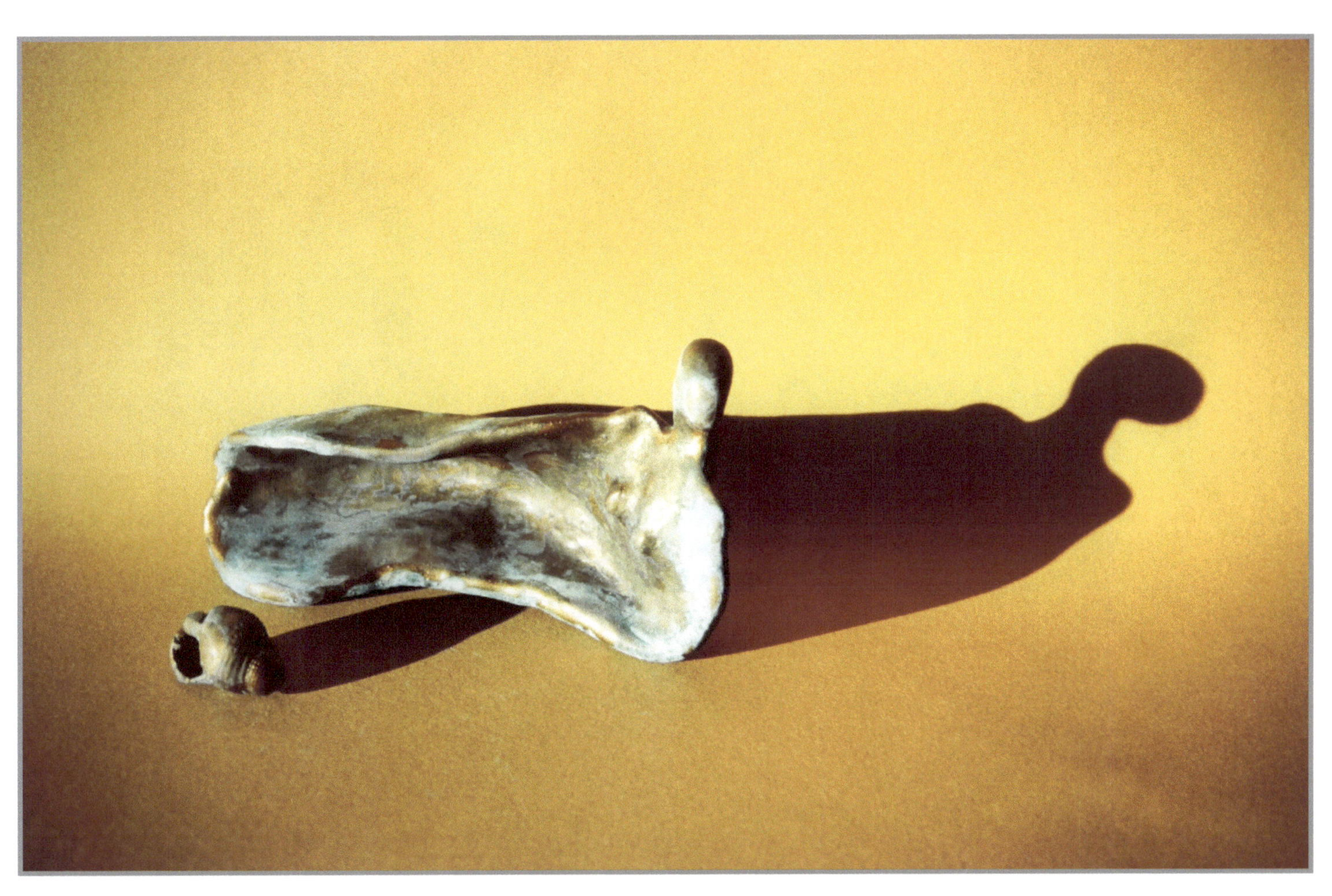

Ceremony with the shell...

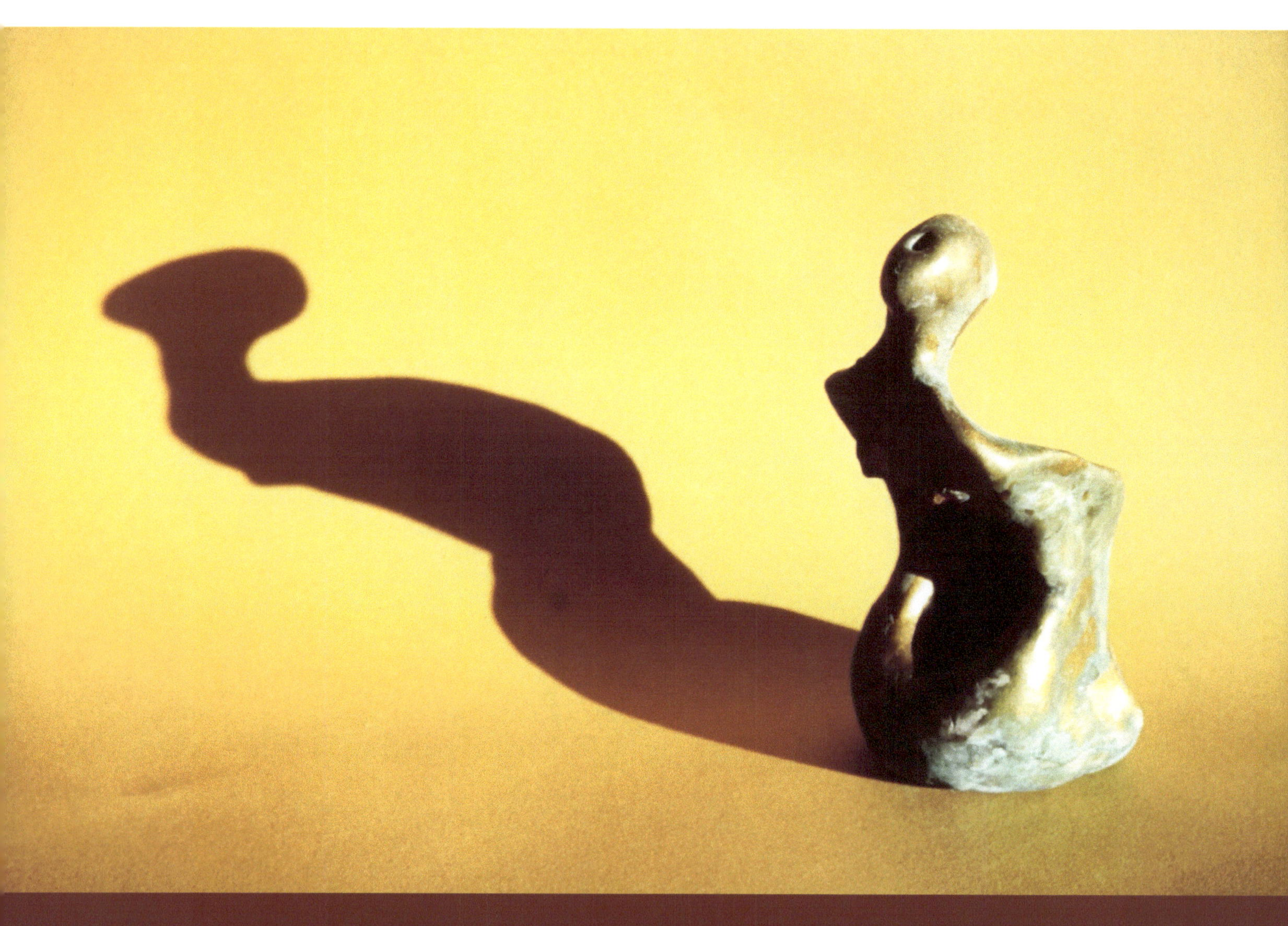

Desert Song-SHE

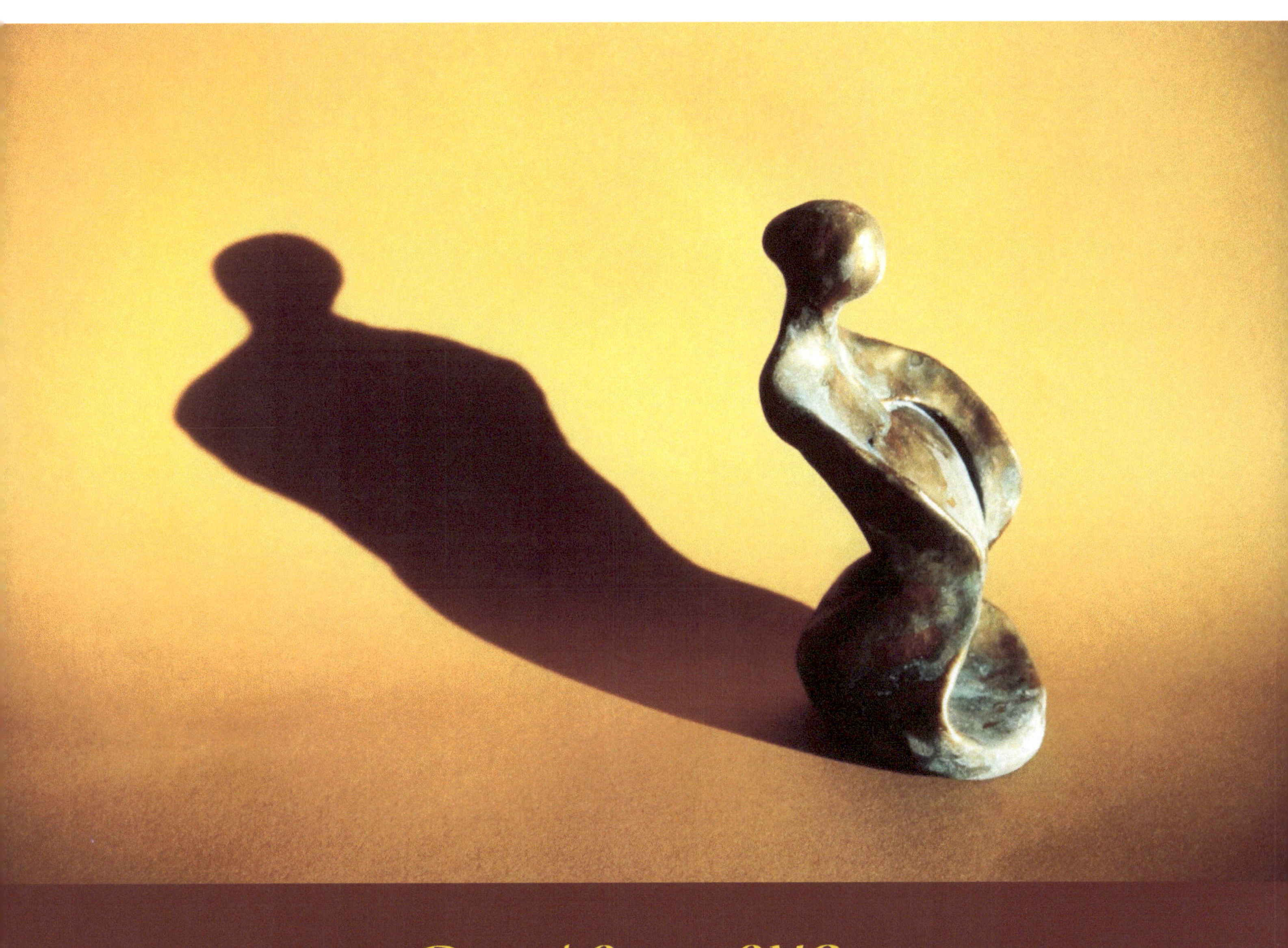

Desert Song-SHE

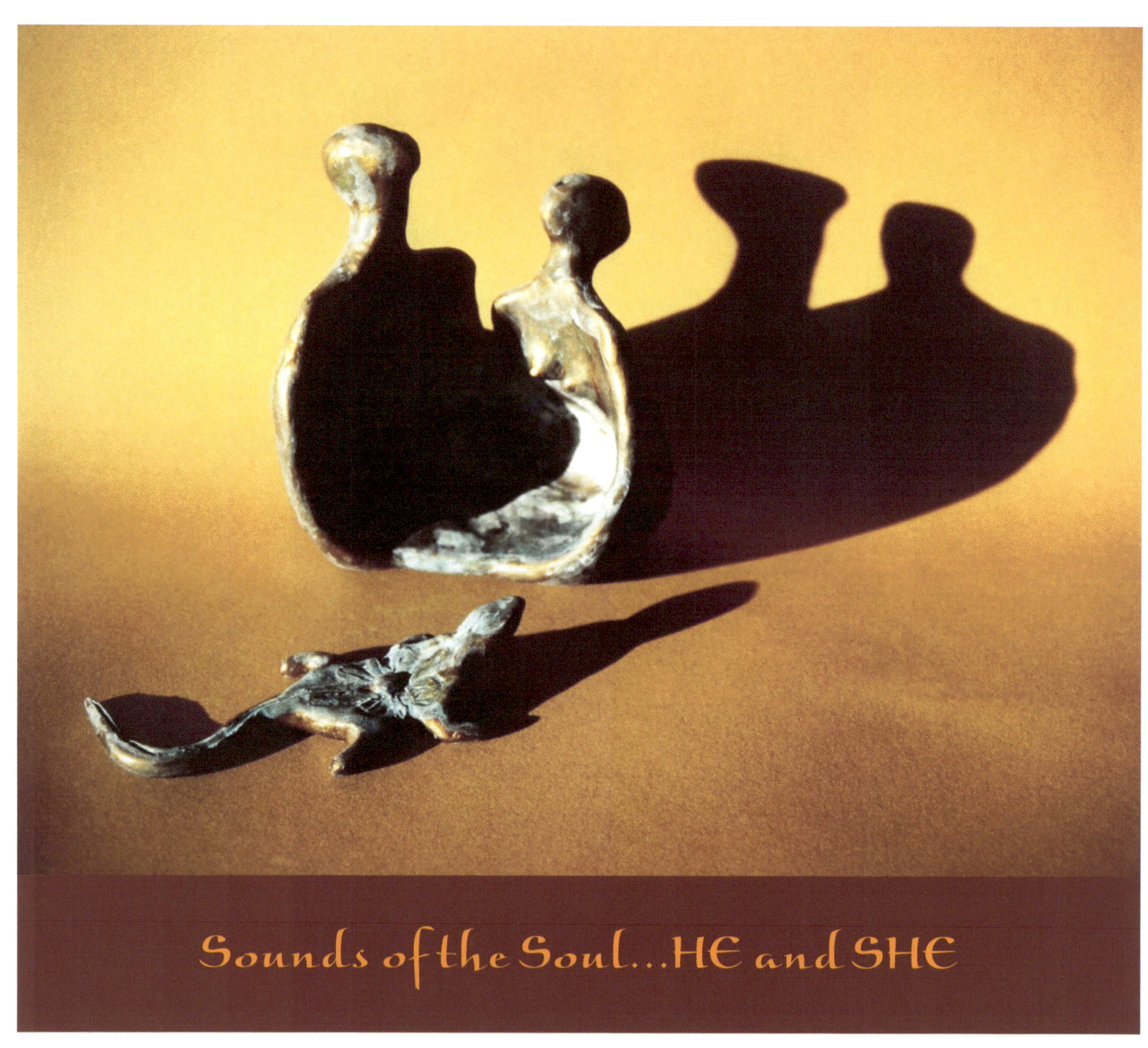

Sounds of the Soul...HE and SHE

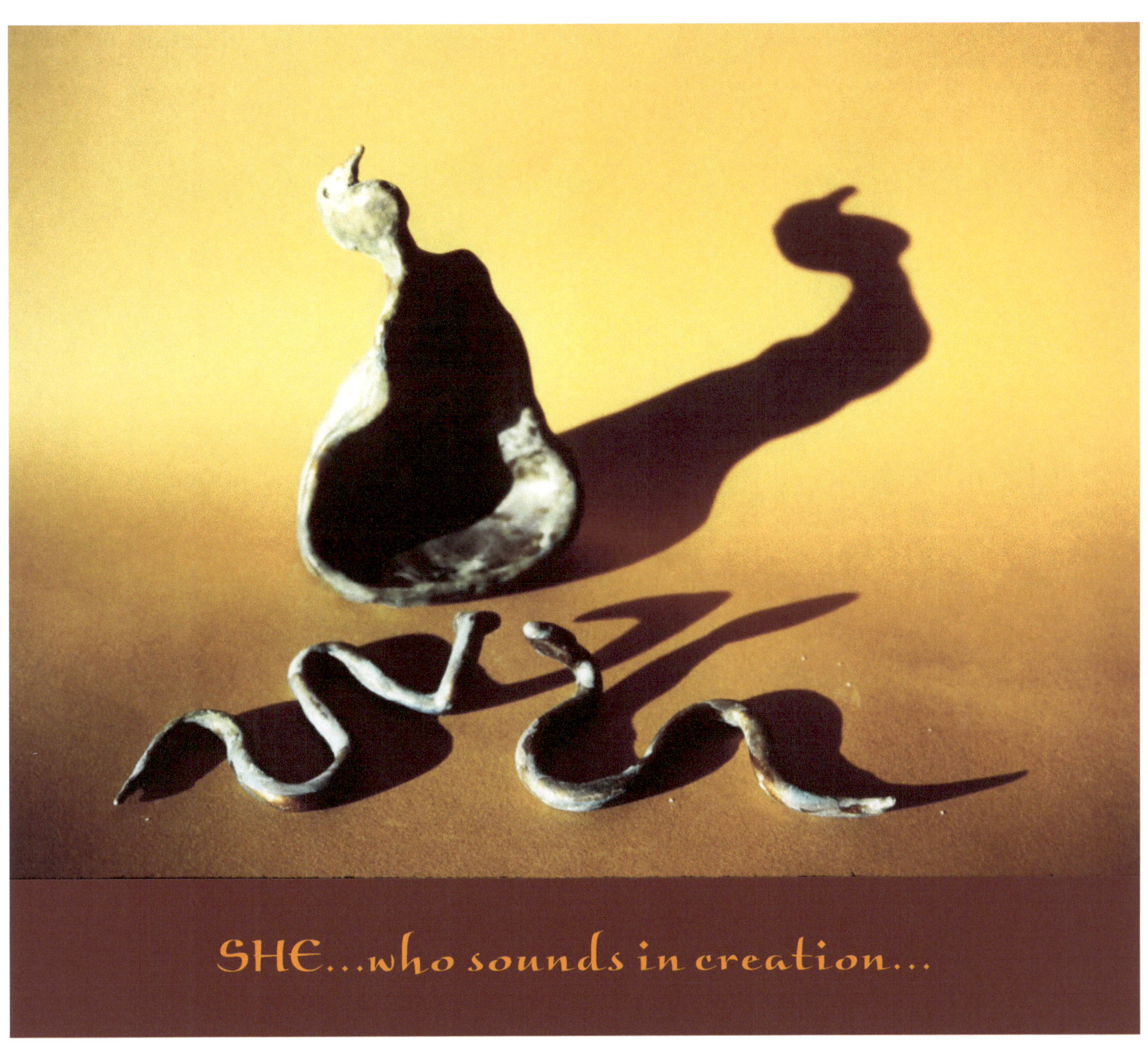

SHE…who sounds in creation…

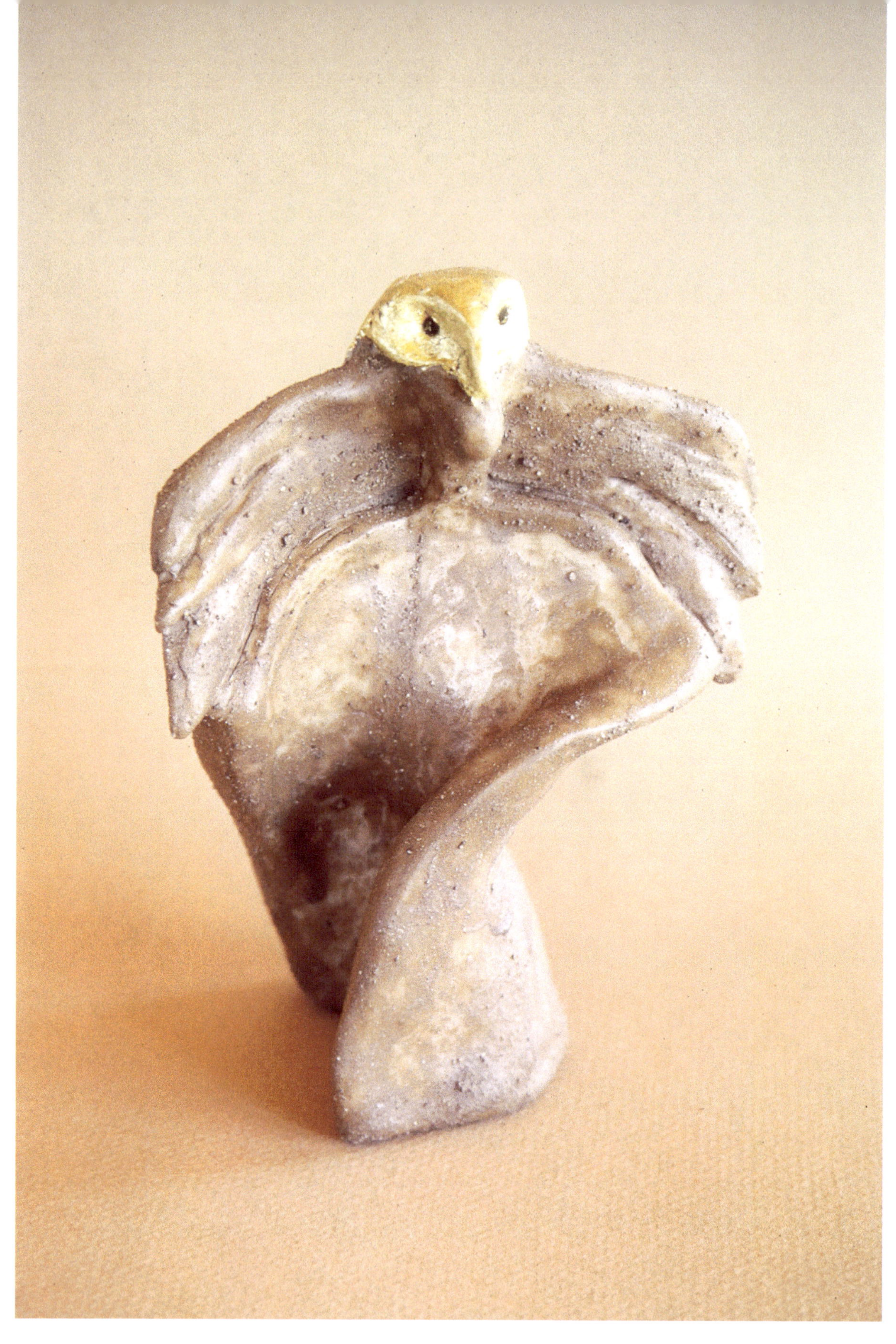

Guardian at the Door

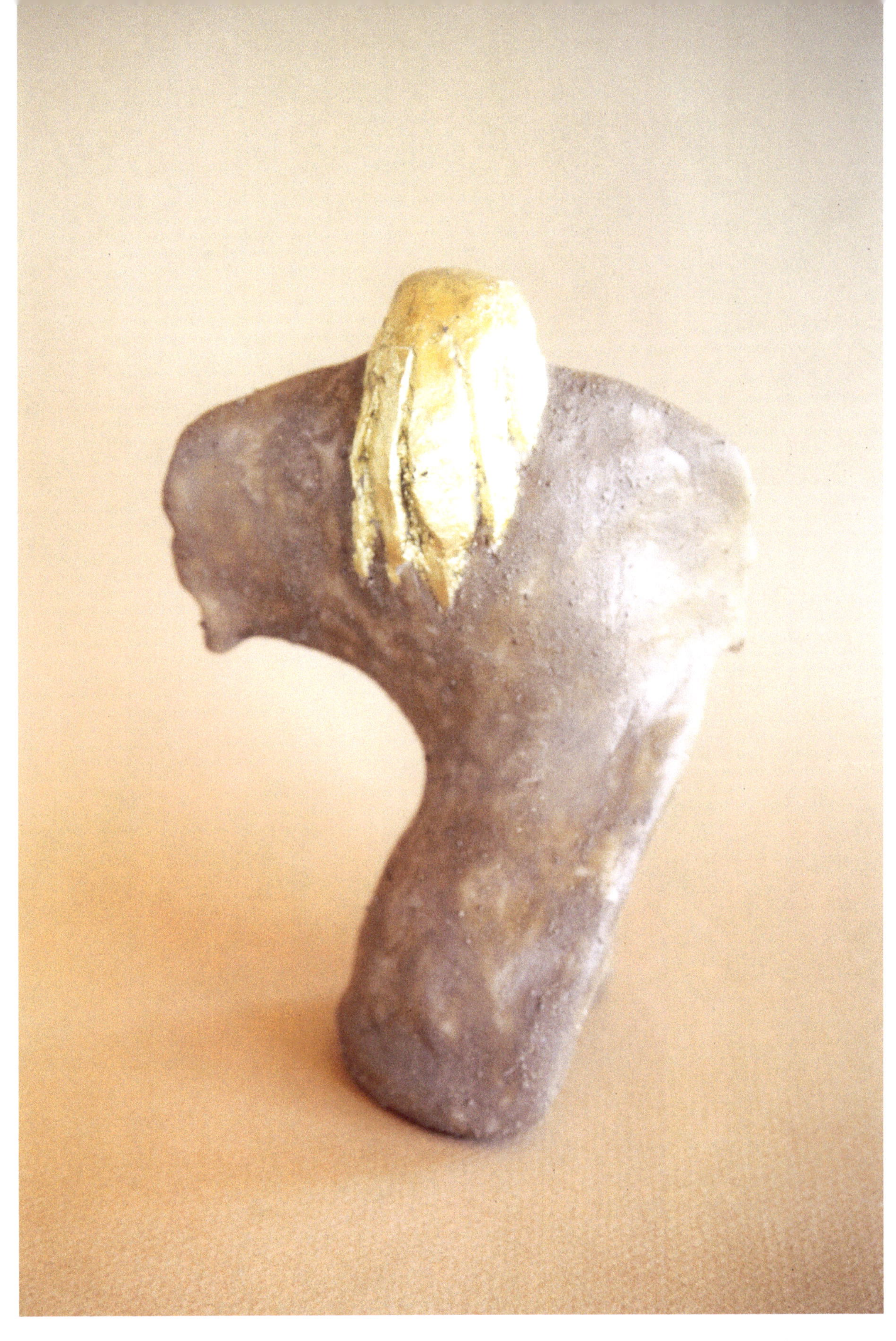

Guardian at the Door

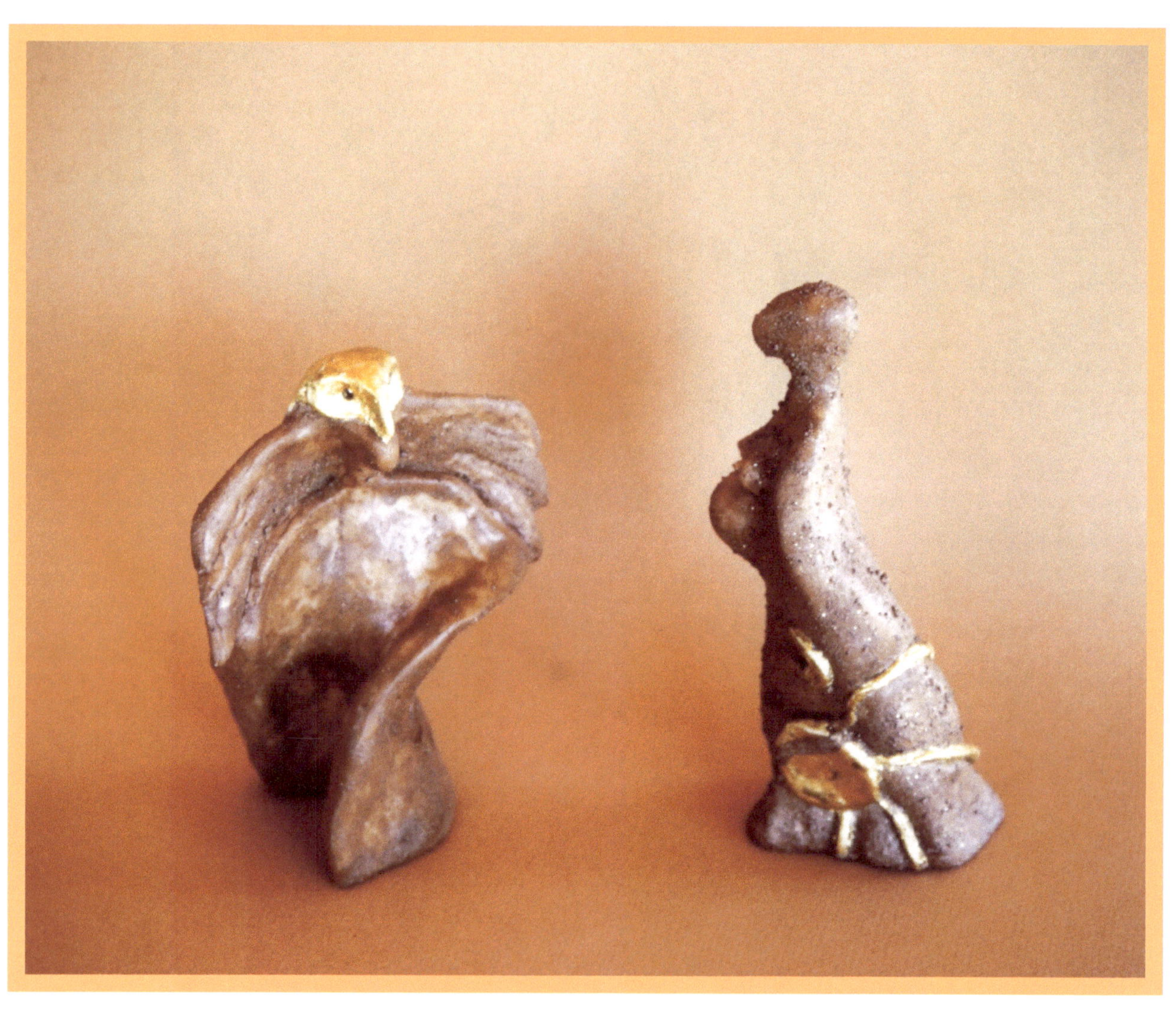

Guardian at the Door
and
Birther of the New Earth

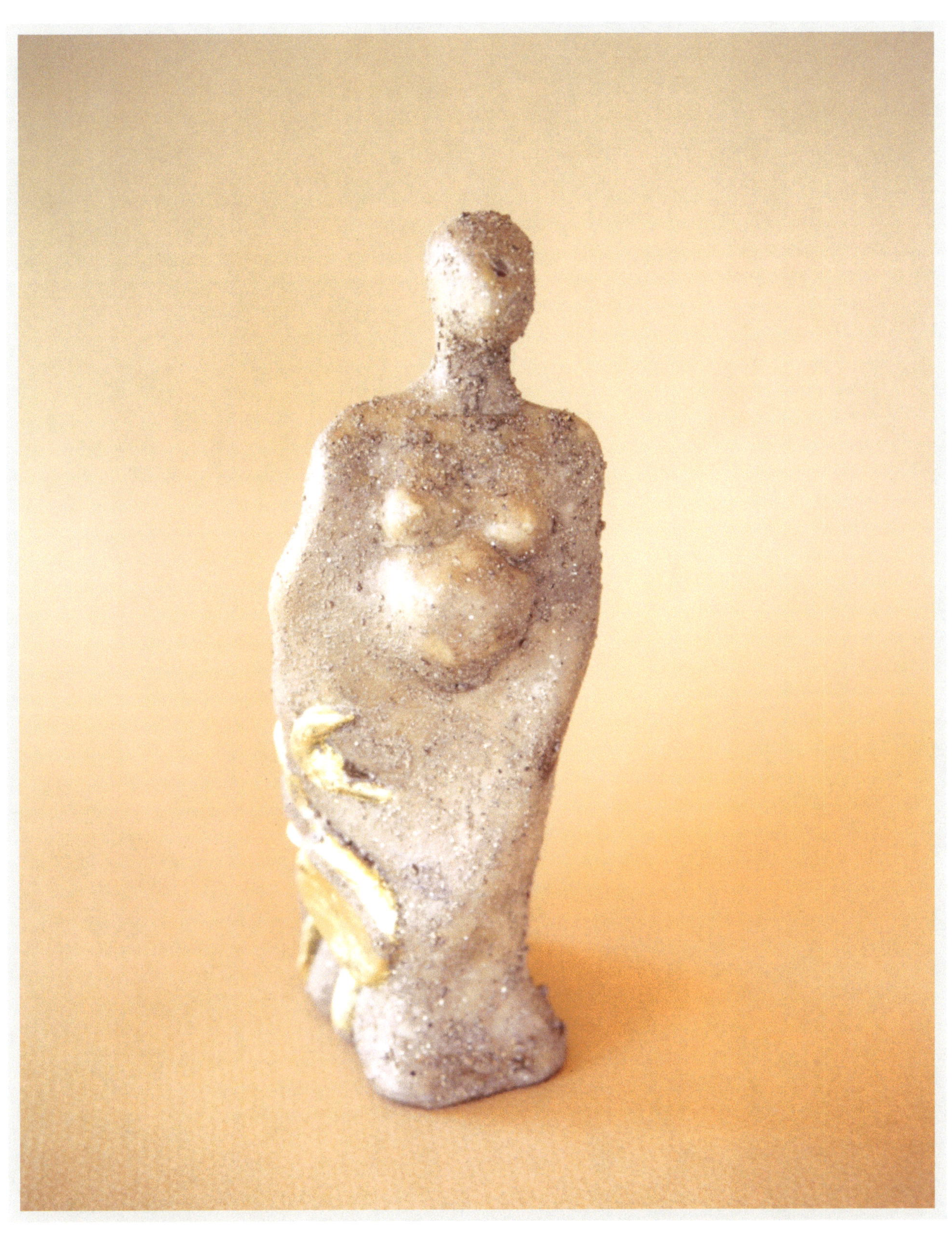

Birther of the New Earth

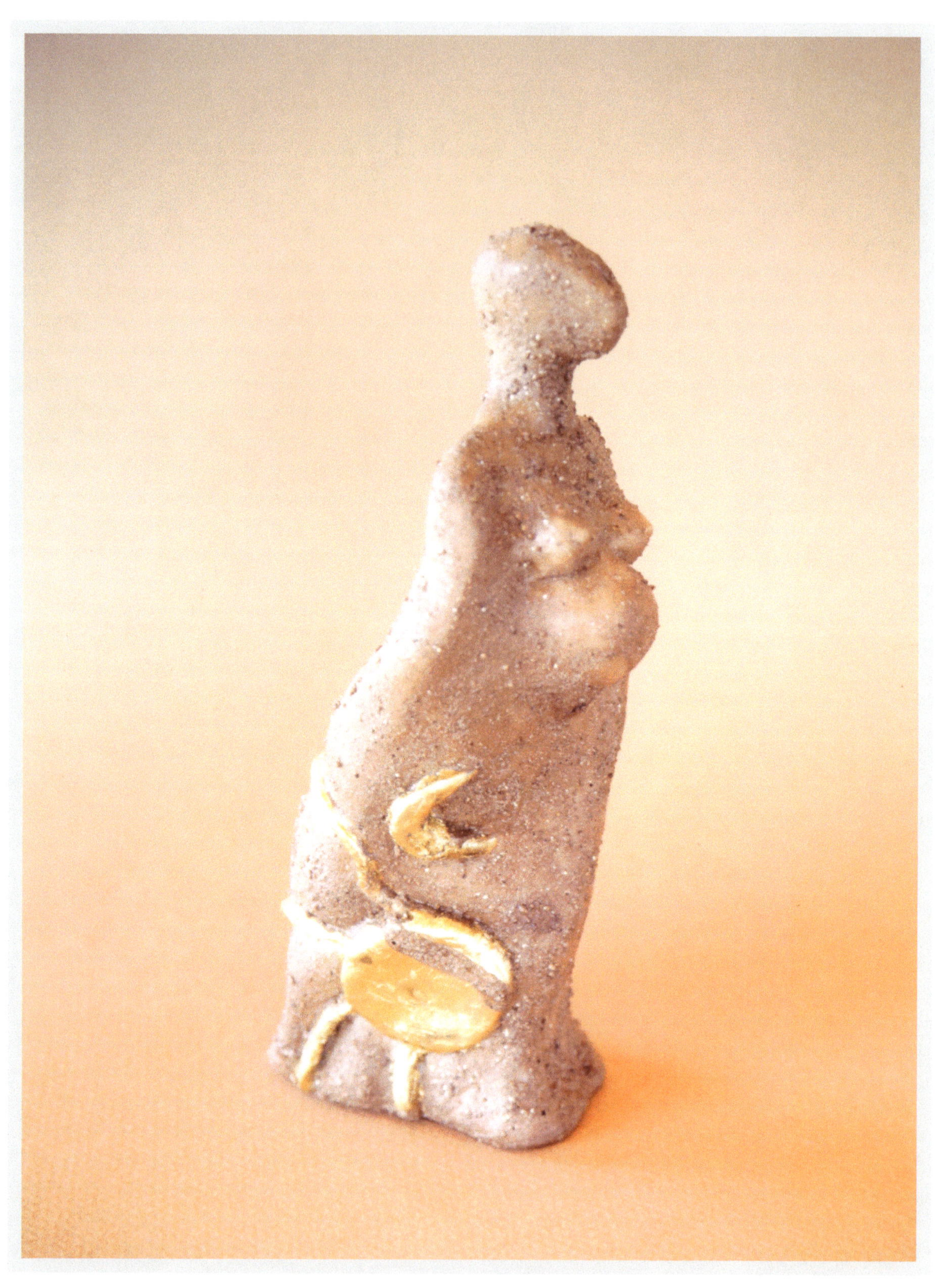

Birther of the New Earth

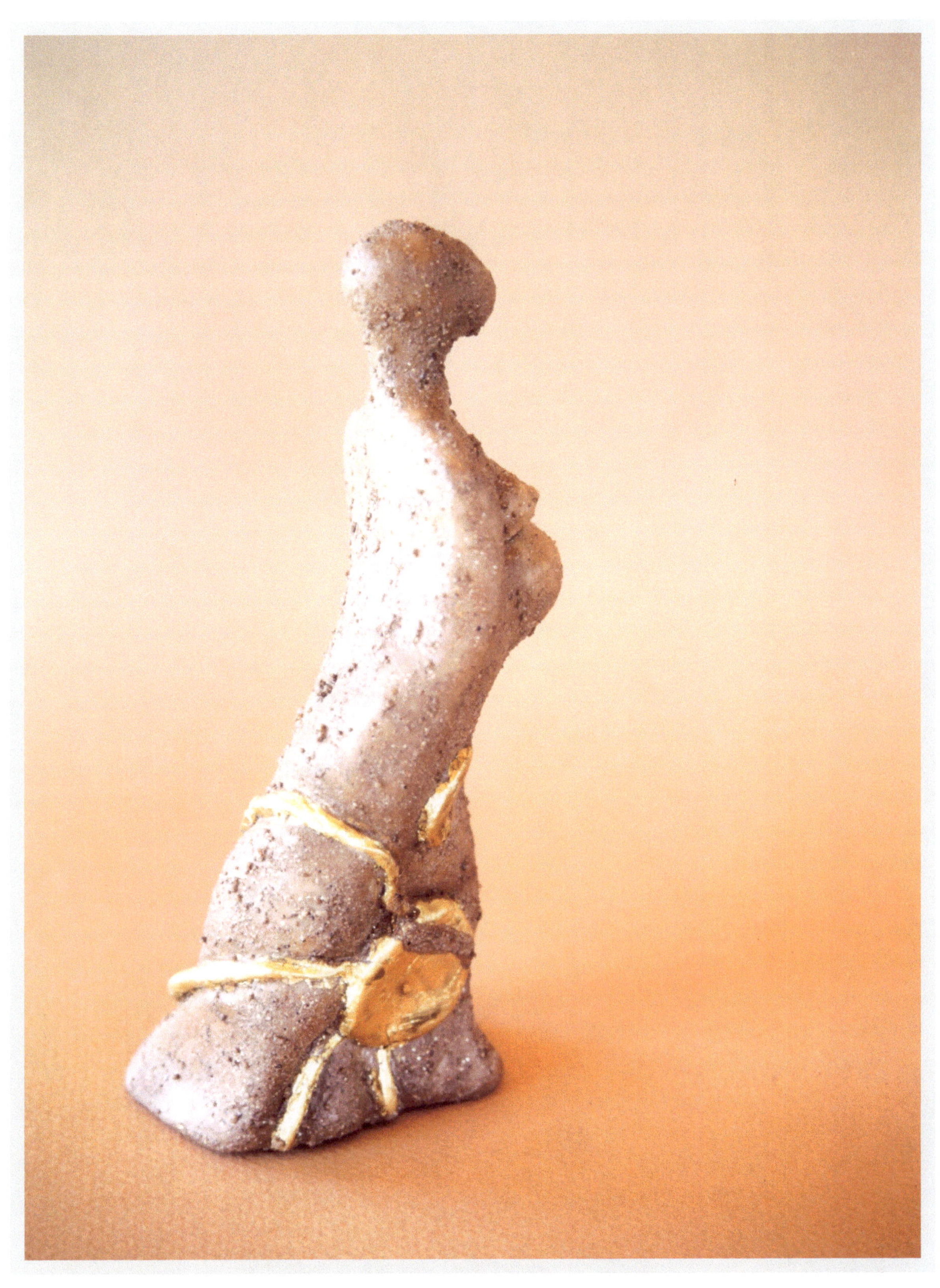

Birther of the New Earth

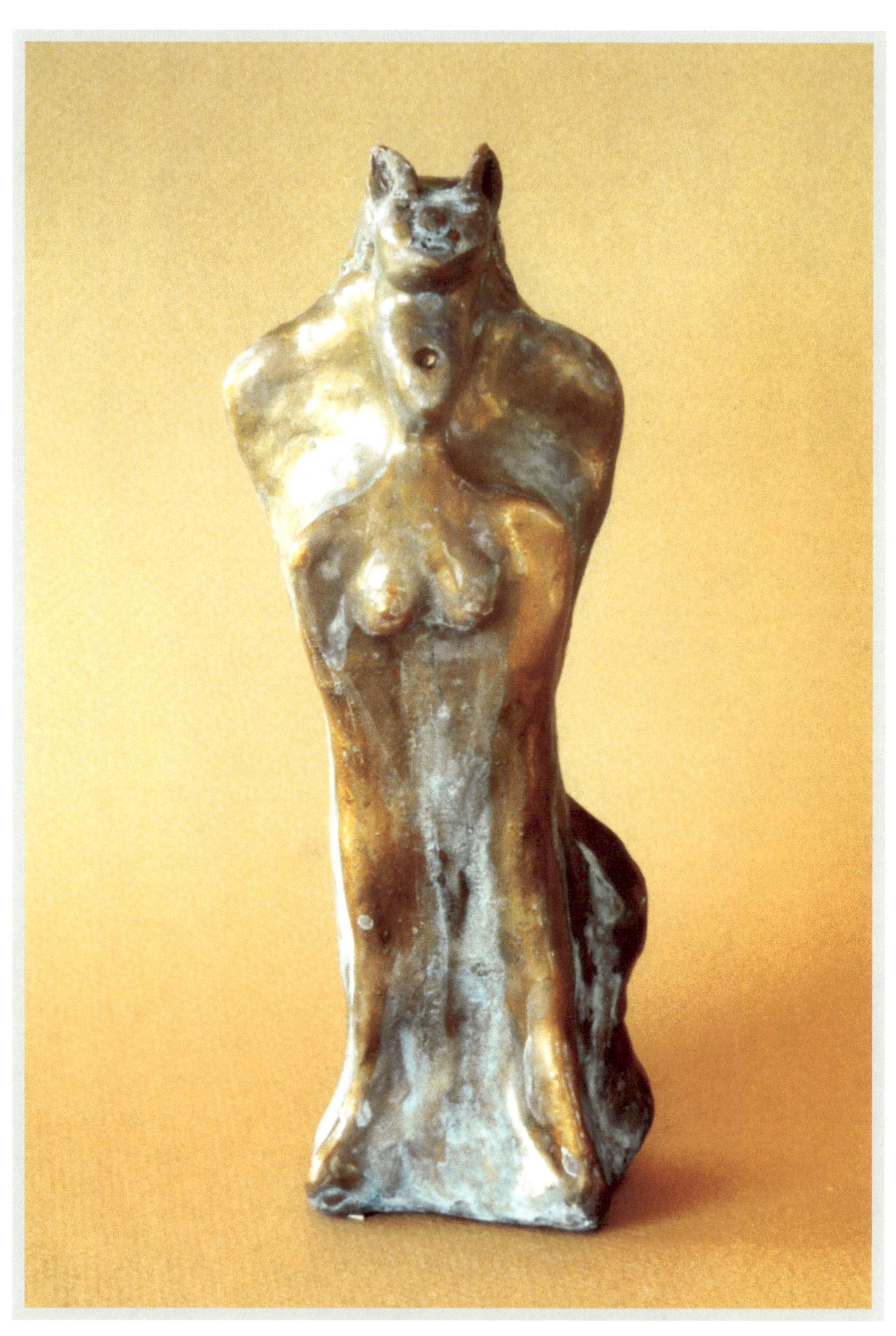

Sphinx-SHE...sounding the mystery...

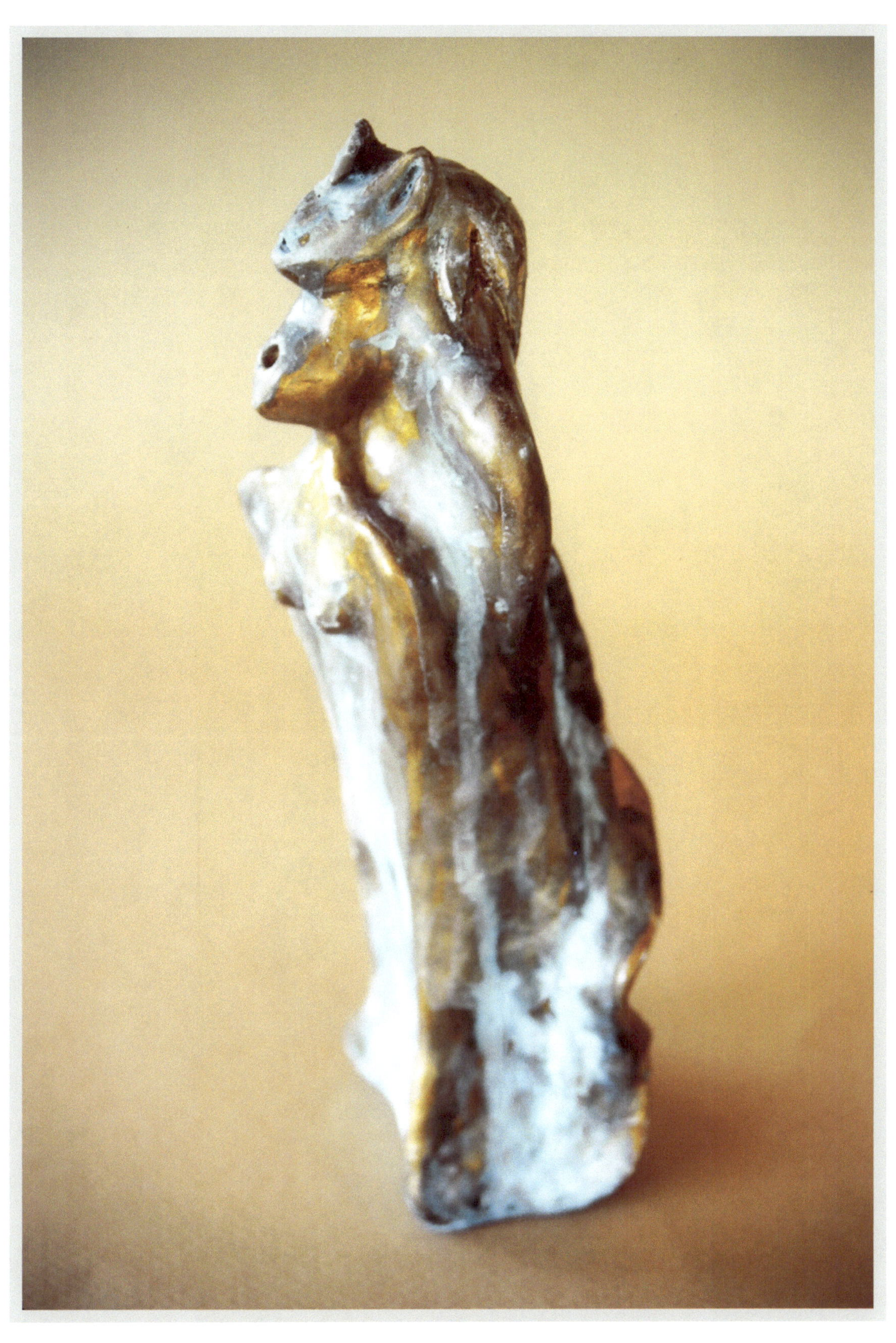

Sphinx-SHE...sounding the mystery...

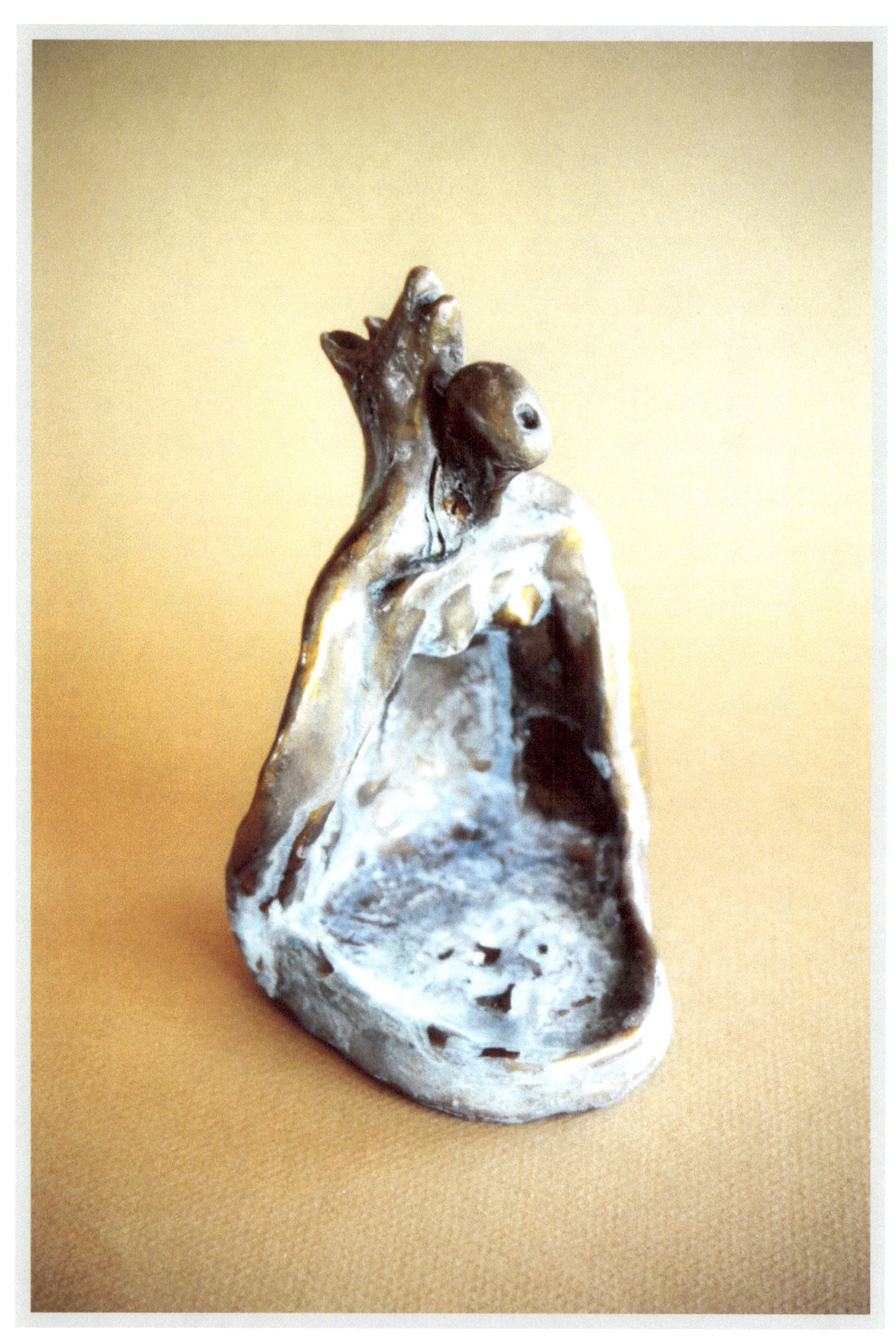

Wolf-Song-SHE

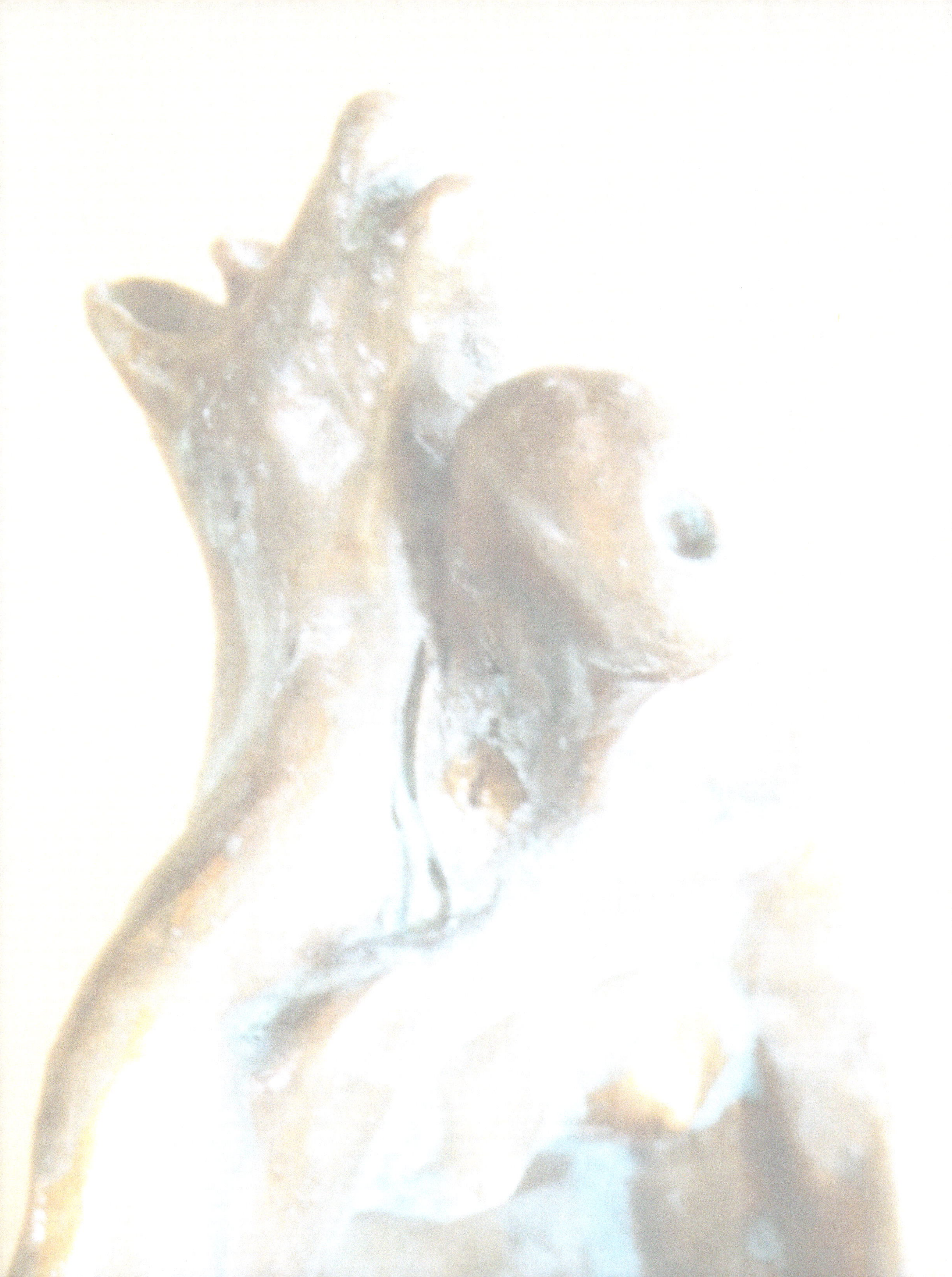

Fourth Phase:
Bronze Kachina Sculpture

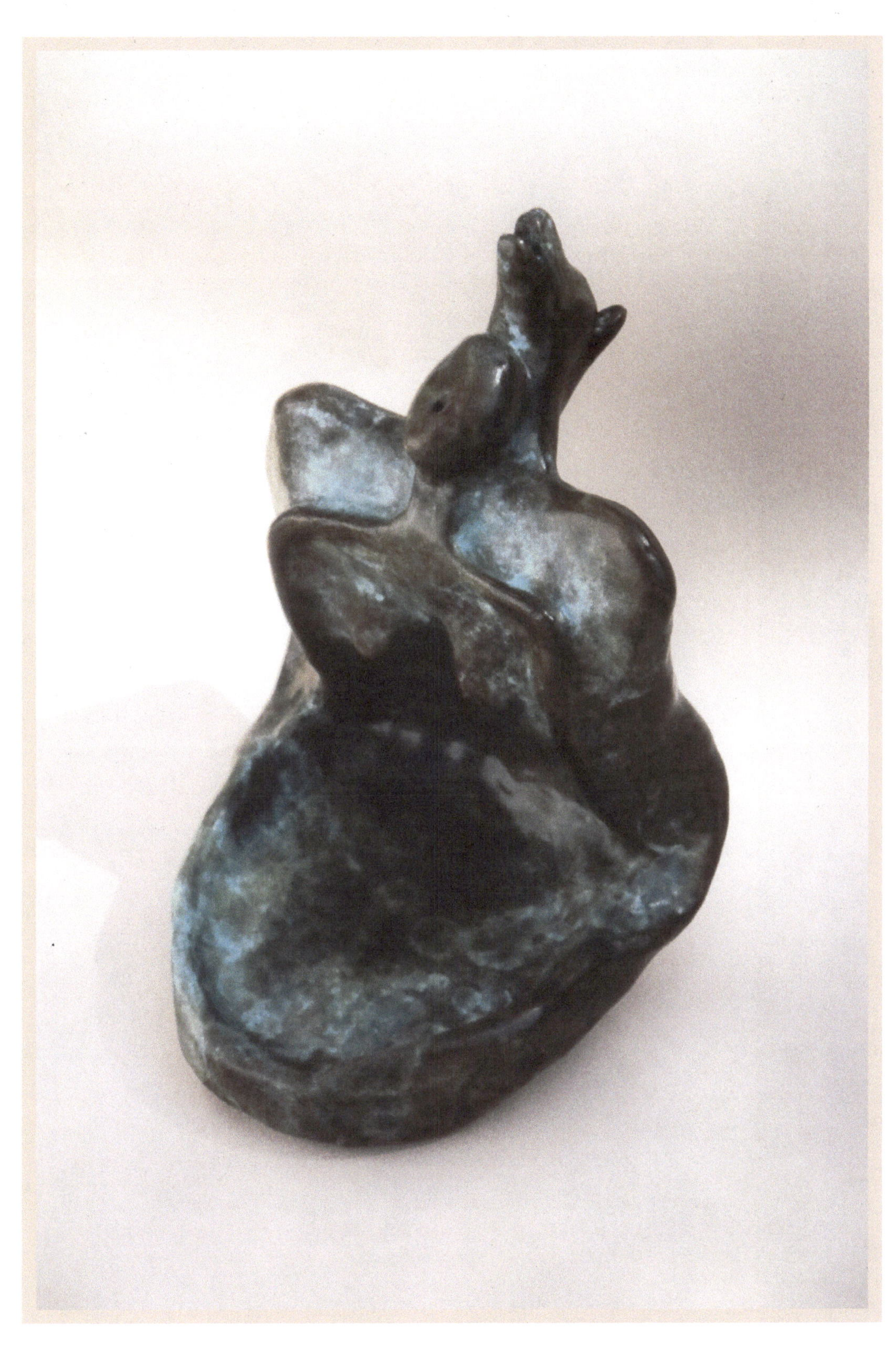

Wolf Dance HE and SHE

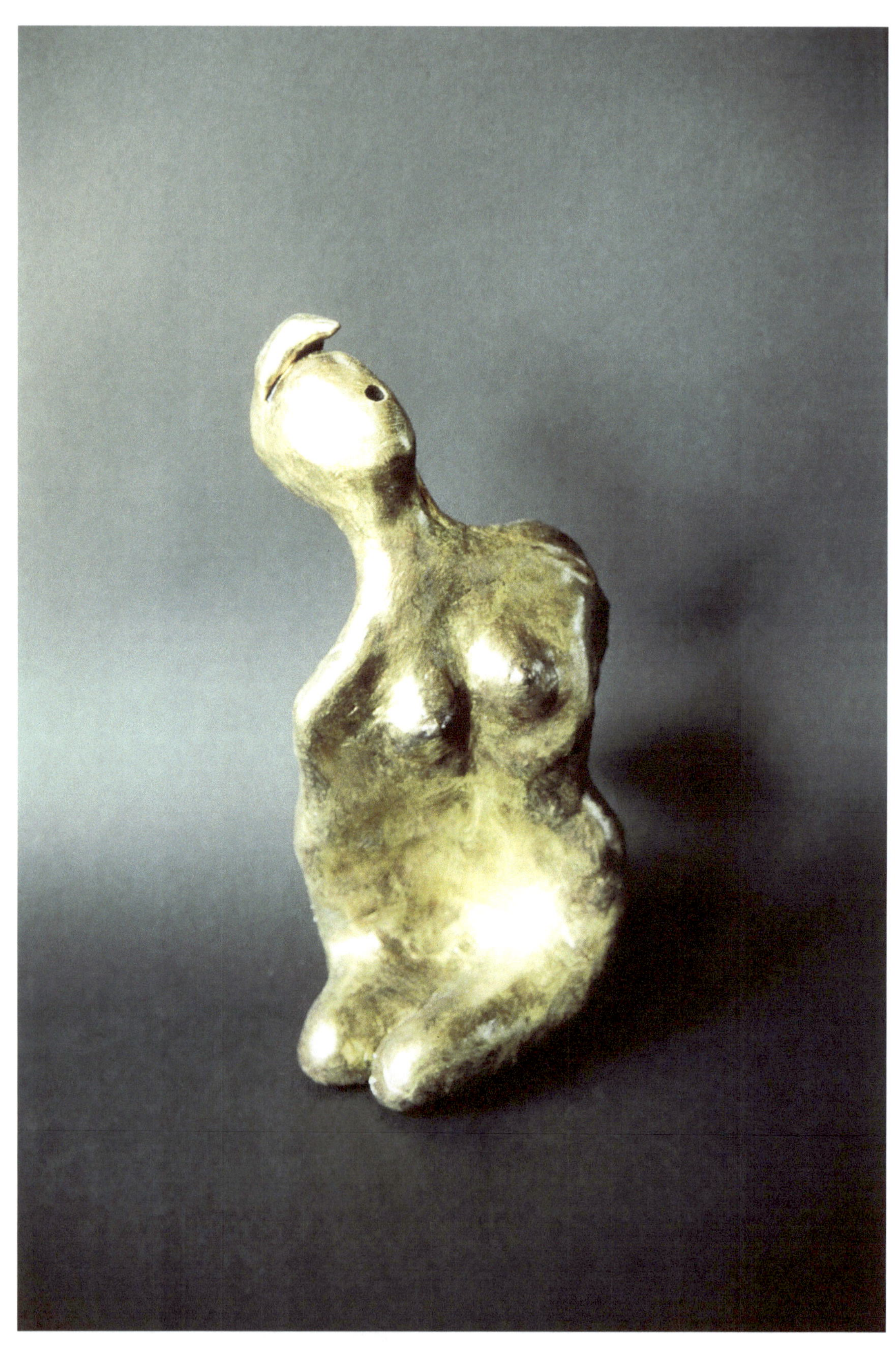

Warrior-Priestess-SHE...in flight...

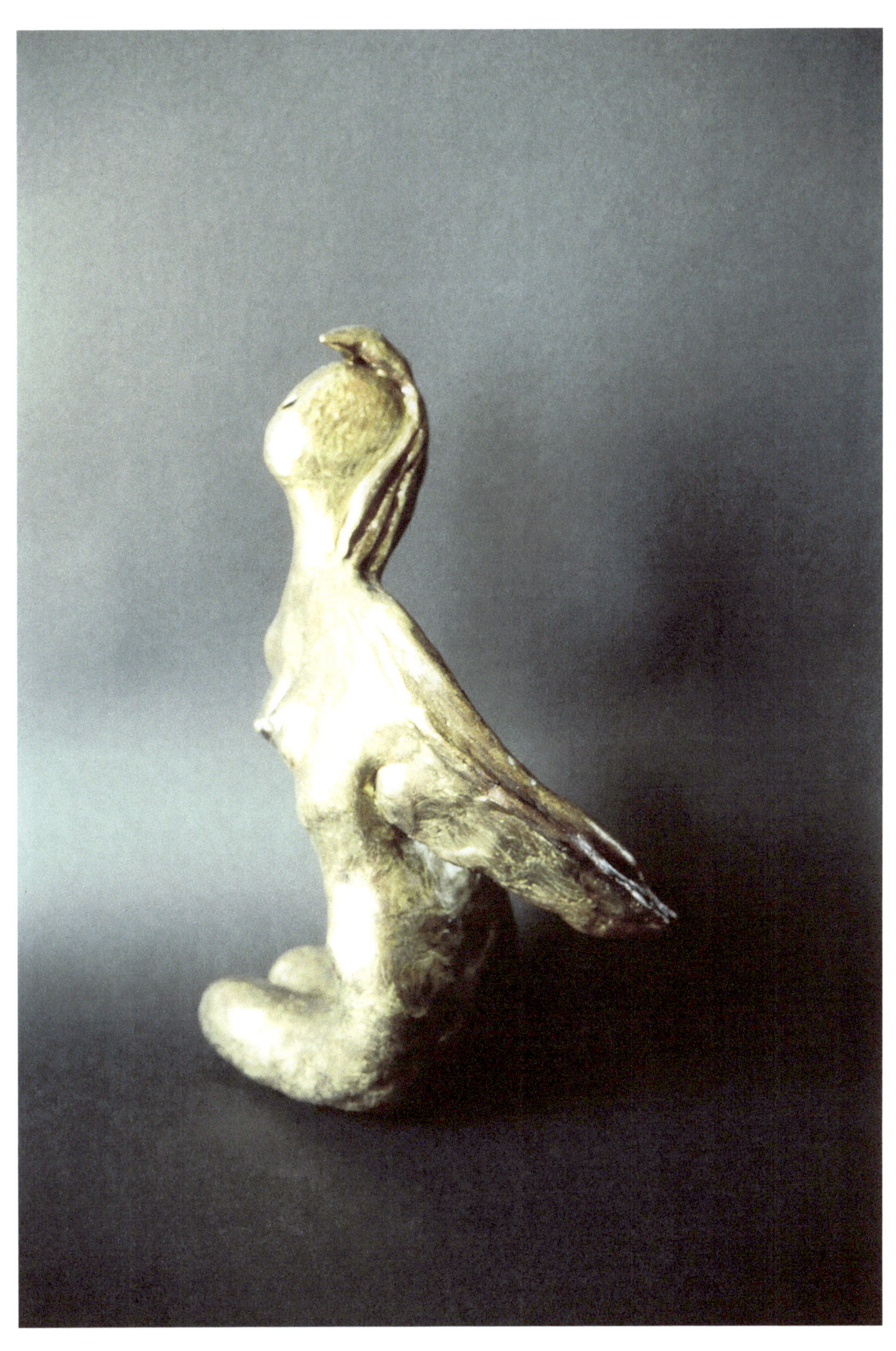

Warrior-Priestess-SHE...in flight...

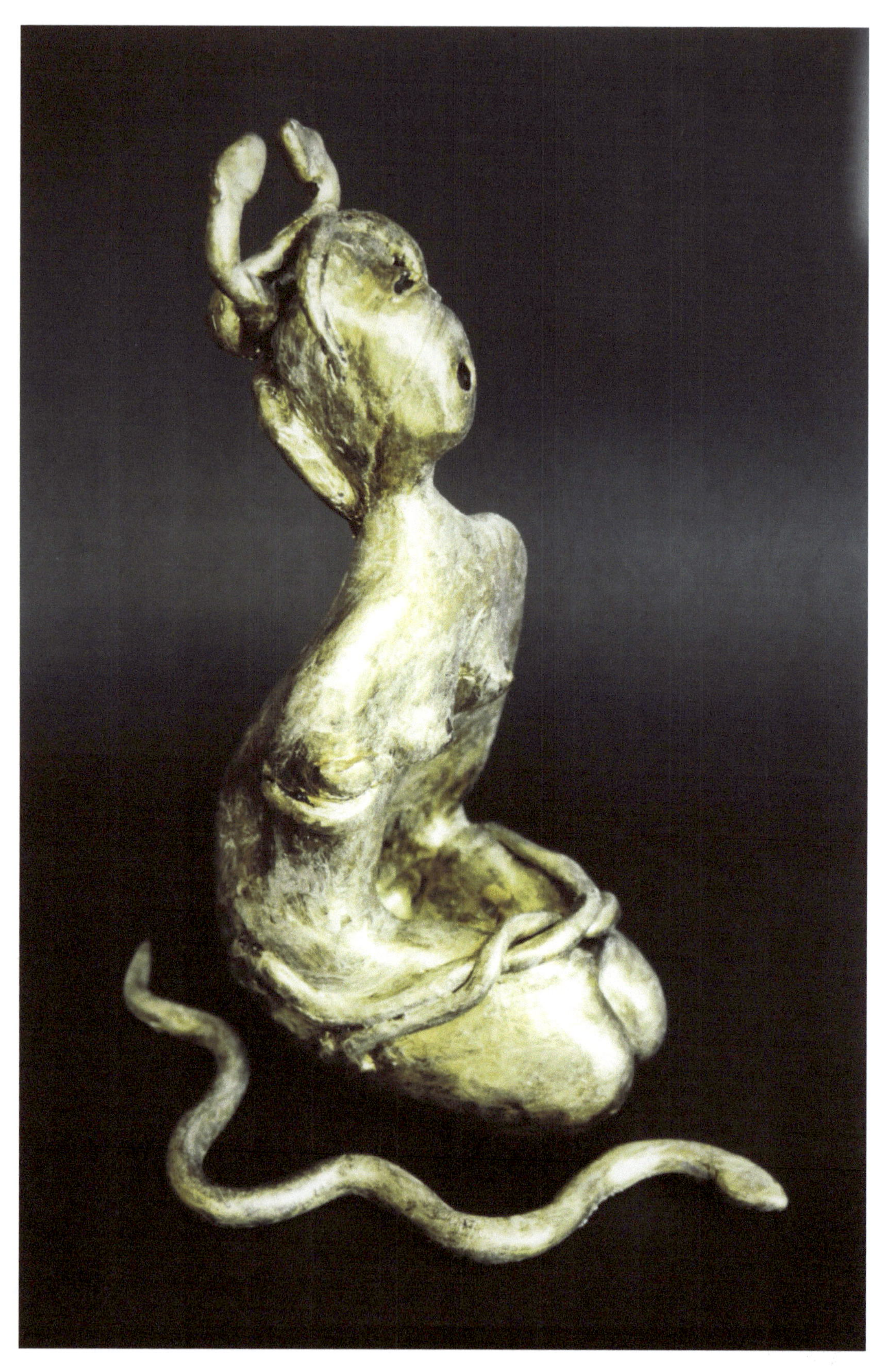

Serpent-Priestess-SHE

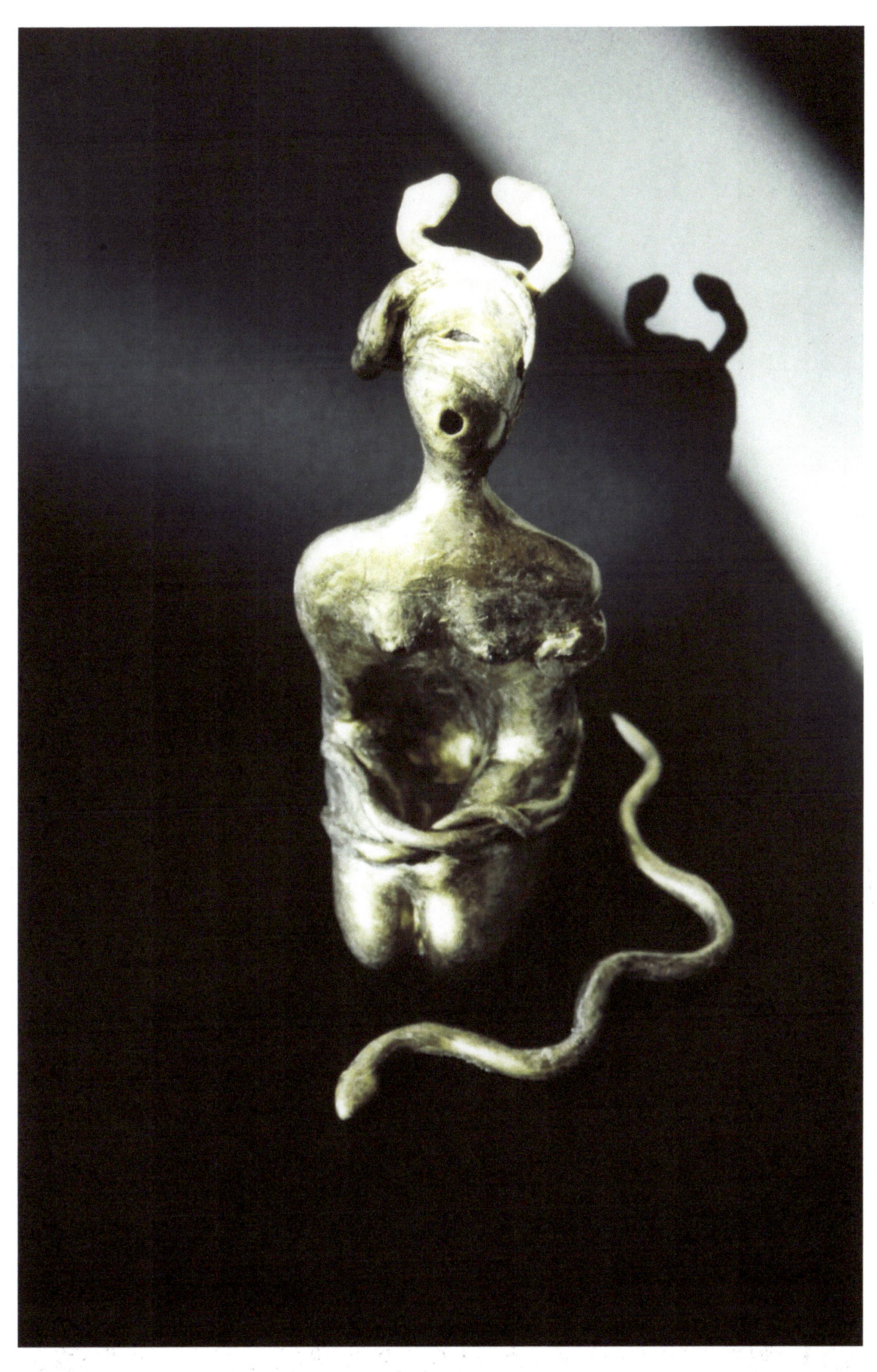

Serpent-Priestess-SHE

Fifth Phase:
Ceramic Kachina Sculpture

a dream of the faceless one

This dream came to me 20 years after the other sculptures in this book.

It is predawn.
A dream is upon me.
I am sculpting.

The clay piece is about 1.5" deep, 7" across, and 10" tall. It is flat, like a plaque. The image is being sculpted in relief. I am sculpting with my thumbs and fingers, using no instrument. I am watching the face being inscribed into the willing, waiting clay. I can see the face clearly.

The face is a powerful face.
It is the Faceless Face of God.
It is alive.
I awaken from the dream. I am instantly aware of these words:
Face of the Faceless One

Not long after the dream, I felt to read the Masks of God series, by Joseph Campbell. History has indeed hidden the Faceless One. For a very long time. I then signed up for a ceramic class and sculpted three small art pieces reflecting the elevated message of the dream. The Face of the Faceless One, in the dream, was bringing a very poignant message about our True Identity as Faceless, Nameless, Wordless and Timeless. Pure Awareness...is our Spiritual Identity. The sculpted figures call to us to drop human identity with the body and mind.

They call to us to realize our God Identity. The I Am Consciousness.
They call to us to feel, know, experience the essence world.
They call to us to realize...the eternal one....

Inspiration comes...
on the wind...in a dream...
in moments beyond the face...

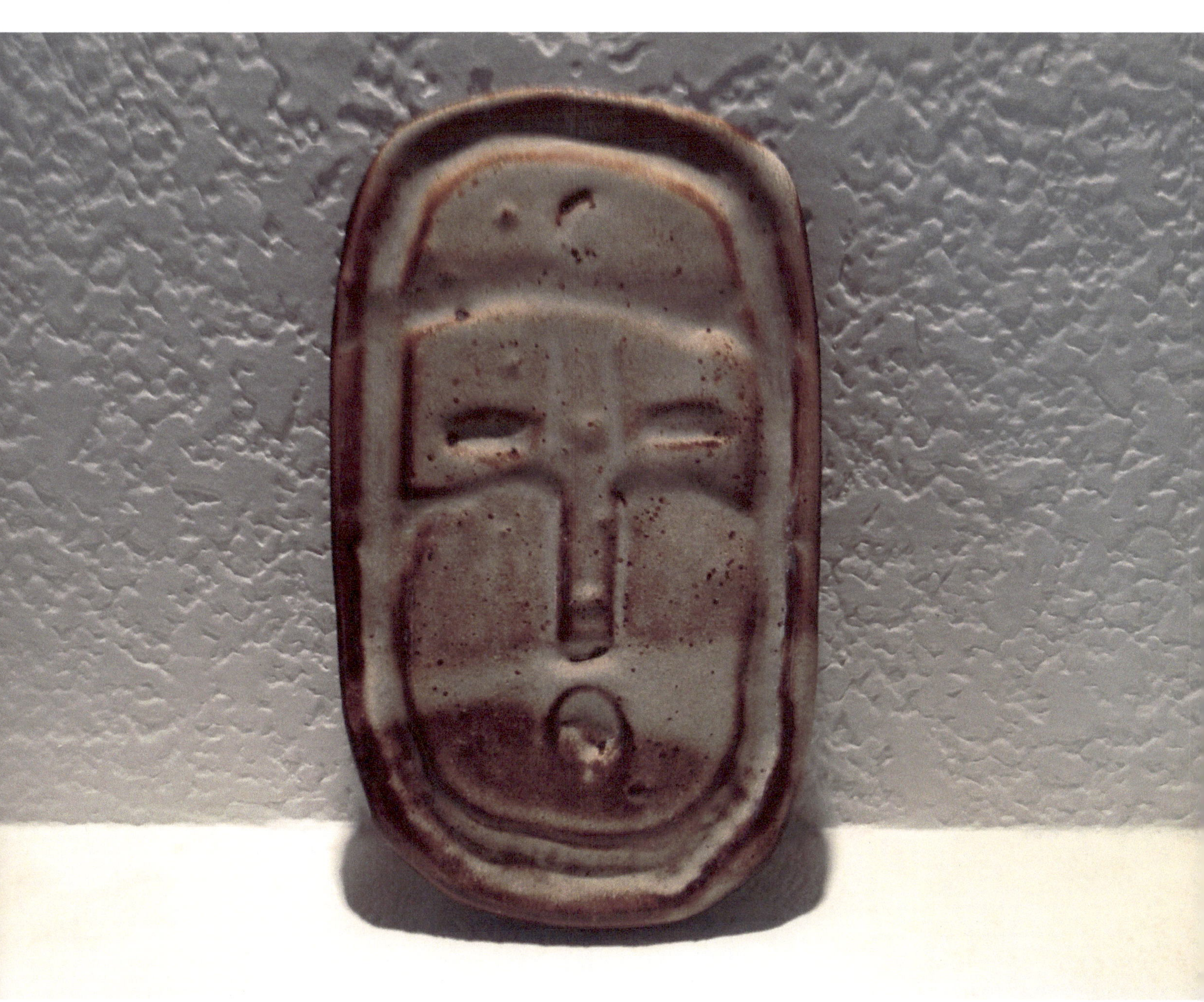

Face of the Faceless One

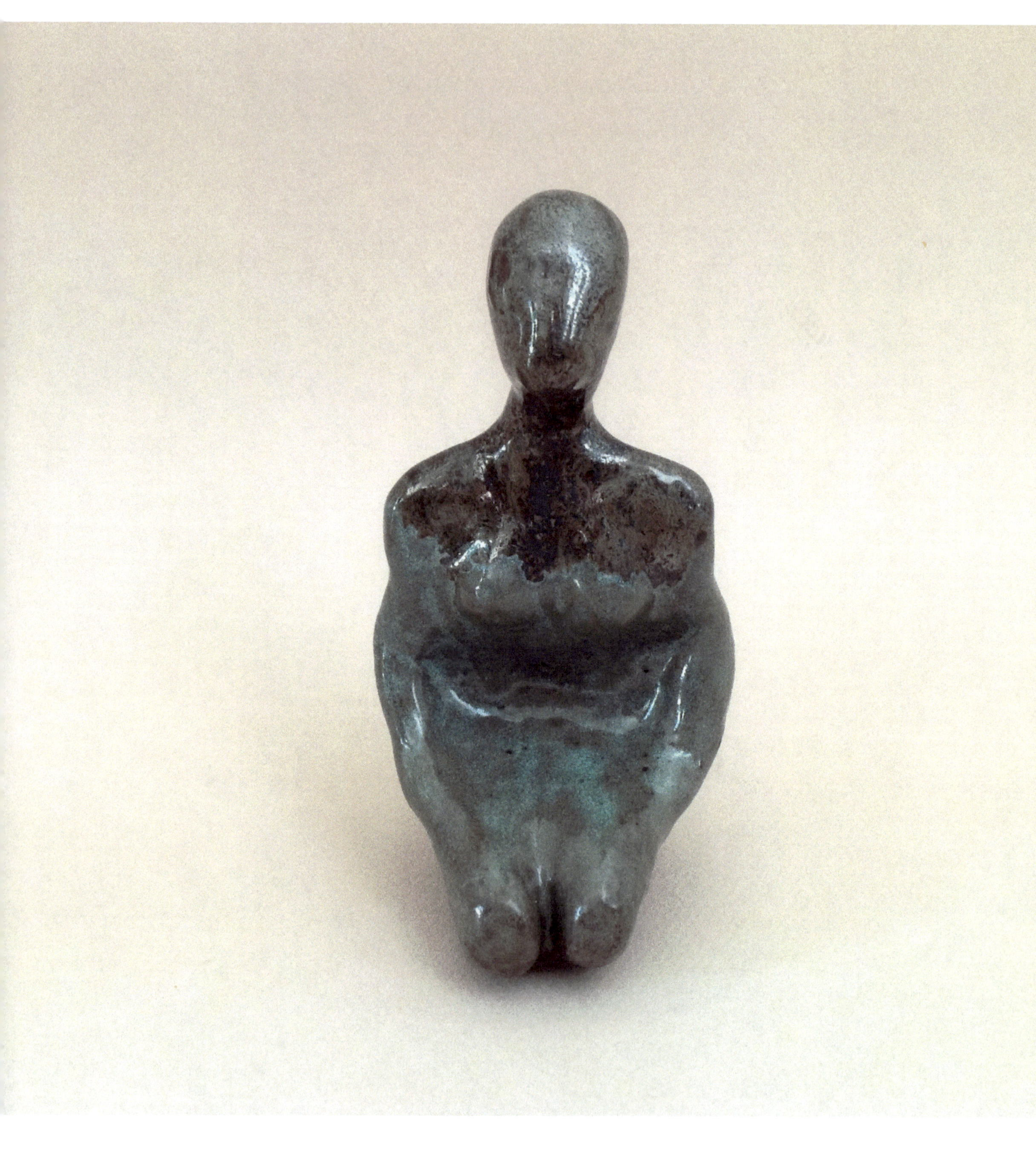

The Faceless One-SHE

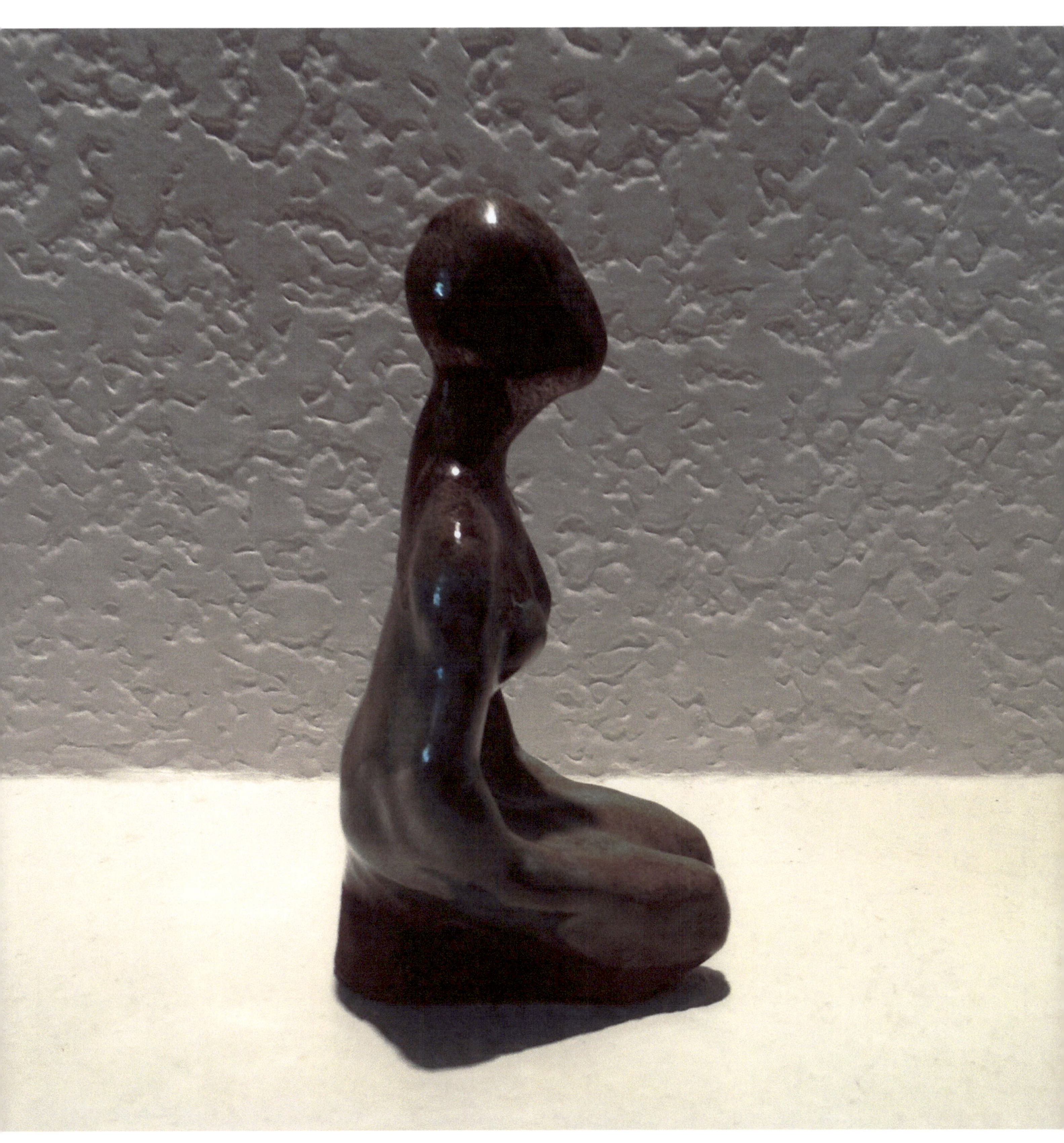

The Faceless One-SHE

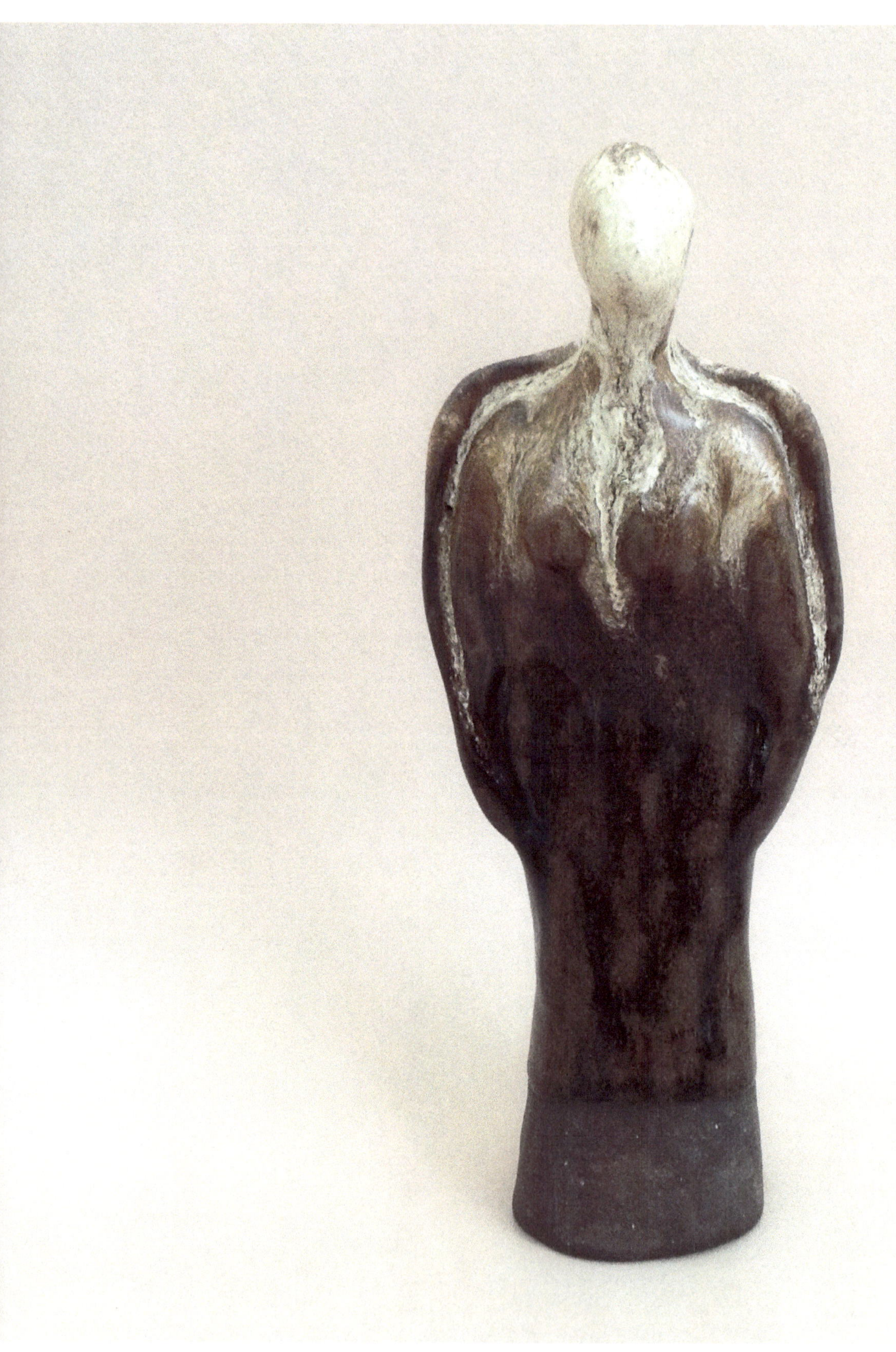

Angel from the Faceless Realm

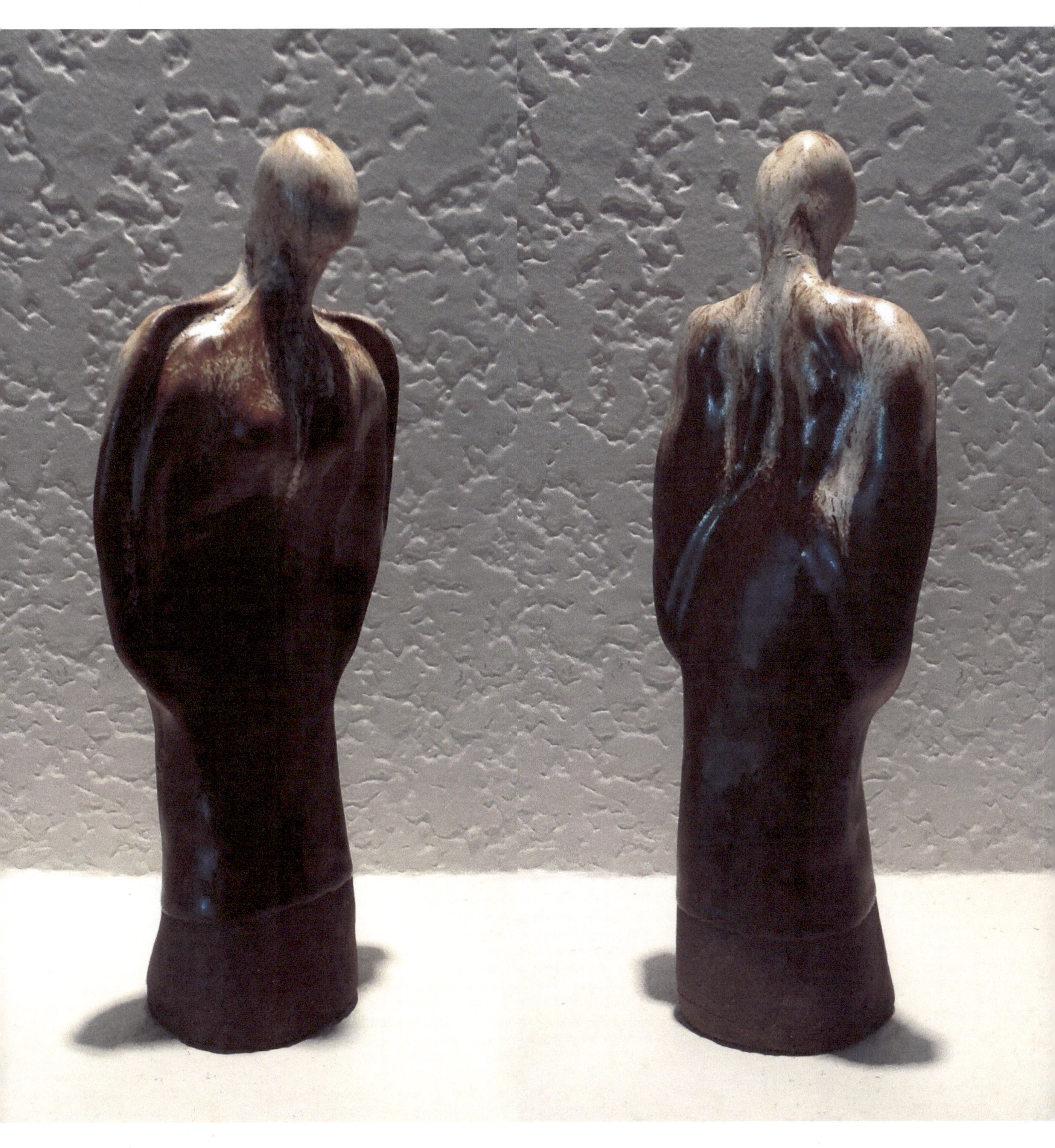

Angel from the Faceless Realm

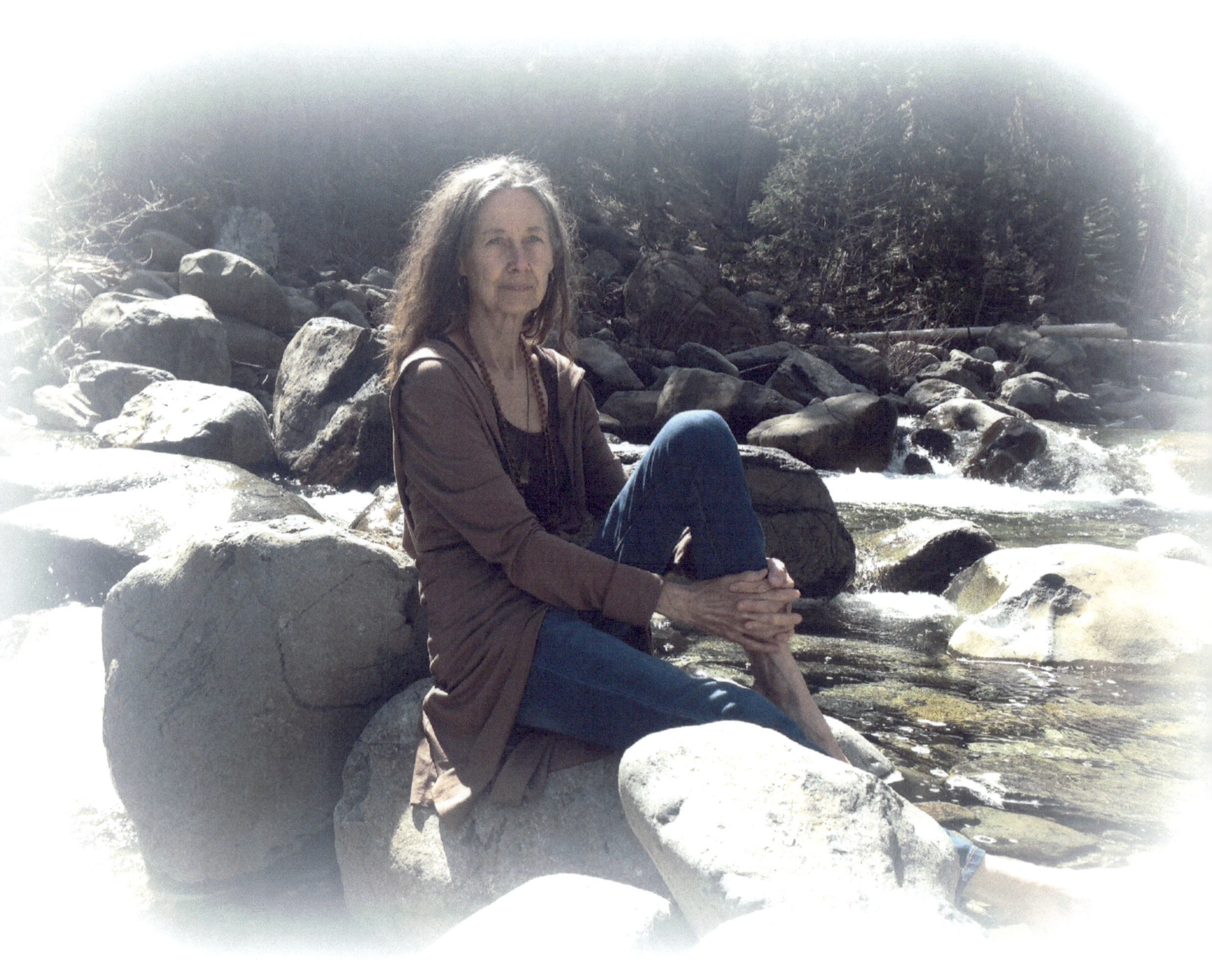

About the Artist/Sculptress/Writer

Mary Saint-Marie has traveled extensively with her Art of the Soul. She began to pioneer visionary art in Salem, Oregon in 1972, after much inspired travel out of the country, feeling the soul of people in many diverse cultures.

Art of the Soul has been viewed and collected in the U.S., in over one hundred and fifty exhibits. Mary's work has been exhibited in galleries, workshops, expositions, holistic faires, conferences, symposiums, spiritual centers, and retreat sites. It has been shown and collected in Europe and the Yucatan, as well.

Art of the Soul is mystic art. It has appeared on calendars, greeting cards, CD covers, books and magazines. *Quest, Mystic Pop, Anemone, Dream Network Journal* and *Crone Chronicles* have all featured Mary's art. This sacred art is also in the books *One Source Sacred Journey*, a collection of 44 international visionary artists, *Songs from the Edge of Everything*, and *The Ways of Spirit*.

Mary's art has appeared on numerous television interviews, such as the Wisdom Channel and Channel 5 in San Francisco. The art was featured on television across Germany and on Bridging Heaven and Earth TV. Most recently, Mary's art was featured in the documentary, *FEMME: Women Healing the World*, which is an award-winning film about Oneness and balance.

The mystic art of Mary Saint-Marie was also the main focus of her multi-media sacred enactment, *SHE...it is who Remembers*, for eight years.

Unexpectedly, Mary wrote a play, while on retreat one weekend. It arose spontaneously from a dream, with no planning. She had no formal training in writing a play. It was a total surprise and a gift. While it is now in book form, it had its genesis as a play about Higher Consciousness. The play, *The Monitor and Laughter of the Gods: Saraswati Comes Swingin' Her Hips*, was produced by Mary, in co-creation with many deeply inspired and gifted actors, dancers, directors, chanters, and ones who coordinated and assisted.

Another recent creation is an Animation Meditation video/short, entitled *Holy Sight for the Earth and for the Sky*. In this one minute animation, there is art, narration, soul sounding by Mary, and a photo of the Earth. The gifted animator brought all the artistic elements together in one powerful transcendent minute to invite realization or remembrance of the One Illumined Self that we are. (See video and credits on YouTube and/or the www.marysaintmarie.com website.)

Mary's art appears on all of her previous ten books, which may be seen on www.marysaintmarie.com. It also appears on her two CDs, *Journey of Consciousness* and *Soul Sounds for World Birth*.

The artist is continually inspired to create, using new forms. After the pen and ink, airbrush, pencil, charcoal, and Prismacolor phases of creating, Mary began multi-media, multi-technique, and multi-dimensional paintings on water color paper.

The artist became inspired with some of the more rare art of William Blake. She began opening to her own form of beautiful textures that would reflect the feeling of both earth and sky. The As Above, So Below. She explored both in nature and in junk yards, seeing the weathered metals with such exquisite textures helped by nature's hand. As Mary opened and allowed, the process began to be revealed from within. It seemed to be a synthesis of all she had done, since multi-media classes at the University of Wisconsin to that moment. The process included many layerings, as had her pencil drawings. It turned into a beautiful living ceremony of creation.

Simultaneously to the creation of these new multi-media paintings, Mary began to sculpt small pieces of altar art. These ceremonial and one of a kind sacred and infused figures remind ones of the sacred in everything. The Oneness. They reflect Life As Living Ceremony.

These small kachina sculptures were created for close to a decade, constantly changing form and materials. Always mirroring the human form as one of the Soul's Expression.

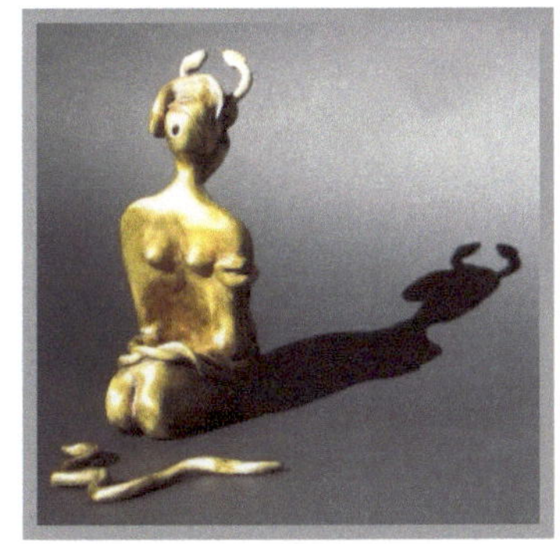

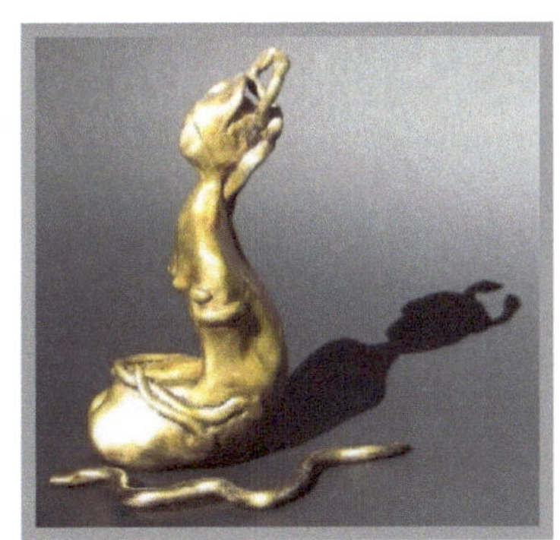

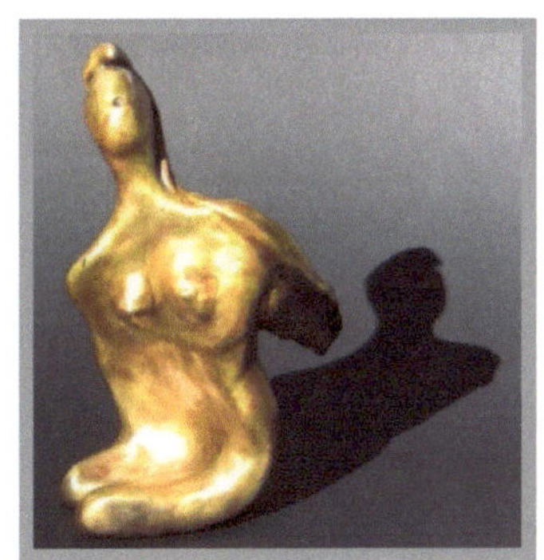

Biography and Education

SINCE 1974, Mary Saint-Marie has lived close to nature, near forests, lakes, rivers, waterfalls, and high desert, mainly in the Northern California mountains. She was guided there via a prayer and a dream.

Mary was a high school English teacher, as well as a coordinator in public educational television. During this time Mary was in Fine Arts at the University of Wisconsin, beginning to explore the life she desired to live. And it was here that she fell in love with multi-media art. She took a position teaching college English in Salem, Oregon. It was here when all changed.

After a near death experience in a car collision, in 1971, Mary began drawing, painting, sculpting, and helping people find their Inner Being. The near death experience catalyzed a journey to Europe, Morocco, the Middle East, and to India and Kashmir to see the soul of others and to begin to experience the inner Life. She began to draw and unknowingly was creating her first three public art exhibits upon her return to the U.S. She began to pioneer visionary art exhibits.

This was followed by 1½ years of traveling around America looking into many new natural and organic lifestyles that were emerging in America. Although everyone called these people hippies, they were way showers of the New Earth that is still emerging...

The near death experience into the Christed Soul Realm initiated a new life and many new expressions that continue to this day.

Mary was now aware of the luminous Universal Oneness. The near death experience exacted a definitive remembering and awareness, for she saw past, present, and future of her own life as one life, here now. She saw her life via the numinous Soul. Via a joy that is unlimited and has no description. After this experience, Mary could see the light of Being around living plants. It was the aura, the Universal Energy. The world experienced during that collision felt more "real" than the world she had been living. There was no turning back.

The artist began to share these rememberings of the Invisible world through numerous visionary forms. The Formless manifest as form. The artist finally awoke to the Manifest as sacred. Holy.

This body of work reveals the sacred life we are all living. The work is multi-cultural, multi-media, and multi-dimensional. Mary shares the Awareness of life as simultaneously unique and individual as well as being a ceremony of the One Life.

This body of work is inspired from within and from experience. It reveals the delicate and sacred balance of the visible and Invisible as One. Here we see the Universal Dance of the One.

This body of work reminds us of the Wholeness that we Already are. The Transcendence. It reminds us that the ordinary and Extraordinary are One. It reminds us that we may attune inwardly and allow ourselves to be danced by the Infinite...for we are the Living Ceremony...

Sculpting

Giving the essence world a form is an elevated experience.

This experience allows one to understand Beauty expressed. But the understanding is not with the mind. It is such a deep inner experience because it is that which is Indescribable.

One is the open vessel through which it happens. So it is experienced in consciousness and on a cellular level.

Simultaneously, there is the awareness of the formless, the form, and the one aware of the creative process. It is Being Creative.

Preparing to Enter the Studio

Preparing to enter the studio space is an expansion of consciousness.

Sometimes one may want or need to walk and/or be in nature before working in the studio. In a silent nature meditation, one may empty out all but a sense of the Infinite Love, the beauty of Being. For the moment, the seemingly external world falls away.

In this silent time in nature, one may have insights about Beauty expressed.

There are many times I have walked or sat for a day or two before beginning to sculpt, paint, or write. It is a meditation that allows one to easily let go of the world. Let go of the pulls of the world and the concerns. It is a meditation that allows one to feel the Emptiness. Or one may simply get silent.

In the passage in this book, Soul Glyphs as Sculpture, I describe how I have created Sounds and Signings of the Soul as a way to feel gestures, postures, frequencies that feel powerful and elevated. Those direct experiences then become the inspiration for starting a new sculptured form. It is a powerful way to feel the exalted state of pure awareness. Devoid of the ever thinking mind. Joyful Emptiness... alone...

Then, as I approach the studio space, I feel the appreciation of having the time and space to create. It is a gift. I feel a reverence that has no words. One becomes the very prayer. Words do not come...

There is an intuitive feeling and knowing when it is time to create. It cannot be explained in words.

Then enter the studio/creation space with deep reverence. Open to the Infinite. Open to nature. Feeling and experiencing.

The Studio

The environment is key to me in creating. A sacred environment is conducive to the creative process. Ones who are sensitive to the external environment give great attention to the space.

The creative environment is a place where I am not interrupted and where I can feel and be close to nature. And I am most creative when I am in solitude.

Solitude allows the inner flow to be easily felt with no disturbances.

Solitude may deeply enhance the inner journey. One becomes very sensitive to just being. Solitary being. The "art and act of sculpting" is the luminous experience. The sculptress and the sculpture almost disappear if one goes in deeply enough.

I begin with an area that is spacious and light filled. I feel expanded.

The actual art environment might be different each time. A candle. Meditative music or silence. Essential oils. The time of day. Dawn.

Before I begin, I have a practice of Being at One with all of the materials being used. I do this by realizing All as light manifest. I allow our energy to touch. I feel the inner essence relationship with the materials and equipment to be used. This can be a very deeply felt experience. Joy filled.

I come into a state of deep appreciation of co-creation. These substances allow me to create on this plane of existence. And I am the one that allows the form to be revealed. This form of gratitude opens up the field of light even more.

All of this preparation heightens the felt sense of the field of light.

Sometimes I have a glimpse of what I am going to create. Or I may just feel the essence of it. Usually I am simply open and in the Emptiness before I begin.

Beginning a Sculpture

My hands work and feel the sculpting compound or clay for some time before there is a feeling of a "direction." I just allow that. I trust that. It is beholding the great mystery within and being a part of the appearance world.

I am listening and feeling with my entire being. My hands take on a knowing consciousness.

Sculpting in this way is ecstatic. It is full of wonder. It is holy.

When the sculpture is complete, there is just a knowing.

During the time that I am sculpting, I journal if something comes to me. The title. An insight.

I find that sculpting allows one to experience oneself as the living revelation.

Life as a Living Ceremony becomes one of the many gifts of sculpting.

Art, Books, CDs, Soul Sessions and Soul Retreats

www.MarySaintMarie.com
www.EarthCareGlobalTV.com

Art:

All art in *Life As Living Ceremony* is available as giclee fine art reproductions.

Please email to find the names of current gallery showings.

*See the website to view videos/YouTubes with art.

Books:

Galactic Shamanism
The Holy Sight
Messages from the Silence
Nectar of Woman
The Sacred Two
The Star-Stone Ones
The Animating Presence
The Monitor and Laughter of the Gods, a play in book form
Art As Consciousness
The Oracle and the Dreamer
Life As Living Ceremony

CDs:

Journey of Consciousness, a meditation
Soul Sounds of World Birth

Recording:

Return to Oneness, a recording giving Voice to the Animals and addressing Rights of Animals (will be made available as a cd)

Soul Sessions and Retreats:

*Please see the website to find out more about the spiritual education for individuals and groups. Mary works both in person and by phone.

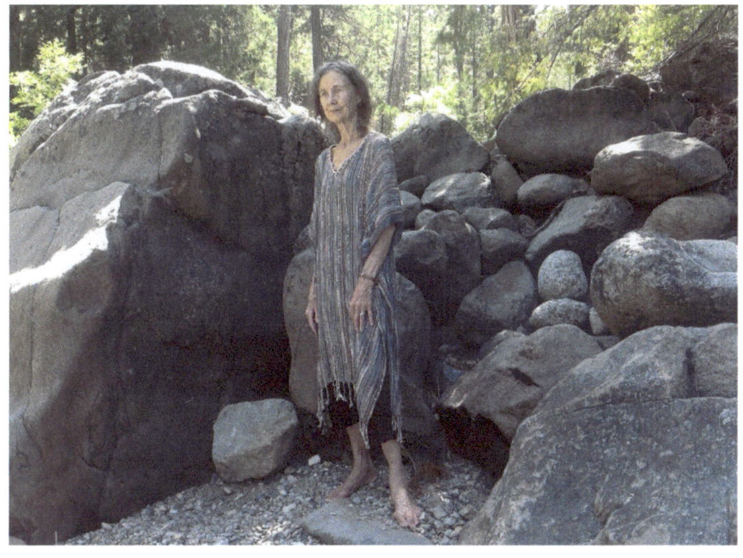

Life As Living Ceremony

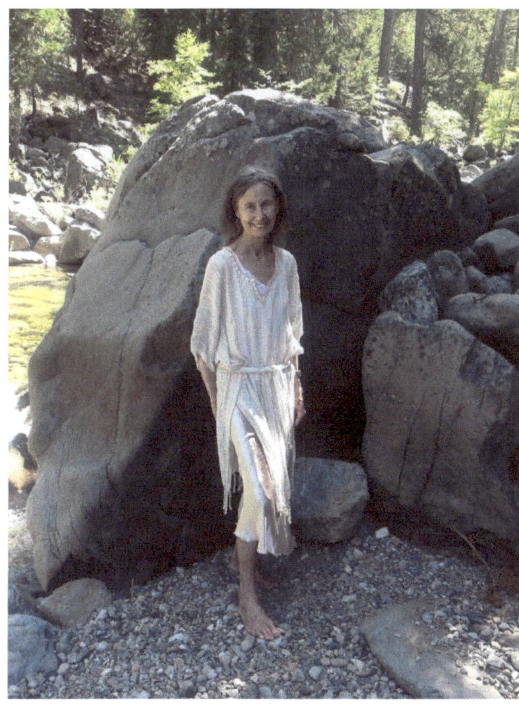

EarthCare Global TV

Please see the website for the full vision of a profound unification of earth care.

EarthCare Global TV has as its purpose to freely educate and inspire people of the world about earth care. It serves to unify ones of like vision through communication and Vision in Action.

EarthCare Global TV sees the understanding of the Universal Law of Balance in all of nature being shared worldwide that the principle may be realized in daily life by all. The vision shares the practical understanding of the need of purity and sustainability.

*Please see the category, Internet TV, on the website, to see the listing of 300+ earth care documentaries. The documentaries are about being a Voice for the Earth. And they are education and inspiration for humanity to choose a new direction: Purity instead of pollution.

*See also the category, Videos, on website to view youtubes about the earth, created with the art of Mary Saint-Marie.

1. earth care, a short video created for The One Minute Shift, to expand awareness of the oneness of everyone, everything and everyplace.

2. *Holy Sight for the Earth and for the Sky*, an animation meditation

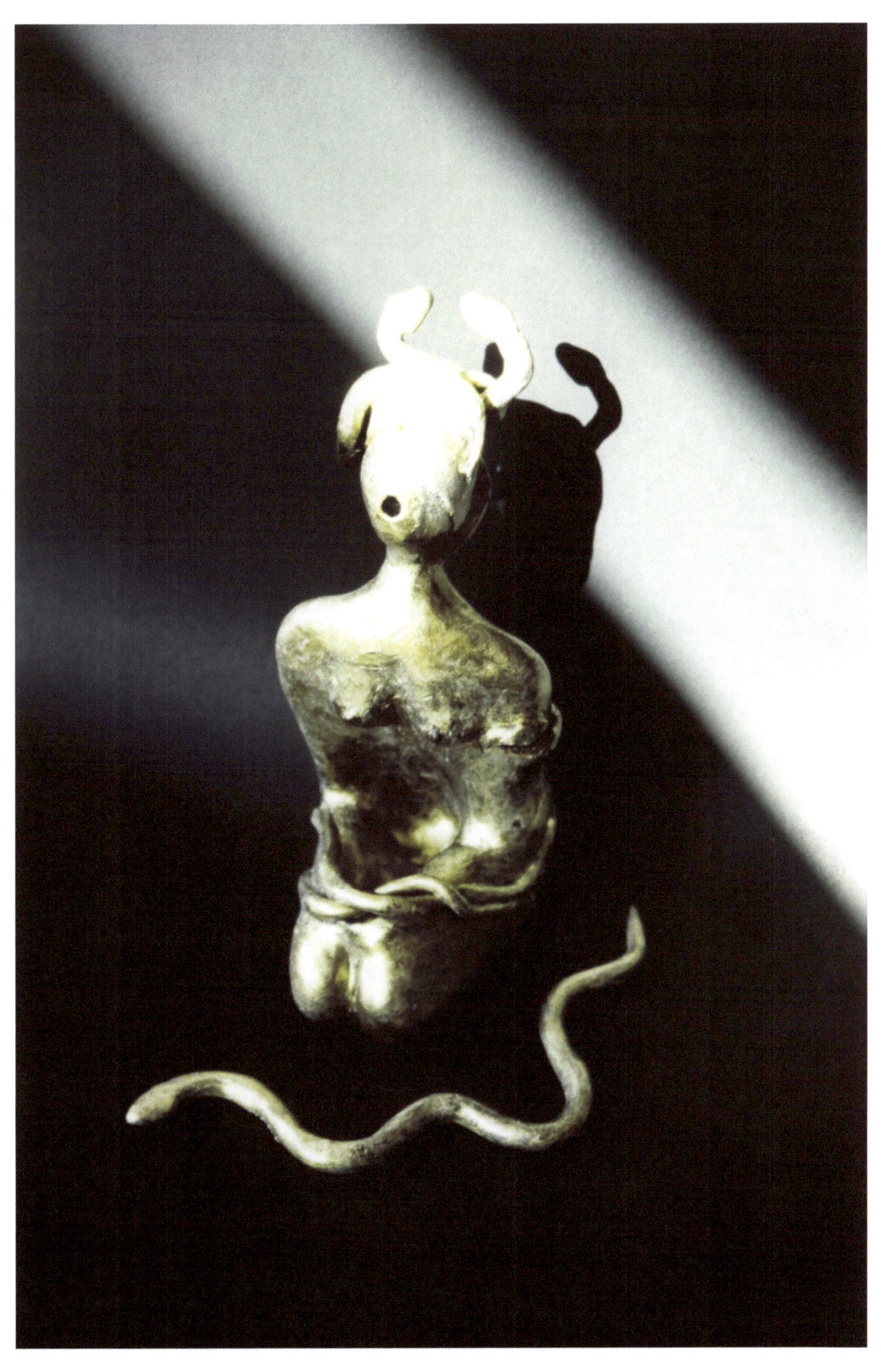

Serpent-Priestess-SHE

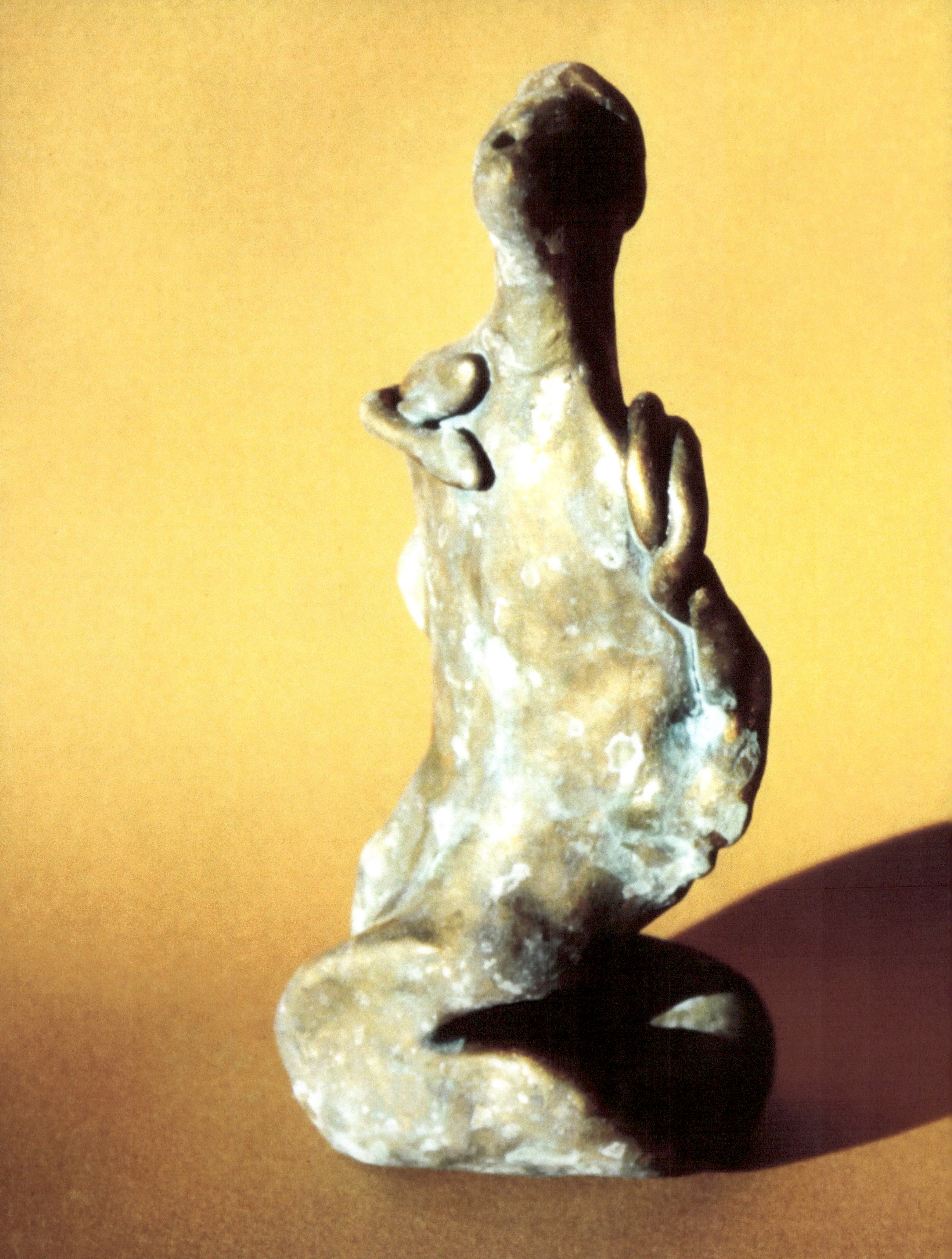

www.ingramcontent.com/pod-product-compliance
Lightning Source LLC
LaVergne TN
LVHW070118110826
845147LV00002B/147

9780692845172